AMERICAN CATHOLICS

and the

MEXICAN REVOLUTION,

1924–1936

AMERICAN CATHOLICS

and the

MEXICAN REVOLUTION, 1924–1936

MATTHEW A. REDINGER

university of notre dame press
notre dame, indiana

Manufactured in the United States of America

Library of Congress Cataloging in-Publication Data

Redinger, Matthew.
    American Catholics and the Mexican Revolution, 1924–1936 /
Matthew A. Redinger.
        p.   cm.
    Includes bibliographical references and index.
    ISBN 0-268-04022-2 (cloth : alk. paper)
    ISBN 0-268-04023-0 (pbk. : alk. paper)
    1. Mexico—Foreign public opinion, American—History—20th century.
2. Catholics—United States—Attitudes—History—20th century.
3. Catholics—United States—Political activity—History—20th century.
4. Mexico—History—Revolution, 1910–1920—Religious aspects—Catholic
Church.   5. Mexico—History—Revolution, 1910–1920—Foreign public opinion,
American.   6. Public opinion—United States—History—20th century.   I. Title.
    E183.8.M6R415   2005
    322'.1097209042—dc22

                                                                                    2005025287

The heartfelt dedication of this study goes to my wife, Ann, and to my children, Elizabeth and Daniel. Without their dedication to the Herculean tasks of forcing me to work when I had to and of calling me to play when I needed it, none of this would have been completed.
This work is for them.

The unhappy truth is that the prevailing public opinion has been destructively wrong at the critical junctures. . . . They [the people] have compelled the governments, which usually knew what would have been wiser, or was necessary, or was more expedient, to be too late with too little, or too long with too much, too pacifist in peace and too bellicose in war, too neutralist or appeasing in negotiation or too intransigent. Mass opinion has acquired mounting power in this century. It has shown itself to be a dangerous master of decisions when the stakes are life and death.

—Walter Lippmann

CONTENTS

PREFACE

GEOGRAPHY BROUGHT THEM TOGETHER, BUT HISTORY DROVE THEM apart. This is the fundamental reality in relations between the United States and Mexico. For Mexico's part, this remains a love-hate relationship, perhaps best memorialized in Porfirio Díaz's quip: "Alas, poor Mexico. So far from God and so near to the United States."

Because of this geographical propinquity, the tremors emanating from south of the Rio Grande cut a wide swath through American society. From oilmen to the American Federation of Labor, many groups in the United States focused their collective attention southward as the Mexican Revolution progressed. Among the most interested groups were Roman Catholics in this country, who became increasingly concerned when the revolutionaries of 1910 sought to re-address the position of the Church in Mexican society by striking out at that single clearest representative, that archetype, of the old order. Catholics in the United States viewed the revolutionary anticlerical agenda as a threat to something at their very soul—their Catholicity. They responded to this challenge by standing up for what they recognized as a truth that lay at the core of their identity as *American* Catholics, the right to worship freely, as an inalienable and universal liberty. As the revolution took on an anticlerical nature through the Constitution of 1917, American Catholics became actively involved in an effort to force the United States government to re-address its relationship to that revolutionary regime.

This study has dual purposes. First, it is an analysis of those efforts of American Catholics as a private interest group to affect change in the public policy of this nation through the creation of an educated, sympathetic public opinion in the United States. As such, it is more than an examination of one country's contact with another. It digs deeper to examine the social context of that international relationship. In exploring these deeper issues, this study achieves its second goal in that it provides an examination of the Catholic Church in the United States as a case study of private interest groups' effort to mold public policy to fit their own particular agendas. This study is an analysis of the ways in which factors from without (the persecution) motivated an interested "public" (Catholics in the United States) to impress upon the policy-making structure (president, secretary of state, and Congress) that public's contention that the foreign policy needed to be altered.

Among those authors who have interested themselves in a study of United States-Mexican relations during the revolutionary years,[1] a few have focused their attention on ways in which American Catholics involved themselves.[2] None of these scholars, however, has examined the Catholic Church in the United States as an interest group bent on creating a public opinion, with which they hoped to influence public policy, as does this study. The present work expands upon the existing literature by analyzing the ways in which an interest group (Catholics in the United States) was motivated by factors from without (the Mexican anticlerical persecution) to influence the policy-making establishment (president, secretary of state, and Congress) to change United States foreign policy (United States–Mexican relations).

It would be logical to begin this examination with a few basic definitions. An "interest group" might best be defined as an organization bound together by a single common element, such as, in this case, a religious denomination. It is important to note, however, that mere membership in a church does not constitute membership in an interest group. The group coalesces only when it finds a cause to embrace and around which it can begin to work as one.[3] Moreover, groups such as churches become *interest* groups when they embrace political agendas.[4]

Second, we need to consider what we mean by "public opinion" as it applies to these interest groups. Inherent in this understanding is an impression of what a particular "public" is. As regards a group as large and extended as the Roman Catholic Church in the United States, it is incumbent upon us to recognize that there are many publics. Indeed, if this study were to contend that all Catholics in the United States believed the same on nearly *any* given subject—save dogmatic issues—it would eviscerate its own efforts at credibility. For the purposes of this work, we need to concentrate on a particular public, that is, those activist Catholics who felt moved into action by Mexican anticlericalism.[5]

With this understanding of the public, we move to the issue of opinion. For much of the twentieth century, scholars strove to understand the phenomenon of public opinion.[6] At its most basic level, public opinion might be viewed as a perspective shared by a community (broadly defined) on a given topic. This, of course, would suffice as a definition, but it would be of little use to this study without a consideration of how public opinion is used. This is where meat meets bone. V. O. Key identified the essential element: the use of public opinion to compel governments to act.[7] It is in this inducement to action that we come to the most intractable of issues, that of "influence." Influence is where we find the linkage between public opinion and public policy.

Social scientists have identified the difficulties of drawing any clear connections between public opinion and public policy. Some, such as James Rosenau, claim that to make any such connection, the scholar must rely on little more than guesswork, the pursuit of which requires an examination of motivational and attitudinal data from which inferences must be drawn. He maintained that to pursue this line of inquiry is to narrow our scope of inquiry so much that it would "shed little light on the opinion-policy relationship."[8] Others disagree. Jean-Guy Vaillancourt casts a significantly broader net in his estimation of the power of public opinion. He defines power as the "capacity to influence or to affect social activities, or as Amitar Etzioni puts it, 'a capacity to overcome part or all of the resistance, to introduce change in the face of opposition.'"[9] Carol Bodensteiner maintains that special interest groups are credible in the political arena only to the extent that they are broadly representative of, and dedicated to, the public interest. This linkage of the group and public interest establishes the relevance of the group's influence.[10] In another context, Douglas Little notes that to fully understand the influence of an interest group, "one must move beyond the realm of crude . . . calculation. . . ."[11]

It seems clear that an analysis of a policy line and the changes in it which may logically have resulted from the efforts of an interested (or "attentive") public to influence the course of that policy line can, indeed, shed light on the relationship between opinion and policy. Although "influence" is not empirically measurable, the results of its exercise can be identified. While this requires that the scholar acknowledge that additional factors might well have contributed to the change of policy, this acknowledgment effectively points to the wondrous complexity inherent in the relationship between public policy and public opinion. I hope that the various categories and methods of analysis I employed in this work are useful for analyzing other groups at other times, and in other contexts.

c h a p t e r   1

MEXICAN CHURCH-STATE CONFLICT AND THE ORIGINS OF CATHOLIC ACTIVISM

Historian Frank Tannenbaum postulated that American foreign policy is, and has been, responsive to public opinion.[1] While various administrations might chart their own courses, in the end, the people assert themselves through Congress and through the "ten thousand agencies of public expression represented by the churches, the trade unions, women's organizations, and spontaneous public bodies that arise in any crisis." Ultimately, they succeed in forming policies "consistent with the special sense of justice and rightness so dominant in American feeling."[2] In the years following the end of World War I, a number of organizations formed to focus attention on foreign policy issues, such as the Council on Foreign Relations (1918) and the Foreign Policy Association (1918). Similar groups arose to assert their will in the arena of international peace. Such groups as the National Council on the Limitation of Armaments and the National Council for the Prevention of War comprised a peace movement which mobilized support behind the naval arms limitation agreements of the 1920s. They sought to exert their will through petitions, speech-making, and intensive lobbying efforts.[3] Within this context of organized expressions of specific interests, this tradition of activism provided the Catholic opposition to the Mexican persecution a firm foundation.

Catholic activism in the United States reflected the new sense of self-assuredness American Catholics experienced in the post–World War I years. In fact, this self-awareness made some uneasy. Mary McGill, associate editor of *The Catholic Girl*, wrote to the editor of *America*, Wilfrid Parsons, SJ, that as Catholics, "We are so SURE. That characteristic would hurt me, if I didn't believe. I think I would hate people who are so certain and set apart, if I were not so favored with our *Supreme Gift*."[4] To a large degree, this self-assuredness arose out of the important contribution American Catholics had made to the war effort. Archbishop James Cardinal Gibbons of Baltimore served as chair of the "League of National Unity," which helped to unify Americans behind the war effort. Father John J. Burke, CSP, served as the chair of the secretary of war's "Committee of Six," comprised of one Catholic (Burke), four Protestants, and a Jew, who advised the secretary on religious and moral issues of the war. For this service, the War Department awarded Burke the Distinguished Service Medal in 1919.[5]

Overall, American Catholic response to the national call was impressive. While Catholics comprised about 16 percent of the American population, they made up nearly 21 percent of those Americans under arms.[6] Clearly, the contribution Catholics made in the war effort helped dispel much of the anti-Catholics' doubts as to their patriotism.

This self-assuredness should not be mistaken for Catholic unity. The American Catholic Church was badly factionalized and fragmented along ethnic, political, and philosophic lines. Examples of this divisiveness include the debate over the American participation in the World Court.[7] Another split was a legacy of the 1890s debate between the St. Paul Archbishop John Ireland's "Americanists," who sought to adapt the Church to American society, and "Europeanists," including New York Archbishop Michael Corrigan's German and Irish Catholics, who sought to hold onto their ethnic diversity.[8] This ethnic diversity, the result of several decades of Catholic immigration, was still, by the 1920s and 1930s, a source of anti-Catholicism and the prevalence of a Catholic subculture.

The American Catholic Church's immigrant-church status helped feed American Catholic dedication to the Mexican Church, by sensitizing American Catholics to religious oppression, both foreign and domestic.[9] For most

Catholics in the United States, a mistaken assumption of the inherent nature of Catholicism in Mexico—borne out of their understanding of history— fired their desire for involvement in the Mexican affair.

The Roman Catholic Church, they knew, from the earliest days of the colonial period in the sixteenth century, had been a major force in the history of Mexico. Catholic missionaries served the *conquistadores* on their voyages of exploration and exploitation, not only in their capacity as evangelizers of the "heathen" natives but also as agents of royal control of the colony itself. Serving in this capacity was incredibly lucrative for the Church. Such institutions as tithes on agricultural produce and perpetual liens on land earned for the Church vast wealth. This wealth was contingent, of course, on maintenance of the colonial status quo. It was because of this traditional position in colonial society that the Church hierarchy remained loyal to the Spanish crown, bringing all Church resources, including its vast wealth, its control of the press, and even the dreaded Inquisition, to bear against the revolutionaries in 1808 in the wars for independence.[10] Since the Church proved to be a barrier to Mexican progress, the revolutionaries who held Mexico's future in their hands began a battle against its position in Mexican society which would last through the first half of the twentieth century.

The roots of the anticlerical movement of the Mexican Revolution lie deep in the nineteenth-century conflict between the landed, pro-cleric Conservatives and the urban, largely mestizo, anticlerical Liberals. Often, Liberal attacks on the Church early in the nineteenth century were purely utilitarian—they sought to weaken the Conservatives by weakening the clergy who supported them. Later, however, fundamental philosophical postures underlay Liberal anticlericalism. Beginning in the 1820s, Liberals and Conservatives vied for dominance, and alternately replaced each other's constitutions with laws that reflected their philosophies. Most influential in laying the groundwork for conditions that would make a revolution necessary in 1910 was the Porfiriato, the thirty-four-year reign of Porfirio Díaz.

The United States government first became actively concerned with the Mexican Revolution in the context of the revolution's reaction to two basic trends of the Porfiriato. First, Díaz worked to modernize Mexico by actively encouraging foreign investment in such sectors as railroads, mining concessions, oil drilling, and public utilities. The result was the domination of Mexico's industrial capacity by foreign interests such as Standard Oil and Texaco, which produced approximately 60 percent of Mexico's oil and owned more land in Mexico than did Mexicans themselves.[11] United States citizens' property rights in Mexico were worth nearly $2 billion by 1910.[12] The United States government's concern for property rights played a prominent role in the ways the Calvin Coolidge and Franklin D. Roosevelt administrations responded to the Mexican church-state struggle.

It was in the context of the revolution's reaction to the second trend of the Porfiriato that American Catholics sought to interest the United States government in the affairs of Mexico. In the years following the coup which swept him into power, Díaz worked to secure his position by playing a double game; he simultaneously courted both the leadership of the Catholic Church in Mexico and those who favored active enforcement of the anticlerical provisions of the liberal Constitution of 1857. The dictator garnered the support of the Liberals by allowing the anticlerical provisions of the Constitution of 1857 to remain on the books. At the same time, his devout wife, Carmen, acted as mediator between the Catholic hierarchy and Díaz. His policies toward the Church, which can best be described as benign neglect, allowed the clergy to more than triple in size during his reign, from some 1,600 in 1878 to nearly 5,000 by the time he left office in 1911.[13] Consequently, the clergy managed to gain back a great degree of the power, wealth, and prestige it had lost under the Liberal regimes of Benito Juárez (1855–1872) and his successor Sebastián Lerdo de Tejada (1872–1876).[14]

Historian Randall Hanson contends that an additional facet to the resurgence of the Catholic Church during the Porfiriato was a rededication, on the part of the Church in Mexico, to "socio-economic activities" that drew inspiration from Pope Leo XIII's 1891 encyclical *Rerum Novarum*. This encyclical initiated an era of reform in which the Church sought to redefine its relationship with the poor and oppressed. In Mexico, this reform effort led to the establishment of mutual aid societies, land distribution proposals, political consolidation, and the foundation of a Catholic trades union, all under the banner of Catholic Social Action.[15]

Very early in the revolution, there was not a clear anticlerical agenda other than a general desire to enforce the liberal Constitution of 1857, which had fallen to disuse under Porfirio Díaz. This lack of an apparent anticlerical agenda is clear in the rush to establish political parties in the heady days following Díaz's 1908 bombshell announcement that he would not seek the presidency again in 1910. Among these new political organizations was the Partído Católico Nacional (PCN). The PCN was typical of political movements of the early revolutionary period in that it embraced a common revolutionary program on anti-reelection, social progress, and labor reform.[16] The clergy feared that the first revolutionary president, Francisco Madero, a spiritualist who was known to consult the Ouija board, would pose a significant threat to the Church. Fortunately, however, Madero was too preoccupied with challenges to his power to undertake reforms in church-state relations. In 1913, General Victoriano Huerta, Díaz's military strongman, led a counter-revolution, overthrowing Madero, thus allowing the clergy to heave a sigh of relief.[17] While the clergy welcomed Huerta with open arms, the violent means with which Huerta came to power alarmed Woodrow Wilson, who refused to legitimize Huerta's regime by granting it diplomatic recognition.[18] William Taft's ambassador to Mexico, Henry Lane Wilson, urged the Wilson administration to recognize Huerta, but the president's private emissaries in Mexico, William Bayard Hale and John Lind, saw little worth recognizing in the tenacious Huerta. On April 21, 1914, Wilson carried out what some consider his "personal vendetta" against Huerta by authorizing the occupation of the port of Veracruz, thereby intensifying the anarchy of civil war.[19]

Out of the anarchy of civil war that erupted following the Veracruz occupation, Venustiano Carranza emerged as the person in relative control of Mexico. With Huerta thus removed, Wilson warmed to the idea of recognition. American Catholics viewed this as a critical juncture, since recognition implied support for the revolutionary government in Mexico. Wilson was less interested in the Mexican succession troubles because he had other concerns, especially that of a war brewing in Europe. He favored conciliation of Carranza rather than forcing him into Germany's open arms. On October 8, 1915, Wilson administration talks with Carranza's representative in Washington, D.C., Eliseo Arredondo, ended with Arredondo addressing one of the concerns that American Catholics considered paramount in any consideration of recognition: the Mexican position on religious freedom. Arredondo's controversial "pledge" was an item of American Catholic debate for the next two decades. As Carranza's representative, he assured the Wilson administration that

> Inasmuch as the re-establishment of peace within order and law is the purpose of the Government of Mr. Venustiano Carranza . . . all the inhabitants of Mexico without exception, whether nationals or foreigners, may equally enjoy the benefits of true justice, and hence . . . the Laws of Reform, which guarantee individual freedom of worship, according to everyone's conscience, shall be strictly observed. Therefore, the Constitutionalist Government will respect everybody's life,

property and religious beliefs, without other limitations than the preservation of public order and the observance of the institutions, in accordance with the laws in force and the Constitution of the Republic.[20]

Arredondo had simply restated basic tenets of Mexican law to which virtually all Mexican leaders clove: that under the Constitution of 1857, all Mexicans were guaranteed religious freedom, so long as the exercise of that freedom does not violate the law of the land. It was, however, the nature of that constitutional law that caused so many debates in the years to come.[21]

Carranza called a constitutional convention into order at Querétaro in 1917 to re-address the provisions of the Constitution of 1857. It was time for a change, and the whole Mexican nation held great hope for constitutional peace after the chaos of revolution. The perception that change was needed crossed ideological lines, as some delegates "clutched Bibles to their breasts while others waved *Das Kapital* enthusiastically."[22] Carranza presented the convention a draft constitution he himself had written, but shortly after the convention began, radical anticlericals took control. These radicals, interested in rapid social change, launched a broad-based attack on the Roman Catholic Church. Some of the radicals' proposals that found a place in the Constitution of 1917 included the secularization of all education and the closing of religious-affiliated schools; the elimination of all public religious ceremonies, that is, those performed outside the confines of a church building; the confiscation of all church property, which was declared to be Mexican national land; the registration of priests, who were now required to be native-born and who were deprived of the right to vote; the abolition of any oaths in the form of religious vows; and the exclusion of religious institutions from legal protection. This constitution alarmed American Catholics, but they were calmed by memories of Arredondo's pledge, and the fact that Carranza did not enforce the anticlerical provisions.[23]

Alvaro Obregón, Carranza's successor, also emphasized the consolidation of his own control of Mexican politics over implementation of anti-religious laws that would cause instability in the Mexican body politic.[24] Obregón did not allow the Church to run roughshod over him, however. On January 11, 1923, a huge throng gathered in Guanajuato to witness Apostolic Delegate Ernesto Filippi dedicate the cornerstone to a monument to Christ the King.[25] Obregón viewed both the ceremony and Mexico City Archbishop José Mora y del Río's pastoral letter, which proclaimed "Jesus Christ is our King, not only in the figurative sense . . . but in the real sense that He has true power to rule man and societies. . . . His kingdom is not of this world, but it is in this world, and it is manifested in a human society, visibly perfect, universal, and eternal, which is the Catholic Church" as grave challenges to the government's primacy over temporal affairs.[26] This assault on governmental authority drove Obregón to expel the apostolic delegate. The president demonstrated a degree of moderation, however, when he retained the secretary of the apostolic delegation to carry on the work of the delegate. Obregón's interest in preserving peace in Mexico through moderation is clear also in a 1924 agreement between his government and the Vatican. The Mexican president authorized his secretary of foreign relations, Aarón Sáenz, to exchange statements with Papal Secretary of State Pietro Cardinal Gasparri in which the Mexican government agreed to allow a new apostolic delegate to serve in Mexico so long as the Vatican promised to appoint only Mexicans who refrained from political involvement as bishops.[27]

Obregón's four-year term ended when his candidate to succeed him as president, fellow Sonoran Plutarco Elías Calles, won handily in the July 1924 elections. Obregón chose Calles as a safe choice, because, as the revolutionary hero noted, Calles "will not overshadow me." Moreover, Obregón considered Calles "the least of my generals."[28]

Calles was keenly aware that his political patron and presidential predecessor held him in low regard. Calles, therefore, tried to forge a political legacy independent of Obregón by concentrating on, as first priorities, agrarian reform (Calles distributed more land to peasants than any earlier revolutionary president), workers' rights (Calles worked to expand the power of the leading labor organization Confederación Regional Obrera Mexicana—CROM), and oil issues (Calles took a firmer stand on oil rights than Obregón by disavowing the 1923 Bucareli Agreements).[29] Similarly, Calles chose to reverse his predecessor's trajectory vis-à-vis the Church by rededicating his government to the full implementation of the anticlerical provisions of the Constitution of 1917. In fact, he publicly maintained that Obregón's complicity with the Vatican had "violated at least the spirit if not the letter of the Constitution."[30] Clearly, Catholics had much to fear from Calles, and they did not have to wait long before Calles began to attack the Church.

In February 1925, just over two months after Calles's inauguration, two defrocked Mexican priests—José Joaquín Pérez and Luis Manuel Monje— backed up by a gang of armed men, seized the church of La Soledad in Mexico City. Most assumed that Calles was behind the plot, and their suspicions proved well grounded. Calles and Luis Morones (his friend and the president of CROM whom Calles had elevated to the cabinet post of minister of industry, commerce and labor) used CROM members, banded together under the title Caballeros de Guadalupe, to guard the schismatics in the church. Morones also met regularly with the schismatic priests, Pérez and Monje. The final piece of evidence that showed Calles's hand in the affair was when he formally gave the church to the ex-priests and authorized them to establish a schismatic Mexican Apostolic Church. Calles and his assistants intended the Mexican Apostolic Church to split the Roman Catholic Church in Mexico, but instead, the Roman Catholics rallied around the Mother Church. Residents of the area around La Soledad protested the loss of their neighborhood church, and signed a petition demanding that the government recognize their constitutional right to freedom of religion.[31] On a broader level, the Asociación Católico de la Joventud Mexicana, or the Mexican Catholic Youth Association, founded the Liga Nacional Defensora de la Libertad Religiosa (National League for the Defense of Religious Freedom—or "Liga") to spearhead Mexican Catholic resistance to the Calles government.[32]

The church-state conflict took on new life in February 1926 when the Mexico City newspaper *El Universal* published comments by Archbishop José Mora y del Río condemning the constitution. Regardless of the fact that these comments were nine years old—he had originally made them in 1917 in the context of an episcopal protest against the anticlerical articles of the new constitution—Mora observed that the truth had not fundamentally changed with the passage of time.[33] Even though Mora claimed that he was aware of no new clerical campaigns to undermine the constitution, Calles considered the comments a broadside attack on the revolution in general and his government in particular: "No road is more wrong than the one that you are following. I want you to understand, once and for all, that not even the agitation that you try to provoke . . . nor any other step that you take . . . will be capable of changing the firm intention of the Federal Government to ensure that what the Supreme Law of the Republic commands is strictly enforced."[34]

Despite the datedness of Mora's comments, Calles had found the pretext he had sought for so long. He ordered Adalberto Tejada, the government's chief lawyer, to try Mora in Mexico City on charges of sedition (the court found Mora innocent). More important than the Mora trial, Calles began his harsh enforcement of the anticlerical provisions of the Constitution of 1917. On July 2, 1926, he passed his new penal code, fully implementing the constitution, and providing for fines and punishments. With the passage of this code, which deported foreign-born priests, nationalized all Church property, and closed all religious schools, convents, and monasteries, American

Catholics dove headfirst into the melee. The Coolidge administration suffered the slings and arrows of Catholics at all levels—national organizations such as the Knights of Columbus and the National Councils of Catholic Men and Women, individual Catholic leaders such as influential bishops and archbishops,[35] the National Catholic Welfare Conference, and strong local responses from lay Catholics—all seeking action on behalf of the Mexican Catholics. Some Catholics demanded that the United States government sever diplomatic relations with Mexico, while others favored a lifting of the bans on the export of arms and ammunition to Mexico. William Howard Taft first imposed this arms embargo on March 4, 1912, restricting the sale of guns to the government forces during the violent "military" phase of the revolution.

In the days and weeks following Calles's order that the anticlerical provisions of the constitution be enforced, Catholic rebels rose in rebellion throughout the western and northern states of Mexico. These were uncoordinated and sporadic rebellions, united only by their battle cry of "¡Viva Cristo Rey!" (hence their common nickname, the Cristeros), their opposition to Calles, and their dedication to the Catholic Church.[36] In September 1926, the Liga began working to organize the rebels into a single force, and began to seek financial aid from the Catholics in the United States. In this effort they failed dismally, principally because the Vatican counseled peace and clearly condemned warfare (although individual Mexican and American prelates enthusiastically endorsed the rebellion).

At the same time the Cristeros were rising to combat the Mexican federal forces, the Mexican hierarchy loudly denounced Calles's crackdown. After they received Vatican approval, the Mexican prelates called on all priests and bishops to close their churches on July 31, 1926. This clerical strike, which the Mexican hierarchy hoped would apply sufficient pressure on the government to force the abolition of the anti-religious laws, was a gross misjudgment on the part of the Church leaders. Contrary to popular perception, the clerical strike was far from uniformly followed. Some dioceses, such as Jalisco, enforced it strictly, while others, such as Chihuahua, largely ignored it. The areas in which the strike was most faithfully enforced—Colima, Guanjuato, Guerrero, Jalisco, Michoacan, and Nayarit—correspond with the heart of the Cristero Rebellion.[37] The Mexican Church languished for three years, until a settlement brought temporary peace between the Church and the Mexican government. This *modus vivendi* of 1929 was an important milestone in the involvement of American Catholics in the Mexican crisis, because two of its most important actors were American priests, Fathers John J. Burke, CSP, and Edmund A. Walsh, SJ.

Following this settlement, peace reigned in Mexico between the Church and the state, at least for a couple years. In mid-1931, the governor of Veracruz decided to renew the revolution and again enforced the constitutional provision empowering him to limit the number of priests who could carry on church services in his state. Shortly thereafter, the Mexican Congress adopted a similar measure for the Federal District, thereby beginning the second phase of the persecution. Pope Pius XI responded to the measures with an encyclical letter, *Acerba Animi,* dated September 29, 1932, in which he expressed his sadness that the *modus vivendi* was truly dead because the Mexican government refused to live up to its word. From the pope's perspective, the reasonable application of the laws that was promised in 1929 turned out to be no less than an increase in the persecution.[38] Mexican President Abelardo Rodríguez interpreted the encyclical as a direct challenge, and once again forced the hierarchy into exile.[39]

Conditions facing Catholics in Mexico did not improve until President Lázaro Cárdenas ousted Calles in a bid to wrest control over the Mexican government away from the older strongman by purging the cabinet on June 19, 1935. Cárdenas announced at that time that the enforcement of the anticlerical laws would end. He clearly sought to turn the revolutionary tide in a new direction when he claimed in a February 16, 1936, speech that it was the government's duty to do "all that may be necessary to carry out the program of the Revolution, the fundamental aspects of which are social and economic in character. . . . It is no concern of the Government to undertake anti-religious campaigns. . . . All our attention must be concentrated upon the great cause of social reform."[40] Instead of continuing the anticlerical agenda, Cárdenas decided that it was more important to unify the Mexican people to face the challenges presented by the global depression of the mid-1930s. As proof that the anticlerical phase of the revolution had passed, Cárdenas's successor, Miguel Avila Camacho, announced during his campaign his position on the persecution: "*Yo soy un católico* (I am a Catholic)," which the press widely misquoted as "*Yo soy creyente* (I am a believer)."[41] Regardless of his exact words, the result was the same—Catholics could once again feel free to express their Catholicity.

The American Catholic attempt to influence United States–Mexican relations in the midst of the persecution of the 1920s and 1930s was a broad-based effort. Not only were the most important prelates in the American hierarchy involved, but the movement also depended upon the grassroots labors of Catholic lay men and women working at the parish level. This is not to say that the effort was unified at all levels or during all phases. Most of the time, certain individual Catholics who either favored the United States government's policy or simply opposed the activism of the Church worked at cross-purposes with their fellow Catholics. Moreover, as is true in most situations, people's attitudes changed from one issue to the next.

In the chapters that follow, this study breaks down the activities of interested Catholics on a number of levels and attempts to chart those changes in attitudes in response to changing conditions in Mexico. Because of the complexity of the activities and attitudes of the different actors in this drama, the following chapters concentrate on different elements of the American Catholics who were involved in the Mexican crisis. Each chapter analyzes their involvement in the effort to influence United States–Mexican relations essentially from their first involvement to the end of their active interest in the Mexican persecution. As a result of this organizational scheme, various elements of this story, such as the Borah resolution of 1935, occur in several chapters, wherein different facets of those subjects come into sharper focus.

Following this introduction, chapter 2 considers the work of the American hierarchy as a whole in its struggle to chart a course for the Church in the United States. The efforts of the hierarchy ranged from prayer to politics, and it was forced to operate within the narrow bounds afforded it by conflicting opinions among the prelates. Chapter 3 then turns from consideration of the hierarchy as a whole to an examination of the activities of a few individual prelates, from the venerable Archbishop of Baltimore James Cardinal Gibbons, the acknowledged head of the hierarchy, and his controversial successor, Michael Cardinal Curley, to Curley's close associate in the hierarchy, the outspoken Francis C. Kelley (Tulsa/Oklahoma City). William Henry Cardinal O'Connell of Boston, and Arthur Drossaerts of San Antonio round out this look at individual prelates.

The work of John J. Burke, CSP, general secretary of the National Catholic Welfare Conference, who exercised considerable influence throughout the period under examination, is the subject of chapter 4. Burke's position and personal charisma made him indispensable in the American Catholic Church's consideration of the Mexican crisis. Not only did he work to foment an educated public opinion among Catholics, but also he employed his talents as a diplomat while dealing with the president of Mexico in the 1920s and as an advisor to Franklin Roosevelt in the 1930s.

Chapter 5 moves from the work of this one well-known priest to the efforts of a variety of lesser-known clerics. Some of these priests used their

positions as editors of Catholic journals to aid in the Catholic effort to address the persecution in Mexico, such as Wilfrid Parsons, SJ, of *America*. One
of the most radical Catholics in relation to the Mexican Revolution was a Jesuit writer, Michael Kenny. He not only advocated activism, but also worked to
support actual rebellion against the Mexican government. Edmund A. Walsh,
SJ, founder of the Georgetown University School of Foreign Service, made use
of his skills as a negotiator to help bring about the settlement between the
Mexican Church and the Mexican government in 1929. This chapter ends with
a look at two officers of the National Catholic Welfare Conference, John A.
Ryan and James H. Ryan. John A. Ryan, director of the National Catholic Welfare Conference's Social Action Department, was one of the leading liberals in
the 1920s and 1930s. His associate, James H. Ryan, assisted Burke and succeeded him as general secretary of the NCWC. Both Ryans took on the liberal
establishment in the American press head-on.

From the examination of the activities of the hierarchy and clergy, this
study then turns to a consideration of the work of lay men and women. Chapter 6 examines the Knights of Columbus, the single largest nationally organized
association of lay Catholics, which succeeded in mobilizing its formidable
membership to foment public protest of the American policy toward the Mexican revolutionary movement. From their offices in New Haven, Connecticut,
the supreme knights in this period, James Flaherty and his successor, Martin
Carmody, orchestrated the work of the Knights in communities throughout
the nation. This was an activist group which was unafraid to make demands,
and they demanded a lot, from the lifting of the arms embargo and a formal
protest from the White House, to the recall of Ambassador Josephus Daniels
and the severance of United States diplomatic relations with what they maintained was a pagan and communistic lair of snakes south of the Rio Grande.

Other laymen, working as individuals and in more organized efforts,
doing whatever they could to aid their Mexican brothers and sisters, are
examined in chapter 7. One key layman, William Montavon, the chief legal
counsel for the National Catholic Welfare Conference, even went so far as to
travel to Mexico twice to secure peace between the Church and state—once
with Burke, and again on his own. He worked tirelessly, through his voluminous writing and hectic speaking schedule, to make the Mexican crisis an
American concern and thus to inflame a strong public opinion. Other Catholics worked from positions somewhat closer to the locus of power in the
United States. Representatives John Boylan (New York), James Gallivan (Massachusetts), and Clare Gerald Fenerty (Pennsylvania), and Senator David I.
Walsh (Massachusetts) proved to be the most active congressional Catholics

during the 1920s and 1930s. They not only used their forum to publicize the harshness of the persecution suffered upon the Mexican Catholics, but they made more concrete contributions, chiefly an interdenominational congressional petition that led Franklin Roosevelt to publicly address the American dedication to the ideal of religious liberty.

On a larger scale, lay men and women, working through a number of organizations, dedicated themselves to the resolution of the Mexican crisis. Some of these organizations garnered official Catholic Church support, such as the National Councils of Catholic Men and Women, the Holy Name Society, and the National Committee for the Protection of Religious Rights in Mexico. Others, such as the more radical Friends of Catholic Mexico, flirted with economic warfare against the Mexican government, beyond the sanction of the Church.

The Church and the religious crisis was certainly not the only Mexican diplomatic conundrum facing the United States government in the 1920s and 1930s. Scholars frequently use the oil crisis under Article 27 of the Constitution of 1917 as an exemplar of private interest group involvement in foreign relations. The concluding chapter of this study draws some key comparisons between the church-state crisis and the conflict over oil concessions in an effort to provide a broader context for the work of activist Catholics on behalf of their Catholic brothers and sisters in Mexico.

This is a story of raw emotion and calculated strategy because it deals with something that touched the core of the people involved—their faith and the free practice of their religion. At first glance, the efforts of all of these people and organizations appear to have been for naught and to have failed dismally if the standard to which they were compared is no more than their stated goals. If, on the other hand, the scope of possible outcomes is widened and a bigger picture comes into view, these activist Catholics and their unnamed and faceless fellow Catholics throughout the United States accomplished a considerable amount. They helped create an atmosphere within which the American government shifted its fundamental stance to one which may be characterized as an active interest in the Mexican situation. It was through this active interest that the American people were able to make clear to the Mexican government, through diplomatic channels, the fact that the United States was committed to the maintenance of the right of all people to worship freely, "not only in the United States but also in all other nations."[42]

chapter 2

THE EFFORTS OF THE AMERICAN
CATHOLIC HIERARCHY AS A WHOLE

THE ROMAN CATHOLIC HIERARCHY OF THE UNITED STATES PLAYED A monumental role in the effort of American Catholics to influence their government's policy toward Mexico in the 1920s and 1930s. The prelates exercised, individually, a multitude of different strategies to exert this influence, from appeals for simple prayer to more mundane attempts to guide Catholic voting patterns. This variety of responses is an indication of the different personalities and political affinities of the bishops and archbishops. Clearly the American hierarchy was analogous of the wider Catholic Church in the United States: both were characterized by a multiplicity of opinions and attitudes.

The hierarchy found itself divided over its role in responding to the challenge presented to the Church in Mexico. Polar examples of opinion might be found in the most vocal opponent of American policy toward Mexico, Archbishop Michael J. Curley of Baltimore, and an archbishop widely viewed as one of Franklin Roosevelt's most loyal backers, George Cardinal Mundelein, archbishop of Chicago. This division in the ranks of the hierarchy should not be interpreted as a difference of opinion over the conditions in Mexico—the hierarchy was united in its condemnation of the persecution. The division becomes evident only when one examines the various ways the prelates sought to remedy that abysmal situation. In this and the following chapter, this study will explore the activities of the Catholic hierarchy as a whole and the National Catholic Welfare Conference, and then those of individual prelates who shone above the rest of their fellow churchmen in trying to influence United States policy toward Mexico.

The assembled bishops' activities concerning the Mexican persecution center on their pastoral letter of 1926 and two other major statements, in 1926 and 1934. In 1926, the hierarchy reacted to the intensification of the anticlerical schemes of President Plutarco Elías Calles with a pastoral letter and a formal enunciation of support for Mexico's Catholics. The hierarchy built on this foundation of activism with a formal statement in 1934, arising out of the appointment of Josephus Daniels as ambassador to Mexico.

The first of these major statements came in September 1926, after Calles instituted his "*Ley Calles,*" which implemented the anticlerical provisions of the Constitution of 1917. The American hierarchy responded to this open threat to the Church with a letter of sympathy and support for their coreligionists in Mexico. The prelates acknowledged that tough times lay ahead for the Church in Mexico, but told the Mexican Catholics to take comfort in the fact that Catholics in the United States—clergy and laymen both— remained fully committed to their struggle for religious liberty, pledging even to stand with the Church in Mexico "to the end."[1]

As the crisis in Mexico deepened with the initiation of armed rebellion in the western states under the Cristero banner, the bishops decided a more active and forceful stance was necessary. The hierarchy announced plans for a pastoral letter on the Mexican situation, but made it clear that the letter would seek not to mold United States–Mexican relations, but would be limited to a statement of constitutional and international law relevant to the controversy in Mexico.[2] A committee of five bishops was organized to draft the pastoral; Bishop Francis C. Kelley of Oklahoma City/Tulsa, as the prelate most thoroughly informed on the Mexican crisis, took up the task of writing the bulk of the letter. At the hierarchy's annual meeting in early December 1926, the prelates promulgated their "Pastoral Letter on Mexico."[3]

The pastoral letter expressed the concerns of the bishops not only as Catholics, but also as citizens steeped in devotion to American institutions.[4] This pastoral letter was composed of two main sections. The first compared the United States and Mexican constitutions and the provisions for basic human rights and religious freedom therein. This comparison resulted in the unsurprising verdict that "no American can accept the Mexican theory of government as being in accord with fundamental justice without repudiating his own traditions and ideals."[5] The second section is a compendium of the contributions the Catholic Church had made to Mexico throughout its history.

The elements of the pastoral that received the most attention were the hierarchy's clear condemnation of the armed rebellion in to Mexico and its denial of trying to become involved in politics. The prelates stated that "Christian principles forbid the Church founded by the Prince of Peace to take up the sword or rely upon such carnal weapons as the inflamed passions of man would select."[6] Both those individuals who sought to aid the Cristeros and those who accused the Church of doing so conveniently overlooked this section.

In keeping with their pledge of September that the pastoral would not try to dictate United States government policy, the bishops claimed that

> What, therefore, we have written is no call on the faithful here or elsewhere to purely human action. It is no interposition of our influence either as Bishops or as citizens to reach those who possess political power anywhere on earth, and least of all in our own country, to the end that they should intervene with armed force in the internal affairs of Mexico for the protection of the Church. Our duty is done when, by telling the story, defending the truth and emphasizing the principles, we sound a warning to Christian civilization that its foundations are again being attacked and undermined. For the rest, God will bring His will to pass in His own good time and in His own good way. Mexico will be saved for her mission whatever it may be.[7]

The December 1926 pastoral, which the *New York World* considered "sober and far sighted counsel" and "an eloquent statement of the church's side of a quarrel which has run on in Mexico for sixty years,"[8] proved extremely useful. The bishops returned to the statement above to belie claims that the Church sought active intervention into the Mexican crisis.

The assembled hierarchy, in their annual meeting of November 14 and 15, 1934, issued their third major statement concerning Mexico. They intended this statement, on "Anti-Christian Tyranny in Mexico,"[9] as a protest against the intensified persecutions of the early 1930s. The prelates outlined the various ways tyranny was manifested in the lives of Mexicans throughout their country. As far as the bishops' interest in the United States was concerned, the statement repeated many of the themes from the 1926 pastoral verbatim. Once again, the prelates spoke not only as Catholics, but as Americans as well. Also, the hierarchy repeated its earlier claim that it was refraining from seeking armed intervention. This, however, is where the similarities end.

Collectively, the bishops had reached a point by late 1934 where a more active approach was both necessary and justified. They sought action from the American public, in the form of popular pressure on Washington to see that religious liberty was restored in Mexico, but couched the request in a general appeal for basic principles—"the fundamental rights of liberty of conscience, freedom of religious worship, freedom of education, freedom of the press, and freedom of assembly and petition"—that rightly ought to be the standard to which the American government might expect the Mexicans to rise. The bishops believed that they were right in calling for this popular pressure because if people really knew what was taking place in Mexico, it would be clear that they were "pleading not only the cause of the Catholic Church, but the cause of human freedom and human liberty for all the nations of the world."[10]

Perhaps the most interesting element of the hierarchy's 1934 statement was its condemnation of unnamed, yet absolutely unambiguous, individuals who had expressed support for the Mexican government. The United States ambassador to Mexico, Josephus Daniels, had seriously blundered, in the eyes of the United States Catholics, when he first occupied the American embassy and presented his credentials to President Abelardo Rodriguez. Daniels praised his new host for the Mexican people's "marked advance in social reform, in public education . . . and in all measures which promote the well-being of your nationals."[11] Further, the ambassador committed a grave error, from American Catholics' perspective, in a speech he delivered on July 26, 1934, before Professor Hubert Herring's American Seminar at the American embassy. In an effort to hold up the American system of free public education as an ideal toward which Mexico was striving, Daniels remarked that the Mexican government recognized that free public education was the best way to form a free people:

> General Calles sees, as Jefferson saw, that no people can be both free and ignorant. Therefore, he and President Rodriguez, President-elect Cárdenas and all forward looking leaders . . . recognize that general Calles issued a challenge that goes to the very root of the settlement of all problems of tomorrow when he said: "We must enter and take possession of the mind of childhood, the mind of youth." That fortress taken, the next generation will see a Mexico that fulfills the dream of Hidalgo, Juarez, Madero and other patriots who loved their country.[12]

Daniels was unaware of the anticlerical nature of Calles's speech when he quoted the former Mexican president. Indeed, he assured his superiors in Washington that the paper that quoted Calles's speech, from which Daniels drew the quote, did not include the entire text of the speech. He claimed that he had never seen the entire speech—and was thus unaware of the anticlerical context within which Calles had delivered it—until he saw the speech in its entirety printed in the *Baltimore Catholic Review*'s call for his recall or resignation.[13] However, not only had Daniels praised Calles, but also Benito Juarez, president during one of the most strident anticlerical eras in the nineteenth century.

While the public-relations firestorm erupted in the United States, Daniels began building a documentary defense of his remarks. Daniels had received a note from the Honorable Ernest Gruening, who was present at Daniels's address: "I had the good fortune and pleasure to be present on this occasion, and if you should desire it, (should the need arise) I should be most happy to testify that nothing seemed more remote from the purport and obvious purpose of that address than the intent with which you were charged."[14] This sort of defense, however, meant little to Catholics who perceived the address as a threat.

Although Daniels had spoken to Americans, and his speech represented values supporting public education in the United States, American Catholics saw this was a blow to Mexican Catholic education from which they feared it would never recover.[15] That the hierarchy made their 1934 statement shortly after the firestorm erupted over Daniels's ill-chosen comments leaves little to the imagination as to whom the bishops intended as the target of their invective. Their interpretation of the impact of Daniels's words is clear in this passage:

> No man's voice should sound an uncertain note. We cannot but deplore the expressions unwittingly offered, at times, of sympathy with and support of governments and policies which are absolutely at variance with our own American principles. They give color to the boast of the supporters of tyrannical policies, that the influence of our American government is favorable to such policies. We do not believe, for a moment, that it is. It could not be.[16]

That the hierarchy's 1934 statement endorsed universal principles is evident in the reception it received in the American press. A number of Protestant and Jewish journals applauded the statement, including *The Christian*

Century, The Living World, the *Christian Science Monitor,* and *American Hebrew.* In fact, the editor of *The Christian Century* went so far as to assert that "the Bishops' statement might well be reprinted in these columns . . . if space permitted."[17]

As a postscript to these three major statements, the assembled hierarchy in Washington made one more effort to foster religious toleration in Mexico. During their annual meeting, November 18–20, 1935, the prelates established the Catholic Bishops' Commission, Inc., for Mexican Relief. The purpose of this commission was to provide financial relief for exiles in the United States; education for Mexican seminarians; support for Catholic schools, colleges, and hospitals; and to seek help for the Mexican people in their struggle for freedom of conscience and religious liberty.[18]

The leaders of this commission created a significant amount of controversy. The chairman of the commission was Archbishop Curley; Archbishop Arthur J. Drossaerts of San Antonio served as his assistant, and Bishop Kelley as secretary treasurer. That Curley and Kelley were vehemently anti-Roosevelt was widely known. To a large degree, it was only to the credit of Michael Francis Doyle, legal counsel for the commission, and a loyal friend of Franklin D. Roosevelt, that the commission did not bog down in discussion of the Roosevelt policy toward Mexico.[19] Although the Vatican secretary of state approved the work of the commission, the new apostolic delegate to the United States, Archbishop Amleto Giovanni Cicognani, opposed the composition of the commission. In a private letter to Fr. John J. Burke, Cicognani wrote of Curley and Kelley that "the former was not honest; the latter had no brains."[20] Eventually, the National Catholic Welfare Conference (NCWC) Administrative Committee came to believe that Curley and Kelley had exceeded their responsibility by forging ahead with fund-raising instead of only preparing a plan for relief. The corporation was therefore dissolved in February 1936, to be re-formed weeks later, in March, with the sole purpose of establishing a seminary for the training of Mexican priests. By early 1937, Mexican seminarians were deep in study at Montezuma Seminary, a thousand-acre site outside of Las Vegas, New Mexico, thanks chiefly to the efforts of this commission.

The National Catholic Welfare Conference

The ruling against Curley and Kelley by the NCWC Administrative Committee demonstrated its authority among the American hierarchy. The NCWC, as the central voice through which the prelates could express their attitudes and concerns, was a powerful tool for the American hierarchy. This organization of bishops was a relatively new institution, founded in 1919 through the efforts of Fr. John J. Burke and others.[21]

During the early days of World War I, a number of influential Catholics became concerned that the Protestants' centrally organized Federal Council of Churches of Christ in America was drowning the Catholic voice out. The principal individuals who grew increasingly concerned about this issue included both priests and laymen. Fr. Lewis O'Hern, CSP, director of the Catholic Army and Navy Chaplains' Bureau; Fr. Burke, editor of *The Catholic World*; Fr. William Kerby, sociology professor at Catholic University of America; and Charles P. Neill, a layman on the War Department's Commission on Training Camp Activities and former United States commissioner of labor, met to express their mutual concerns about the lack of a central organization to oversee the American Catholic response to the war.[22] Together, the four conceived of a National Catholic War Council, and took the idea to Archbishop James Cardinal Gibbons, the recognized head of the American hierarchy.[23]

The seed of the idea for the War Council found fertile soil in Gibbons. He recognized the need for a national level of organization for the Catholic Church. According to Gibbons, "the Catholic Church in America, partly through defective organization, [was] not exerting the influence which it ought to exert in proportion to [Catholic] numbers and the individual prominence" of many Catholics. Although the Church was well organized on the local level, it lacked a clearly articulated Catholic voice, which was absolutely necessary in responding to the war crisis.[24] Under Gibbons's signature, Burke called a meeting of the bishops of the United States to meet at the Catholic University of America in Washington, D.C., in August 1917.

Burke and Gibbons were most surprised by the level of enthusiasm for the plan. More than one hundred delegates from sixty-eight dioceses and Catholic societies voted to establish the National Catholic War Council, composed of priests and laymen working under a bishops' administrative committee, with Bishop Peter J. Muldoon of Rockford, Illinois, as the first chairman of the Administrative Committee. The War Council facilitated American Catholic participation in war-bond drives and in sending aid to chaplains overseas.

The success of the War Council in expressing Catholic patriotism and support for Wilson's war effort inspired chairman Bishop Muldoon to call for a more permanent organization to lead the Church following the end of the war. He framed his reasons for establishing a more permanent organization in political terms: "We do not hesitate to say that some representative body could accomplish untold good by directing editors, teachers, and even the clergy, on general matters pertaining to the welfare of the Church. There is an incessant demand for instruction on 'how to act' on many bills that are now before the legislatures of the country."[25]

Burke and others also recognized that the War Council was involved in a number of concerns at war's end. Since the hierarchy was neither willing nor able to take on the responsibility of running the community centers and social work schools founded by the War Council's Women's Committee, a new organization was needed.

February 20, 1919, when seventy prelates met in Washington to celebrate Cardinal Gibbons's golden episcopal jubilee (commemorating fifty years as a bishop), was a perfect opportunity for the establishment of such an organization. A letter of congratulations from Pope Benedict XV provided the stimulus. In his letter, he expressed his appreciation of the War Council work and addressed the peacetime needs that could be met by a permanent national Catholic council. Archbishop John T. McNicholas of Cincinnati considered the celebration as "really the birthday of the National Catholic Welfare Council."[26]

On September 24, 1919, 92 of America's 101 prelates met at Catholic University and founded the National Catholic Welfare Council.[27] Cardinal Gibbons presided over the meeting, and outlined the purpose of the council. It would provide "a comprehensive and efficient organization of the episcopal body" in order "to further the religious, educational and social well being of the Catholic Church in the United States."[28] The assembled bishops chose Archbishop Edward Hanna of San Francisco to serve as the first chairman of the Administrative Committee, and elected Burke to serve as general secretary.[29]

The NCWC was designed along strictly Americanist lines by emphasizing voluntary action; no bishops, archbishops, priests, or laypersons were required to participate. Moreover, the council's ruling or votes carried no binding authority. President Warren Harding and Congress favored the establishment of the NCWC so the administration could more accurately gauge Catholic sentiment. According to Burke's biographer, John B. Sheerin, Congress even considered the National Catholic Welfare Council as "authoritative."[30]

This perception about the authoritative nature of the NCWC made some bishops anxious. They feared that the council's authority would empower it to interfere with their jurisdiction over their own dioceses. Driven by this fear, they appealed to Rome, and their anxiety fell upon sympathetic ears in the Curia (the pope's inner circle of advisors), including Gaetano Cardinal De Lai, the secretary of the Constitorial Congregation. De Lai's incredible influence is clear in his ability to convince Pope Benedict XV, who formerly saw a great future for the NCWC, to withdraw his support. Benedict had drafted a decree calling for the dissolution of the NCWC but died before he had a chance to sign it. His successor, Pope Pius XI, considered the decree "unfinished business" and signed it on February 25, 1922. The shocked NCWC Administrative Committee sent Bishop Joseph Schrembs of Cleveland to Rome to argue its case. By June 23, Schrembs had proved his case, and a new decree drafted July 2, 1922, instituted a permanent National Catholic Welfare Council. In 1922, the name changed to the National Catholic Welfare Conference because of the technical definition of the term "council" under Canon Law.[31] The NCWC so convinced Rome of its worth that the Vatican later held it up as a model for organization of hierarchies from other countries.

The NCWC's work dealing with the persecution in Mexico did not begin in earnest until after Obregón's expulsion of Apostolic Delegate Ernesto Filippi in 1923. The Administrative Committee recognized that in order to respond most effectively to the conditions in Mexico, it needed additional information on the crisis, and therefore planned to have a reputable individual dig deeper to discover the truth about the persecution. The Administrative Committee sent Charles Phillips, a noted Notre Dame professor and occasional essayist in Catholic journals, to Mexico in 1925 to investigate the attitudes of the Mexican hierarchy. The result of this investigation was that while the Mexican bishops wanted the facts of the conditions in Mexico to be made known, they did not want the American Church to become involved. They believed that any public protest by American Catholics would accomplish little other than making life more difficult by sparking a new crackdown on the Mexican Church.

Phillips did not personally believe that American Catholics needed to remain outside the controversy. In a speech in San Francisco on December 24, 1927, he claimed that the United States stood "before the civilized world as the sponsors of democracy on the American continents. More than that, . . . our own democratic safety, the preservation of our own ideals of human liberty, in our own country, depends in great measure on the preservation of those ideals in the whole western world." Phillips maintained that Americans had to educate themselves as to the truth about the Mexican problem. Failing this, we shall weaken our own morale, grow indifferent to the ideals of political freedom . . . and in the end become, like the unhappy Mexican people themselves, victims of lawlessness and slaves of a gun-running minority. If it means nothing to us today that human liberty is destroyed in Mexico, tomorrow it will mean nothing to us that human liberty will disappear from the face of our own land. . . . Shall we Americans remain ignorant and indifferent about Mexico? Not if we know our own good."[32]

By the spring of 1926, however, conditions for the Church in Mexico had begun a precipitous decline. In June, Archbishop George Caruana, an American citizen and apostolic delegate to Mexico, had been expelled under extremely questionable pretenses. Later in June, Calles authorized increased persecution against the Catholic Church, including narrow restrictions on qualifications for the clergy and extremely limited numbers of priests. Armed resistance under the Cristero banner loomed in several states. Archbishop José Mora y del Río of Mexico City sought a more active American protest.[33] The NCWC organized a full agenda of activities, including a condemnatory public statement against the Calles regime; public protest meetings under the auspices of the lay arms of the conference, the National Councils of Catholic Men and Women (NCCM and NCCW, respectively); a program of education to support those meetings; and a letter of protest to President Coolidge.[34]

In the public statement, the NCWC sought to accomplish two goals: to make a statement about Mexico's responsibilities, and to issue a call to action by American Catholics. The NCWC maintained that the diplomatic recognition of the new Mexican government under Calles was based on international conditions established in 1915. These conditions, "which underlie all negotiations between civilized governments" stood as "premises to the agreements which were later on entered into by both governments." The Administrative Committee felt not only justified, but obliged to insist that the United States government demand that the original conditions for recognition be met, that is, the conditions spelled out in the Arredondo Pledge whereby the Carranza government promised to guarantee religious liberty to all in Mexico.[35] It is important to note that this protest was based primarily on an erroneous interpretation of the negotiations preceding the Wilson administration's recognition of the Carranza government. The bishops interpreted informal discussions on religious freedom in Mexico as requisite for continued recognition. The NCWC also used the statement to carry out the second of its goals.

The Administrative Committee called on Catholics to meet together and with non-Catholics to protest, so that the United States government would effectively use its influence in the hemisphere to guarantee the Mexican people's religious and educational liberties.[36] The committee sought to mobilize the NCCM and the NCCW to sponsor these protest meetings and to initiate grassroots protests against the policies of the Mexican government and also, by extension, of American policies that supported that government. Education was the foundation of the planned protests. The committee wanted the NCCM and the NCCW to be conduits through which this education—among Catholics and non-Catholics alike—could take place.[37] In August 1926, the Administrative Committee issued the following call to the local chapters of the NCCM and the NCCW for massive organization against the persecution in Mexico:

> To help secure the rights of religious worship for our fellow Catholics in Mexico is a most urgent duty of the Catholics in the United States. The persecution of the Church by the present Mexican Government is being intensified. Immediate and emphatic action is demanded.
>
> We write to your council and the members of your council to ask them to send by telegram or by letter a protest against the expulsion from Mexico by the Mexican Government of the present Apostolic Delegate to Mexico, Archbishop Caruana. . . .
>
> We will soon issue a handbook that will be of information to all and of help particularly to public speakers on the Mexican situation. But kindly take immediate action in answer to our request: send your protest and secure the protest of others, direct to the President of the United States, to the Secretary of State, to your Congressmen and to your Senators. We will appreciate word of what action you take.[38]

Clearly, the Administrative Committee viewed a broad-based protest as crucial to evoke any changes in the situation in Mexico. To expand the base even beyond the NCWC's organizations, the NCWC Administrative Committee endeavored to form a national committee of laypersons dedicated to fomenting a moral public opinion against which Calles simply could not prevail.[39] The result of these efforts was the National Committee for the Protection of Religious Rights in Mexico (NCPRRM), chaired by prominent Catholic Judge Morgan J. O'Brien. Burke solicited participation in the committee's work by sending form letters to prominent Catholics throughout the United States seeking members. Besides the publishing and distribution of pamphlets explaining the situation in Mexico, the committee planned and promoted public meetings throughout the nation where the persecution would be discussed by well-informed panels.[40]

The NCWC Administrative Committee carried out the final element of their agenda with an April 1926 letter of protest to President Coolidge. In the letter, the NCWC requested clarification of the United States' position on religious freedom in Mexico. A key feature of the letter was the insistence that through the aforementioned Arredondo Pledge, the Carranza government "promised in most formal and solemn terms to respect scrupulously the religious rights of every citizen of Mexico."[41] Prior to publishing the letter, or presenting it directly to Coolidge, the Administrative Committee delegated Burke to submit the letter to Kellogg for his consideration. The secretary of state lodged a strenuous request that the bishops revise the letter to remove the most offensive passages, which Kellogg believed would only anger the Mexican government. One of the most notable errors, from Kellogg's perspective, was the observation that Wilson had granted recognition only after receiving the assurance of Carranza's representative that religious freedom would be guaranteed in Mexico. Kellogg noted that the original pledge assured religious freedom under the Constitution of 1857, then in force.[42] Moreover, any allusion to future law changes (referring here to the anticlerical provisions of the Constitution of 1917) could not possibly be construed as a pre-recognition promise from an as yet unrecognized, unofficial government.[43]

The revised letter, while couched in more calm terms, was still a strong protest. The committee wrapped the hammer in velvet cloth, however, by noting that the prelates were aware of the limits of diplomacy and the degree of influence one government can exercise over another. Moreover, the bishops acknowledged past work by the United States government "to advance American principles whenever suitable opportunity presented itself."[44] The NCWC Administrative Committee took Kellogg's advice to heart, as the revised version omitted any reference to the Carranza government's pledge to respect Mexican citizens' religious rights.[45] Burke and Chairman Hanna considered the letter vital, because American Catholics depended upon the hierarchy as their advocates. Burke asserted, therefore, that "the bishops could not leave the Catholic body with the impression that nothing could be done by them."[46]

Undersecretary of State Franklin Mott Gunther, head of Mexican affairs in the State Department, still had specific problems with the revised letter. He believed it would only anger the Mexican government, which would not help the Mexican Catholics.[47] Gunther, however, refrained from telling the NCWC whether or not it could publish the letter, since publication was a matter "of policy which the Archbishops must decide for themselves."[48] Burke and the committee believed that the letter was too important to allow it to wither on the vine, so they published it in spite of Gunther's objections in a press release dated May 18, 1926.[49]

One of the reasons the Administrative Committee needed to appear to be taking action on the persecution in Mexico was to maintain a prominent position, vis-à-vis the Protestants, in the eyes of the American people. After recognizing the growing influence of Protestant denominations in Mexico, American Consul Alexander W. Weddell in Mexico City noted that these denominations had sought to capitalize on the Catholics' misery. Clearly, the Protestants in the United States could not resist the "temptation to fish in troubled waters." Local papers in Mexico City reported that the Commission of International Justice and Goodwill of the Federal Council of Churches had sent a letter of congratulations to Calles as he began his second year in office. The commission "believed that the friendship and mutual understanding of the two peoples and their intellectual relations [had] become perceptibly closer" since Calles entered office. Weddell editorialized that "the absurdity of this declaration must be obvious to any student of Mexican affairs in the recent past."[50] As the American hierarchy witnessed Protestants profiting from Catholic hardships, the prelates waxed poetic: "Let it not be said, to our reproach . . . that others have entered in to reap where Catholic hands have planted, perchance where Catholic blood had watered the soil."[51]

Efforts to cease the shedding of blood in Mexico, Catholic as well as Protestant, were priorities for the NCWC leadership. Following the assassination of President-elect Alvaro Obregón in July 1928, Chairman Hanna of the NCWC Administrative Committee condemned the murder as an outrage against the very basis of civilization. In an attempted countermeasure to Calles's initial claim that the assassination was the hatchling of a Mexican hierarchy plot, Hanna claimed that the act was one of "a demented fanatic, committed on his own responsibility and not as the outcome of a plot by any faction in Mexico."[52] Similarly, the NCWC moved to distance itself from the smoldering Cristero Rebellion. The NCWC called on all Catholics in the United States to refrain from providing either material or even moral support to the cause. To further erode support for the rebels, the NCWC's official organ, the *N.C.W.C. Bulletin,* reported that the Cristero leaders were complicit in the murder of at least one prominent priest.[53]

From 1929 until 1931, the NCWC remained quiet on the anticlerical issue, as the *modus vivendi* of 1929 brought relative peace to Mexico. As the persecution of Catholics in Mexico intensified in late 1931, however, the NCWC Administrative Committee began to mobilize public sentiment in the United States. Chairman Hanna justified the NCWC's effort to guide and encourage this sentiment by claiming that the values of the movement—freedom of religion and worship—were self-evident, and as American citizens, Catholics in the United States should see themselves as guarantors of these liberties for the people of Mexico.[54] To foment this public sentiment, the NCWC rededicated itself to education, through the 1934 publication of a pamphlet written by the NCWC's legal counsel, William F. Montavon, titled "The Church in Mexico Protests." In reviewing this pamphlet, the editor of the *N.C.W.C. Bulletin*'s successor, *Catholic Action,* drew close connections between the situation in Mexico and the United States: "Mexico is our nearest neighbor. Affecting as it does the national life of Mexico, the struggle of the Catholic people to defend their rights affects the national life in our own country. The importance of an enlightened public opinion in this matter is evident."[55] A second matter caught the attention of the NCWC in January 1935 that was intimately linked to its effort to guide public opinion and influence Roosevelt.

In mid-January 1935, several Catholic senators, including Senators Patrick A. McCarran (Nevada), David I. Walsh (Massachusetts), Joseph C. O'Mahoney (Wyoming), Augustine Lonergan (Connecticut), Francis T. Maloney (Connecticut), Richard L. Murphy (Iowa), and James C. Murray (Montana), met with a group of Knights of Columbus officials to plan coordinated action among the senators. By the end of January, these senators had convinced Senator William Borah of Idaho, the ranking minority member of the Senate Foreign Relations Committee, to sponsor a Senate resolution which authorized the Senate to embark on a full-scale investigation into the persecution in Mexico, and which included a provision condemning Mexico based on the anticipated results of that investigation.[56] Borah was a logical choice, since he had long been interested in the Mexican Catholics. In 1915, when a "friend in Boise" sought the senator's support for action on behalf of the Mexican Catholics, Borah responded that the Monroe Doctrine had claimed for the United States government the responsibility for fighting for basic liberties in the hemisphere.[57] As for his hopes for a resolution to the United

States–Mexican tensions, Borah claimed "God has made us neighbors, let justice make us friends."[58]

Borah explained his interest in the proposed 1935 investigation by claiming that the crisis was not confined to Mexico. Borah maintained that there was "ample evidence" to prove that Americans' rights were being abrogated in Mexico.[59] After he had introduced the legislation on January 31, the *New York Times* noted that Borah, formerly a staunch isolationist, had become "a screaming eagle of intervention in the domestic affairs of another nation."[60]

The Roosevelt administration's opposition to the resolution was immediate. Secretary of State Cordell Hull formulated four arguments against the measure. First, if the resolution were adopted as written, the resolution would initiate an investigation, but would also have the Senate render a decision before the investigation was completed. The Senate, according to the resolution, "deems it fitting and proper to protest the anti-religious campaign and practices of the present rulers of Mexico"; it "strongly condemns the cruelties and brutalities that have accompanied the campaign of the present Mexican Government . . ."; and the Senate would demand that the Mexican government "cease denying fundamental and inalienable rights to those of our nationals who may be resident in Mexico regardless of religious convictions."[61] Hull cautioned that such a heavy-handed and premature judgment of a friendly government would be highly damaging to the United States.[62] Hull's second objection to the bill was that it would force the United States Senate to determine United States foreign policy, without involving the president or the House, which caused a grave constitutional problem. Third, there was a general understanding in the State Department that sovereign states could control their own internal affairs. As much as the State Department wanted Americans to enjoy all their freedoms in other lands, Hull recognized that his department was powerless to force the issue. Finally, Hull provided several historical precedents to defend the State Department's position. For example, on October 22, 1845, Secretary of State James Buchanan said of the situation in Sardinia: "They have their system and we have ours; and it has ever been the policy of this Government not to interfere with the internal regulations of foreign government, more especially in questions of religion."[63] Moreover, there was no hard evidence any American citizen's home, person, or civil liberties had suffered at the hands of the Mexican government.[64] With all of these criticisms in mind, Hull expressed his opinion that while the United States government in no way condoned persecution or any limitation of religious liberty, there was a keen difference between policies this country would have liked the Mexican government to embrace and what the United States government could actually demand.[65]

Roosevelt had numerous supporters in his opposition to the Borah resolution. Protestant groups, including the Federal Council of Churches of Christ in America, the National Council of the Protestant Episcopal Church, and the Methodist Episcopal Church's foreign missions board, all condemned Catholic attempts to interfere.[66] Professor Edwin M. Borchard of the Yale School of Law, Borah's longtime international law advisor, counseled that, based on his recent trip to Mexico, the Church's concentration on the violation of human rights was terribly skewed, since what was in danger was not a true expression of religious freedom, but rather the Catholic Church's inability "to undermine the state by their hold upon ignorant Indians and others."[67]

Many Catholics were among those who opposed the Borah resolution. *El Hombre Libre,* a Mexican Catholic newspaper, rejected any plans for interference from the North: "we earnestly beg our sympathizers to leave us alone in our task of remedying the evils which assail us." Even Mexico's primate, Archbishop Díaz, claimed that any such United States intervention "would be very injurious to the interests of the Church in Mexico."[68] Burke, himself, agreed with Roosevelt and Hull that such a public pronouncement as the Borah resolution would only cause an insulted Mexico to step up the persecutions. In the end, Roosevelt's influence on Capitol Hill doomed the resolution, and it was never reported out of the Senate Foreign Relations Committee.

In response to the committee's consideration of the resolution, the Mexican government, through the embassy in Washington, issued a statement claiming that "there is no religious persecution in Mexico."[69] The statement outraged the NCWC. In his official capacity as general secretary of the NCWC, Burke responded to the Mexican embassy report with a terse press release. Burke asserted that "the statement issued yesterday by the Mexican Embassy at Washington is absolutely contrary to fact [and was] purposely worded to mislead the people of the United States and of other nations." Burke continued his statement by identifying the specific points of Mexican law by which the persecution was carried out. Burke conveyed the NCWC's concern that in Oaxaca, where more than 1 million Catholics resided, there was but one priest, and in Durango, there were two priests to minister to 1.2 million Catholics spread over forty thousand square miles. These restrictions fed the fears of the NCWC Administrative Committee that the Mexican government hoped to crush out the last vestiges of the Church in the lives of the Mexican people.[70] This fear spurred the NCWC on to further action. One element of that new activism was the insistence that Roosevelt make it crystal clear to the Mexican government that the American people supported the ideal of religious freedom for all as a basic, inalienable right.

In March 1935, Roosevelt decided privately to comply with the Administrative Committee's wishes that he make his position known to the Mexicans. On March 5, 1935, Secretary of State Hull met with Mexican Ambassador Francisco Castille Najera, and asked him to advise his government of Roosevelt's wishes that the Mexican government avoid taking courses of action that would certainly stir up protests in the United States.[71] Clearly, this gesture was far short of what the NCWC expected. In May 1935, during the NCWC Administrative Committee's annual meeting, the committee authorized a public protest of the president's refusal to stand up for universal principles. After once again insisting that the United States first recognized the leaders of Mexico who initiated the harshest persecutions, the Administrative Committee moved to an appeal for general principles and asked that

> our government be consistent and live up to its own set policy. We ask our government to defend before its own people the principles upon which our government is founded. The traditional policy of our government does not permit it to remain silent at the present moment and in the present crisis. We may not interfere with the internal affairs of another nation. But freedom of conscience, freedom of religious worship, freedom of education are principles on which even for the sake of the least gifted of humanity, our government was never silent.... Persecution does not cease to be persecution when invested with the dignity of constitutional or statute law.[72]

In a press release publicizing the statement, the Administrative Committee pledged to continue to insist that the government press the Mexican government on the issue of religious rights, but also to encourage American Catholics to keep up the pressure on their own government to assume "the role of the good neighbor, it use its good offices" to convince the Cárdenas government to "restore religious liberty to its fifteen million citizens."[73]

In May 1935, the Administrative Committee decided to send General Secretary Burke to meet with Roosevelt to try to evoke a more forceful statement. During his meeting with the president, Burke noted that he represented the NCWC, and that the committee had sent him to remind the president of his promise to issue a statement, which he had not yet done in spite of the worsening conditions in Mexico. Chief among the grievances of the NCWC was that

Mexico refused to accept the appointment of an apostolic delegate. Although Rome had appointed Ruiz acting apostolic delegate in May 1929 for the purposes of the upcoming *modus vivendi* negotiations, the Mexican government had never recognized him officially as apostolic delegate.[74] Moreover, the Vatican maintained that Fumasoni-Biondi retained official authority, that Ruiz was only acting apostolic delegate, and that it intended to name a different permanent delegate.[75] Roosevelt empathized with the frustration of the prelates over the conditions in Mexico, and finally agreed to meet informally and unofficially with Najera himself to discuss the possibility of Mexico accepting an apostolic delegate.[76]

Najera had already proven to be receptive to the attitudes of the American Catholics. He dutifully transmitted the results of the March meeting with Hull to his government. In April, Najera had met with Roosevelt's personal representative, Sumner Welles, and had informed him that the Mexican government was prepared to exhibit a degree of goodwill toward the Mexican Catholics. According to the ambassador, Archbishop Pascual Díaz of Mexico City should forward a petition of protest to the Mexican Supreme Court, identifying those Mexican states in which priests were refused the right to worship. Najera assured Welles that the Mexican Supreme Court would look favorably on this petition.[77]

In mid-May, Roosevelt kept his promise to Burke and the NCWC and met with the Mexican ambassador. The president informed Najera of his displeasure with the unrest that the persecution was stirring up in the United States. After Najera informed Roosevelt of the plan to have Díaz present his petition, Roosevelt asked for more. In particular, he sought the ambassador's reaction to the NCWC's appeal for an apostolic delegate. Welles, who sat in on the conference, asserted that Roosevelt had gone "as far as a President of the United States could go" in pursuit of an expression of sympathy for the Catholic Church in Mexico. Shortly after his meeting with the president, Najera left the United States to convey Roosevelt's attitudes to his own government. Roosevelt strengthened his hand by playing a second card. He consulted with Ambassador Daniels, who was in the United States for a short time. Roosevelt authorized Daniels to return to Mexico and privately discuss the earnest desire of the United States government for the security of religious freedom in Mexico.[78]

While both Najera and Daniels were in Mexico, Roosevelt began to consider the merits of making a public statement. The president's secretary, Marvin McIntyre, informed General Secretary Burke of Roosevelt's plans to consult with Martin Carmody, supreme knight of the Knights of Columbus, since the Knights had been vocal in their demands that such a public pronouncement be made. Burke, alarmed by the precedent this consultation would set, urged Roosevelt to refrain from this plan. He maintained that to confer with the Knights on issues which rightly were the concerns of the hierarchy would be taken as a serious snub, which the American prelates would not take lightly.[79]

During his time in Mexico, Ambassador Najera met with President Cárdenas's foreign minister, former President Portes Gil. Najera complied with Roosevelt's request and briefed Portes Gil on the attitude of the United States government and on the unrest among Catholics in the United States. Daniels met with the foreign minister shortly after Najera, and expressed Roosevelt's concern that Mexico's prestige in the United States was badly damaged by the continued persecution. Portes Gil assured Daniels that the Church issue was at the top of the Mexican president's agenda.[80]

With the Najera and Daniels meetings fresh in mind, Portes Gil met with Cárdenas. The political fallout of this meeting in Mexico was more widespread than anyone could have anticipated. The Cárdenas cabinet resigned, and the president purged the government of all of Calles's handpicked ideologues and installed his own supporters. After Najera returned to Washington, D.C., he confided with Welles that the Calles-Cárdenas break centered around the former president's continued vindictiveness against the Church. Najera reported to Welles that he had met with Calles, the former power behind the Mexican government, and that the ambassador recognized that Calles retained a visceral hatred of the Catholic Church and was dead-set against any permanent church-state settlement.[81] Of most importance to United States–Mexican relations, Cárdenas informed Najera that "the opinion of the United States should be for the Mexican Government the keystone of [Mexico's] both foreign and domestic policy."[82]

In an attempt to capitalize on this apparent victory for the Church in Mexico, the NCWC redoubled its effort to mold that public opinion through the publication of pamphlets. Late in 1935, the NCWC authorized the printing of two pamphlets, "Mexican Bishops' Pastoral" (in which the Mexican prelates claimed to seek only to advance Mexico's social condition, but that this required freedom of action denied them) and "Mexico—Text of Decree on Nationalization of Church Property—Appeal of the Bishops of Mexico," with a foreword by Burke. Burke called Cárdenas's August 31, 1935, decree reserving for the government the sole right to determine which Church properties could be used for worship a "mockery of law," not founded on principles of order, freedom, or justice, but rather no more than "arbitrary tyranny."[83]

It was with statements such as these, and the representations made to the United States government through letters, statements, and personal interviews, that the NCWC did what it could to aid the Catholics of Mexico in their time of need. The NCWC, at the beginning of its involvement with the Mexican persecution, was expected to have an influential role to play in the attitudes of the Catholics of America. The editor of the *N.C.W.C. Bulletin* believed that the organization was uniquely positioned to advocate for Roman Catholics in the United States. The NCWC had great potential. It could "strengthen the bonds of unity among our people in every section of the country" and "become the swift athlete in the cause of Christ's Church. It can be an air squadron, flying to meet any emergency, and all this as an auxiliary organization carrying on its work at the invitation and with the blessing of the bishop or bishops whom it serves."[84] The NCWC, however, proved largely incapable of meeting these high expectations. The opposition of powerful prelates, including Archbishop Michael Cardinal Curley and Archbishop William Cardinal O'Connell (both discussed in chapter 3), the voluntary nature of the organization, and its unwillingness to act until events forced it to, limited its effectiveness in uniting the Catholics. Its educational program did, however, succeed in placing the conditions that faced Mexican Catholics before the American Catholic public. Also, the organization's leaders proved ready and willing to undertake activities which could remedy the situation, such as its willingness to assign Burke to carry on the Church's side of the negotiations over the *modus vivendi* of 1929.

The larger accomplishments of the NCWC resulted from the organization's very existence. The Catholic hierarchy had formed a body that could stand toe-to-toe with the Protestant Federal Council of Churches of Christ. By securing a central, national voice for the Catholic Church in the United States, the establishment of the NCWC was of central importance for the future of the Catholic Church in the United States, and fundamentally compromised the relative power of Protestant denominations.[85] Pope Pius XI also recognized the value of the NCWC. In a 1927 letter to the hierarchy, Pius claimed that the NCWC was "not only useful but necessary" for the unification of Catholic activities in the United States.[86] As such, the NCWC presents arguably the best mechanism through which this private interest group could coordinate the efforts of its internal leadership to work to align public policy with its own agendas.

In the next chapter, this study moves from an examination of the collective hierarchy to a consideration of the work of individual prelates, and in doing so, will explore the incredible diversity of opinion in the American hierarchy vis-à-vis the Mexican situation.

c h a p t e r 3

LEADING VOICES AMONG
THE HIERARCHY

In DISCUSSING THE HIERARCHY AND THE NATIONAL CATHOLIC WELFARE
Conference (NCWC), this study has not yet endeavored to dispel the popular belief that Catholicism is monolithic—that Catholics should be expected
to follow a set guideline in dealing with issues such as the Mexican persecution. If the Church as a whole, including millions of laypersons, was expected
to act in a certain way, the hierarchy, as the spiritual leadership of the Church
in the United States, would have been much more so. But this most definitely
was not the case. An analysis of several of the individual bishops will demonstrate how that group was clearly divided amongst themselves as to the proper
position the Catholics of the United States, and in fact the United States government, should take on the persecution in Mexico. This examination will
begin with the first real leader among the prelates on responding to the Mexican Revolution, Archbishop James Cardinal Gibbons, and continue on with
his successor, Archbishop Michael Cardinal Curley, and several other prominent prelates.

James Cardinal Gibbons, Archbishop of Baltimore

Archbishop Gibbons became interested in the plight of Mexico's Catholics early in that country's revolution. Up to mid-1914, he backed the initiatives of President Woodrow Wilson, particularly Wilson's policy of "watchful waiting" while the Mexican Revolution progressed. Both Gibbons and Wilson were anxious to see what kind of government would emerge from the crucible of war. The course of the revolution, however, and the United States government's response to it, gradually convinced Gibbons that change was necessary in the United States' policies toward Mexico.

Gibbons's support of Wilson's policy of attentive inaction reflected his broad scope of vision. He was convinced that any strong opposition on the part of the United States Catholics would be premature, since the Mexican situation was still in flux. Moreover, the administration had plenty of other issues to be concerned about, not the least of which was the war brewing in Europe. Gibbons believed that constant attacks on Wilson would "probably result, not in securing any assistance in our cause, but in setting the entire Administration against us."[1]

Catholics who advocated strong, immediate action challenged Gibbons because of his backing Wilson's wait-and-see policy. Fr. Francis C. Kelley, editor of *Extension* magazine, insisted that Catholics must press on for religious freedom in the face of this Mexican assault, its future in Mexico was in jeopardy. Others joined Kelley. Archbishop Sebastian G. Messmer of Milwaukee asked Gibbons to consider a joint statement of protest with the other two American cardinals (Denis Cardinal Dougherty of Philadelphia and Patrick Cardinal Hayes of New York). Gibbons, however continued to insist that directing such a statement to the Mexican government would do no good, and directing it to Washington would certainly do harm.[2] Events conspired to erode Gibbons's conviction that Catholics should refrain from direct action.

During a summer trip to New Orleans in 1914, Gibbons met with Archbishop Mora of Mexico City and other exiled prelates, who informed Gibbons of the nature of the persecutions. This new perspective convinced Gibbons to grant an interview with the Baltimore *American* newspaper on July 23, 1914. In the interview, Gibbons expressed shock over the harshness of the persecution and counseled the Constitutionalist leaders to chart their course carefully, for full recognition by the United States hung in the balance. Gibbons also noted that this position of the United States, as arbiter through the power of recognition, was "forced" upon this country "by circumstances" whereby the United States "must practically speak for the rest of the world." This decision over the recognition of Mexico was wrapped up in a number of issues, not least of which was the treatment of Catholics in Mexico. According to Gibbons, "nothing will shock the civilized world more than punitive or vindictive action towards priests or ministers of any church, whether Catholic or Protestant" and that "the treatment already said to have been accorded priests has had a most unfortunate effect upon opinion outside of Mexico."[3]

The White House was intimately interested in Gibbons's views. Wilson sent Senator Blair Lee of Maryland to reassure the cardinal that the Church's rights in Mexico remained a priority for the Wilson administration, and that the president had sent a dispatch to Generals Pancho Villa and Venustiano Carranza to that effect. Carranza, who had responded to the statement through an agent, sought to assure Wilson and Gibbons that Church rights and property would, indeed, be respected.[4]

Gibbons's interview with the Baltimore *American,* which clearly evoked the attention the cardinal sought, marked the real beginning of his activism on the situation in Mexico. He continued this tack by pressing Fr. Arthur J. Maas, the Jesuit provincial, about ways Gibbons could help the Mexican prelates. Maas responded that the Mexican hierarchy wanted Gibbons to force the United States government to push the Mexican revolutionary government to guarantee for all Mexicans—lay and religious—rights to life and property. Maas was confident that a strong statement to that effect from Wilson would go far toward securing religious liberty in Mexico.[5]

Gibbons hoped that his reputation of support for Wilson's policies would bolster his assurances to the president that he was working to quiet the Catholic rumblings; however, those advocating action demanded that the prelate do something. Gibbons used his respected position with the Wilson administration, gained through his past support, to appeal to the president for some sign that Washington was concerned about the Mexicans. Furthermore, Gibbons felt the growing body of evidence of persecution by the Constitutionalists forced his hand in calling for a strong statement from Washington. Gibbons assured Wilson that "one word from you to the constitutionalist leaders would have a great affect and would relieve the sad condition of affairs."[6] Wilson's reply to Gibbons was fraught with the president's frustration. Wilson informed Gibbons that the prelate was mistaken in his estimation of the president's influence over the Mexican situation: "Alas, I am sorry to say that it is not true that 'one word from me to the constitutionalist leaders would have a great affect and would relieve the sad condition of affairs' in Mexico with regard to the treatment of priests, for I have spoken that word again and again."[7] Secretary of State William Jennings Bryan likewise notified Gibbons that the State Department had for weeks been advising Carranza against continued harsh treatment of priests.[8] Armed with the assurances of both the Wilson administration and the Constitutionalist leader that religious liberty was an item of high priority for both governments, Gibbons favored sitting back and giving Carranza room to make good on his word.

Many activist Catholics greeted Wilson's and Gibbons's return to what appeared to be a policy of watchful waiting with great consternation. Kelley, in *Extension,* charged that the United States and its agents were actually responsible for the crisis in Mexico. Gibbons responded to this accusation by demanding that Kelley refrain from making such inflammatory statements unless he could produce proper documentation.[9] Kelley, convinced that Wilson was "deliberately misinformed" about the actual conditions in Mexico, assured Gibbons that he possessed photographs, affidavits, news clippings, and other materials which portrayed the true situation in Mexico.[10]

In spite of his efforts to rein in Kelley, Gibbons was not content to do absolutely nothing. Although he wanted to give Carranza a chance to prove himself, he and Apostolic Delegate John Bonzano recognized the importance of expressing the support of the United States hierarchy for their Mexican brothers.[11] It became clear over the next few months, however, that these expressions of support for the Mexican prelates were insufficient to stem the rising tide of unrest and continued persecutions. As the plight of the Mexican Catholics worsened, Gibbons became increasingly frustrated. In one statement, Gibbons captured what he believed to be the essence of what perplexed Catholics across the United States: "Let a missionary be threatened, and the United States will send a gun to see that American lives are protected. Yet there are many lives being snuffed out in Mexico and we take no action."[12] After the Mexican government promulgated the Queretaro Constitution of 1917, Gibbons focused his considerable energies on the cause of actively aiding the Catholics of Mexico.

In April 1917, Gibbons met with Archbishop Henry J. Moeller of Cincinnati, and Philadelphia lawyer Walter G. Smith. Together, the three formed a committee to draft a protest to the government of Mexico condemning the anti-religious clauses of the new constitution. Smith favored sending the protest straight to Wilson, but Gibbons wanted to spare the president, whom he considered to be under extreme pressure over the war in Europe. Moreover, Gibbons insisted that there were two possible responses Wilson could make to the protest. First, if he reacted favorably, he risked offending the Mexican government, and Wilson did not need a hostile government to the south as he tried to deal with war in Europe. Second, if Wilson reacted unfavorably, he would surely offend large segments of the Catholic population who would feel as if the president were ignoring the cries of one-fifth of the nation's citizens.[13] Instead of forwarding the protest straight to Wilson, Gibbons had the protest published in the organ of the Archdiocese of Baltimore, the *Baltimore Catholic Review*.

The protest letter of the prelates on the Constitution of 1917 indicated first that the hierarchy did not want to step beyond the bounds of their authority. They did, nonetheless, note that the United States government had formally recognized a government that had promulgated a constitution that denied the people of Mexico such basic rights as religious liberty and freedom of religious education. Consequently, the prelates found it incumbent upon them to lodge a strong protest on behalf of the Catholics of Mexico. The protest, which consisted mostly of a condemnation of the anti-religious nature of the Constitution of 1917, did not explicitly lay the responsibility for the persecution squarely on the Wilson administration, as Kelley had done and as others would do in the 1920s and 1930s. It did, however, amount to the strongest statement yet of Gibbons's growing displeasure with the administration's response to the persecution.

As the specter of World War I came to dominate his energies, this protest was Gibbons's last effort to aid the Catholics of Mexico. After the United States entered the war, Gibbons turned to rallying the Catholic response to the demands of the conflict. Catholics, in response, sprang to his call, filling up nearly 35 percent of the army's ranks while comprising barely 16 percent of the population.[14] Also, Burke and others approached Gibbons with their plans for a national Catholic body. This was a cause into which Gibbons threw himself. Gibbons knew that the time had come for the Catholics to have a central voice on a national level. He believed that if the hierarchy did not form such a body as that which Burke, O'Hern, Kirby, and Neill had proposed, Catholics would be forced to resort to partisan politics, thereby inflaming the passions of those who feared "bloc" voting dominated by Rome.[15]

Archbishop James Cardinal Gibbons, as a prince of the Church and a leader of the Catholic Church in the United States, was undoubtedly the most important Catholic voice in this country in the first two decades of the twentieth century. He clearly had respect for the power he wielded, as evidenced by how sparingly he exercised it. When he did make use of that power, whether in an appeal on behalf of his Mexican co-religionists, or when he called on

Catholics to rally around the flag, Archbishop Gibbons got results. Among those who recognized Gibbons's position in the United States was Theodore Roosevelt. In 1917, Roosevelt assured the "dear Cardinal" that "taking your life as a whole, I think you now occupy the position of being the most respected, and venerated, and useful citizen of our country."[16] Gibbons's successor to the archbishopric of Baltimore, Michael (later Cardinal) Curley, certainly garnered less support among the Catholics of the United States, yet he strove to use his position in the Premier See to press for policies he believed would end the persecution of Mexican Catholics.

Michael Cardinal Curley, Archbishop of Baltimore

Michael Curley ascended to the archbishopric of Baltimore upon the death of Cardinal Gibbons in 1921. Almost immediately after being named archbishop, Catholic activists approached him for his help in furthering the cause of the Mexican Catholics. Fr. Francis Kelley, of *Extension,* asked Curley to lend the prestige that accompanied his name and office to a new proposal for a settlement of the church-state conflict. Curley refused to voice support for the proposal, which subsequently died. Kelley, sowing seeds of future cooperation, thought better of antagonizing the new archbishop, and wrote that he respected Curley's wishes, for he did not want "to give the enemies of the Church any basis for the charge that American Catholics [were] interfering in Mexican affairs."[17] Curley's resolve to stay out of the Mexican issue rapidly melted away as persecutions intensified under President Plutarco Elías Calles in 1926.

Once Curley became interested in involving himself and his office in the Mexican crisis, the radical differences between Curley and Gibbons emerged in their attitudes toward the United States government. Whereas Gibbons was deferential and attempted cooperation, Curley attacked the administration without mercy. He made excellent use of the Archdiocese of Baltimore's official organ, the *Baltimore Catholic Review,* in his attacks on the chief executive.

It was under Curley's administration of the *Review* that the journal turned the corner from reporting the conditions in Mexico to front-page editorializing. Curley claimed personal responsibility for examining everything that went into the journal, and although he may not come across as "the actual fighter in its columns," he did "have [his] hand in it."[18] Curley's biting sense of humor, or more appropriately, his sense of tragedy, comes through in his articles. As he critiqued the provisions of the Constitution of 1917, he noted that "in order to preach the Gospel of Jesus Christ in Mexico one must be a

Mexican by birth. If the Savior of the world came back to Mexico He would be exiled forthwith by Calles, the President, because He is not born Mexican."[19] The general goal of his articles, published in 1926 in book form as *Mexican Tyranny and the Catholic Church,* was to discredit the Mexican government, to force the withdrawal of diplomatic recognition of that government, and to place the blame for the persecution squarely on the shoulders of the United States government.[20]

As previously noted, the National Catholic Welfare Conference authorized Notre Dame professor Charles Phillips to investigate the attitudes of the Mexican hierarchy. The result of this investigation was that while the Mexican bishops wanted the facts of the conditions in Mexico to be made known, they did not want the American Church to become involved. Curley evidently either misunderstood the Mexican hierarchy's position, or he believed that Phillips's representation of their desires did not accurately reflect the needs of the Church in Mexico. Curley was of the opinion that only if the Catholics of the United States mobilized would the United States government be obliged to act on their behalf to improve the conditions facing Catholics in Mexico. At a February 19, 1926, dinner for the Knights of Columbus of the Washington, D.C., area, Curley made it clear that he planned to chart a different course than that of Burke and Phillips: "some there are in this capital city who are supine and who believe in reticence, but not the archbishop of Baltimore, not the Knights of Columbus of Washington, not Americans who want action when action is needed and when outspokenness should be the order of the day." To assuage the fears of those who opposed action that might be misconstrued as calling for the unity of church and state, Curley made it clear that neither the archdiocese nor the Knights of Columbus were meddling in politics.[21] Dedication to the doctrine of separation of church and state, however, certainly did not absolve the Church of its higher obligation to speak out and act against tyranny. The sort of action and outspokenness Curley demanded of Catholics was collective:

> I feel that at least twenty million Catholics of this country ought to raise their voices in protest against the Bolshevistic vandalism of our neighboring republic. It is no more worthy of the name of a republic than is Soviet Russia. . . . [O]ur standing amongst nations of the earth would be nobler and higher if we were to raise our voices in protest against the shocking violation of human rights that is now going on in Mexico. . . . If politicians are silent, that is no reason why twenty

million Catholics in America should be voiceless. . . . In the name of three hundred thousand Catholics in this small Archdiocese of Baltimore, and, I might add, in the name of millions of fair-minded Americans of every form of belief in this Republic of ours, I protest against the persecution of religion in Mexico. . . . The whole thing is a stench in the nostrils of fair-minded Americans.[22]

More than simply calling on Catholics to act, he criticized those who failed to do so. He feared that the silence of Catholics would prove to the Mexican and the United States governments that they were resigned to their plight.

Curley's frequent allusion to Bolshevism and the Communistic nature of the Mexican government was a clear indication of his times. Within the context of the Red Scare then infecting the United States, these words had a particularly hard-hitting quality as he raised the alarm about the "Bolshevistic vandalism" rending Mexico[23] and the "Bolshevistic" Constitution of 1917 which "was framed for the purpose of destroying the Church in Mexico just as much as the Bolshevists aim to wreck all religion in Russia."[24] Curley's legal counsel testified before the House Committee on Foreign Affairs on behalf of the archbishop that the Mexican Bolsheviks were working to eliminate morality and religion in Mexico. Curley chose his words carefully, and he managed to capture the essence of what Americans feared most in the years following the Bolshevik Revolution, and in doing so, he had "awakened this country as it [had] not been awakened in years."[25]

The nature of the beast Curley had awakened was manifest in the March 11, 1926, mass meeting organized by the Knights of Columbus in response to Curley's challenge of February 19. It was a protest meeting that transcended denominational and political lines, as Catholics, Protestants, and Jews met to voice their concern over the persecutions in Mexico. Curley gloried in the efforts of other Catholic groups to initiate protests against the persecution. He praised the Holy Name Society for its "manly" protest and at the same time criticized the "spineless" and "cowardly" lack of organized action from the other national Catholic organizations. Most annoying for Curley was the fact that the growing protest movement did not as yet include the NCWC. Curley was angered that the self-proclaimed "central voice" of the Church in the United States had not been counted among those who protested the persecution. Curley even appealed to the apostolic delegate, Archbishop Pietro Fumasoni-Biondi, to get the NCWC involved: "it might be well to get the N.C.W.C. into action. At times like this, one does not know just who or what the N.C.W.C. is. In its ultimate analysis, it seems to be Father John Burke and nobody else."[26]

One of the issues that interested Curley most was the diplomatic recognition of Mexico, and the benefits that went along with it. For Curley, the most effective tool was the general American opposition to the recognition of the Soviet Union. Curley used this opposition to bring into question the basis for the United States' recognition of Mexico. According to Curley, consistency of policy meant that recognition of Mexico required recognition of Bolshevik Russia, because "Mexico and Russia are equally red." Recognition by the United States had brought Carranza and Obregón to power, which Curley considered untoward intervention. It was this recognition that implicated the United States in the persecution, and placed the blame for the atrocities squarely on the shoulders of the United States government. After all, if the United States were to withdraw that recognition, Calles's government would quickly fall.[27]

Curley's strident cries alarmed the administration of Calvin Coolidge. Through Secretary of State Frank Kellogg, Coolidge sought the help of the vice president of Georgetown University, Fr. Edmund Walsh, SJ, to silence Curley. Walsh complied with the president's wishes, and privately implored Curley to stop attacking Coolidge's Mexican policy.[28] If anything, this meeting only spurred Curley on. The archbishop was convinced that the United States government had bedded down with the "monied interests" that sought to rob Mexico of her wealth, at the cost of that country's soul. Curley believed that the Coolidge administration had clearly sold out, so protests directed at the government were a waste of time. Therefore, he decided to take the movement to the public. He believed that "an appeal to the conscience of our American people is far more effective than an appeal to what [takes] the place of conscience in our politicians."[29]

Curley suspected that more than the monied interests had become intimate with the president. The archbishop was ruthless in his public accusations that Coolidge was under the influence of prominent Protestants, especially the Methodist bishops. Methodist Bishop James Cannon had been in the forefront of the effort to reduce Catholic power in Mexico, and Curley was sure that Coolidge was sympathetic to the Methodists' cause. He posited that if it were a few Methodists who were expelled by the Mexican government as was Archbishop George Caruana in July 1926, the United States government would have sprung into action in protest, instead of the deafening silence that fell upon the ears of Catholics searching in vain for an official protest to Caruana's expulsion. Curley used the pages of the *Baltimore Catho-*

lic Review to carry out this campaign of inter-religious hatred. In a long editorial, Curley asked: "What is the matter with the Administration? Is it afraid of the Methodist bishops? . . . The Methodists have asked Mr. Coolidge to keep hands off until the job is done [i.e., until the power of the Catholic Church is destroyed in Mexico]. Surely our President is not playing the game of the Methodists in Mexico."[30] Curley evidently believed that Coolidge's endorsement of the archbishop's program would not amount to the president "playing the game" of the *Catholics* in Mexico, but would instead mean that Coolidge would be harkening to higher principles.

Curley hoped that these higher principles were the objectives of the 1927–1929 *modus vivendi* negotiations between Ambassador Dwight Morrow, representatives of the Mexican Catholics, and the Calles administration, so he refrained from taking steps that could jeopardize the process. In fact, like the full hierarchy and the NCWC, he was relatively silent on the Mexican situation until the Mexican government stepped up the persecutions in the early 1930s. However, once he rededicated himself to the job of trying to nudge the United States' foreign policy toward recognition of what he understood to be universal principles, he proved himself relentless in his quest.

After Josephus Daniels's gaffe in quoting Calles on the Mexican system of socialistic education in 1934, Curley returned to the familiar pages of the *Baltimore Catholic Review,* and to his effort to spur Catholic groups to act. In October 1934, Curley had a letter published in the *Review* calling for Daniels's recall, and also inviting President Roosevelt to read the journal's "exposé of the bestial, pederastic and sodomistic campaign of socialistic education which has gone on in alliance with other methods of warfare against God, Religion and Common Decency in Mexico."[31] Curley found a ready audience from whom he could broaden his protests in a 1934 gathering of Catholics in Washington to honor Christ the King. Before a throng of forty thousand, Curley issued this clarion call:

> With all the vigor and indignation we can command we protest against the persecution of the Catholics of Mexico; we protest against the attempts to tear religion from the hearts of the little ones; we protest against the action of the official representative of our country in indorsing the program of pagan education and in placing himself as a friend of the enemies of the Catholic Church. We want Washington to know our protest. We want these words of indignant protest to reach our nation's capital.[32]

The Borah resolution of late January 1935 provided Curley a standard around which he hoped American Catholics would rally, to bring the official indignation of the whole nation to bear on the Mexican government's persecution of Catholics. In a February 14 editorial in the *Washington Post*, Curley supported the Borah resolution by citing familiar precedents wherein past secretaries of state had intervened in other countries in the interest of protecting religious groups overseas. Curley maintained that any attention to our own history would provide support to such action at the present. Clearly, according to Curley, history proved that not only common sense, but also international law justified passage of the Borah resolution. Curley's further description of the resolution highlighted one of the principal problems with the resolution: "all this resolution asks is an opportunity to learn the truth about Mexico. Then, if [he actually meant "when"] the facts justify it, we can decide whether or not we want to remain silent before a genuine persecution of religion, as well as an assault on American lives and property."[33]

Curley was dumbfounded when he received a letter from Archbishop Edward Hanna, the chair of the NCWC Administrative Committee, which notified Curley that the committee had unanimously decided not to endorse the Borah resolution, and that the results of the committee's vote was to be kept secret.[34] This was one more instance, from Curley's perspective, when the NCWC had assumed powers and influence that it did not merit. In a letter to Hanna, Curley raged that "the Administrative Committee [had] no right whatsoever to speak [his] mind nor the mind of any other Bishop on a matter on which we have not been consulted." Curley maintained that the Administrative Committee's actions sent the message that "the 114 Cardinals, Archbishops and Bishops of the United States are not interested in the persecution in Mexico, and are perfectly willing to have conditions continue as they are."[35] In a confidential letter to Fr. Michael Kenny, the author of numerous scathing articles in the *Baltimore Catholic Review*, Curley laid out his plans to undermine the authority and credibility of the NCWC. The lack of consultation with the prelates, and worse, the implication of official clerical unconcern over the persecution in Mexico, justified a bold initiative such as a press release. In such a public statement, Curley would assert that the NCWC had as much authority or right to speak for the prelates as it did for "the man in the moon." Curley was aware that such a statement would amount to "attacking the N.C.W.C. at its roots. . . ."[36]

This conflict with the NCWC fueled a running feud between the Administrative Committee and the archbishop. In this context, Curley was more than ready to find fault for failed initiatives. Therefore, since the *modus vivendi* had accomplished little good for the Mexican people, Curley blamed Burke for that failure:

> In 1928 a mild-mannered priest [Burke] had gone from the United States to Mexico to engage in conversations with Calles. The next year, another mild-mannered priest [Walsh] went from this country to Mexico to engage in further conversations with Calles. They found Mr. Calles charming, sincere. These two embryonic, sacerdotal ambassadors were assured by Mr. Calles everything would be made all right. There was the law and there was the Constitution of Queretar[o]. But if the *Cristeros* would lay down their arms, there would be no more suffering for the Church in Mexico. The laws would not be enforced. 'Yes, Mr. Calles,' said the embryonic, sacerdotal ambassadors.
>
> The first things Calles did after the peace had been made was to shoot down 500 *Cristero* leaders. . . . The Mexicans hold the names of these two priests in malediction. Let Mexicans deal with Mexicans and do not send innocent Americans to do the work.[37]

Curley believed that Burke was not strong enough to stand up to Calles, and was taken in by the Mexican president. If the occasion for a settlement should arise in the future, Curley asked, patronizingly, that "our gentle, sacerdotal diplomats in this country stay home."[38]

A letter Curley received from a Catholic layman, Charles J. Mahan, seemed to initiate a change in the archbishop's tactics. While Curley had done a great job of encouraging Catholics who had been "waiting in vain for a President to quell the Herodian massacres" in Mexico, Mahan was concerned that the apparent divisions among the hierarchy would doom any coherent advocacy. Unity among the prelates would motivate Protestant legislators to be "mighty quick to cooperate with Catholics" in protests against the persecution.[39] Shortly after Curley received this letter, his tactics changed and he redirected his attacks away from the NCWC, and focused his energies on President Franklin Roosevelt himself.

Curley's attacks on the president were not new—he had opposed Roosevelt's Latin American policy from early in the administration. From March and April of 1935 to the end of the Mexican crisis in 1937, Curley's attacks on Roosevelt took on a new intensity as Curley redirected his invective. The archbishop believed Roosevelt was responsible for the ultimate death of the

Borah resolution. The president's instruction that the resolution should not leave the Senate Foreign Relations Committee proved to Curley that Roosevelt did not take Catholic power seriously. In a speech before the Washington D.C. Sodality Union (a lay devotional society), Curley blasted a shot across the bow of the ship of state that caused many to sit up and take notice.

Curley used the address to the Sodality Union to establish the bases for his attack on, and warning to, the Roosevelt administration. In light of what he considered the administration's long-standing disregard for the Catholics in the United States, Curley claimed that the time had come to let the president know with whom he was fooling:

> The Administration may think it can ignore the 20,000,000 Catholics in the United States today. It may think it can ignore the Knights of Columbus, the millions of sodalists, the 2,000,000 Holy Name men in this country in this year 1935. But these millions of Catholic American citizens will have a chance to vote in 1936. They may then express as they see fit their opinion of this present administration's determination to block all legislation in behalf of Mexico.

Curley went on to address the lack of action from the State Department, claiming that the department's inactivity was inexcusable, and that "20,000,000 American Catholics are getting pretty tired of the indifference shown by the administration in this matter and they want action." In spite of the tone of these comments, Curley wanted to make it clear that he was *not* making a threat. He claimed to be merely pointing out the collective power Catholics could wield.[40] Curley's forceful address before the Sodality Union was met with wild applause from the crowd.

In April 1935, Curley continued both his attacks on Roosevelt's policies and the allusion to the latent political power of the Catholics of the United States. On Roosevelt's Latin American policy, Curley caricatured the Good Neighbor policy by portraying Neighbor Mexico as a wife-beating, child-abusing drunk. According to Curley, Neighbor United States needed to inform Neighbor Mexico that this behavior was simply unacceptable and it jeopardized their good relations. He also observed that other organized denominations — such as American Jews — could get favorable responses from the Roosevelt White House, and that they ought to be applauded for that. The 20 million Catholics of the United States, however, had been ignored. Curley was certain that the inactivity on behalf of Catholics was a product of their disorganization. That, he hinted, would end soon.[41]

Curley's attempt to hit the president in the ballot box quickly struck a resonant chord in Congress. Representative Clare Gerald Fenerty loosed even a less-veiled political threat than had Curley. Fenerty provided Roosevelt with options: "If, as a statesman, he will not think of human rights, let him, as a politician, think of the next election."[42]

Not all Catholics supported Curley in his political effort to unseat Roosevelt. There was a growing realization that if Curley chose to push the issue, it would surely fail. An example of this realization is a letter from S. A. McManus to Curley in March 1935. McManus intimated that if Curley believed that "several million Catholics in this country" would band together to remove Roosevelt from office, he was gravely mistaken. History had shown, according to McManus, that the effort would fail, and he wanted to avoid the pitfalls that had claimed others. He claimed that the Methodists had gained publicity, but also ridicule for "parking themselves up on Capital Hill and trying to mix their religion with Politics until eventually they were preaching Politics from their pulpits."[43]

That Catholic laymen were divided over the issue of the proper response to the Mexican issue was presumably not a surprise for Curley. That he found such opposition among his own prelate brethren, however, must have been a bit of a shock. The lack of clear leadership among the prelates disturbed Curley, especially when the issue was involvement in the government. Curley observed that "a great number of the members of the American Hierarchy have the idea that it is a mortal sin to offend the Government."[44] By far the more serious sin, Curley warned, would be the American prelates "leaving the solution to the Mexican question to the Mexican Hierarchy and the Mexican people."[45] This division among the prelates did not go unnoticed by lay Catholics. Jerome P. Holland wrote to Curley lamenting the fact that lay Catholics could not count on the hierarchy to provide leadership. Holland feared that lay Catholics would interpret the prelates' silence on the Mexican situation as "merely stupidity, cowardice and dumbness, together with a narrowness and provincialism in their outlook."[46]

Early in 1936, Curley's declining health, marked by skyrocketing blood pressure and failing eyesight, forced his resignation from both the NCWC and from national prominence. The news of Curley's illness greatly disturbed Burke. He wrote Curley that the news filled him with great sadness, mostly because of Curley's invaluable work on behalf of the Catholic Church in the United States.[47] In a sign of extreme humility, Curley responded that he "never was . . . of any importance whatsoever to the Church in America."[48]

Curley was wrong. He was of incalculable importance to the Catholics of the United States in the 1920s and 1930s. He stood as one of the two most strident advocates of the Mexican Catholics in the American hierarchy. His call, following Phillips's claim that the Mexican hierarchy opposed American activism, began a wave of unrest that swept across the country. He steadfastly stood against the prelates who favored accommodation with the Mexican government, and he led the charge to force Roosevelt into action. He failed, however, in his effort to use the threat of a Catholic bloc vote as a weapon against Roosevelt in 1936. Whether or not he was successful in evoking change in the overall policy toward Mexico is more difficult to determine. Undoubtedly, the positions he advocated and the opinions he inflamed had some degree of influence in convincing Roosevelt to make the moves he did to ameliorate the conditions suffered by the Catholics of Mexico. The fact that Roosevelt was receiving mixed signals from other Catholics, however, mitigated Curley's considerable efforts. Nonetheless, the fact remains that Curley was very influential in molding American Catholics' opinion on the Mexican situation. Fortunately for him, he was not alone—his work resonated with the efforts of other prelates who fought to win for the Mexican Catholics the right to worship freely. Bishop Francis Clement Kelley of Oklahoma City and Tulsa proved to be one of the most outspoken of those outspoken prelates.

Francis C. Kelley, Bishop of Oklahoma City and Tulsa

Bishop Francis C. Kelley's first impression of Mexico was that it was no more than "a colored space on the map" at the bottom of North America, but later, he understood it as "an upturned diplomatic tack on the American Presidential chair."[49] By 1914, Kelley had emerged as perhaps the one who turned that tack to such a position as to evoke the most immediate action from the American chief executive and the State Department. His two major published works, the first published while he was editor of *Extension* magazine, *The Book of Red and Yellow* (1915), and the second after he had become a bishop, *Blood-Drenched Altars* (1935), encapsulate his involvement with the Mexican persecution. These two works stand as parentheses around a career of activism and boldness in advocating the position of the Mexican Catholics. Kelley spared no expense, in time, energy, or finances, in his effort to aid his persecuted Mexican co-religionists, both south of the Rio Grande and those exiles and refugees in the United States. He also demonstrated no sympathy to the United States government when he believed that the government was neglecting its duty in fostering religious freedom abroad as well as at home. While Kelley's first book predates the period in which this study concentrates, it provides essential context for the bishop's later work.

The catalyst for Kelley's initial interest in Mexico was the announcement of Woodrow Wilson's policy regarding the Mexican Revolution. Kelley's opposition to the watchful waiting policy garnered him tremendous support, including that of one of the most popular personalities in the nation, former President Theodore Roosevelt. Kelley took advantage of both Roosevelt's interests and a rapidly growing corpus of evidence of the persecution in Mexico. Together, Kelley and Roosevelt pored over a collection of affidavits and other evidence of horrendous suffering by Mexican Catholics. The result of this study was an article by the former president in the *New York Times,* in which Roosevelt condemned the Wilson administration for its lack of forceful policy toward Mexico. The tenor of the article was that Wilson's meddling in Mexican affairs actually caused the "terrible outrages committed by the victorious revolutionists on hundreds of religious people of both sexes." Wilson was responsible, in the final analysis, for the suffering of Mexico, because of his "officious and mischievous meddling."[50] Kelley at the same time struck at the administration for the outrages, but placed the blame more on the whole American public for not speaking out against the persecution: "Who has brought this state of things about? Ourselves! Who insisted upon the non-recognition of a government lawfully in charge according to the Constitution of Mexico [Huerta's]? Ourselves! Who upheld the hands of Carranza and Villa? Ourselves! Who foisted this iniquity upon the decent people of Mexico? Ourselves!"[51]

Kelley built on the momentum Roosevelt's article began by publishing his first book, *The Book of Red and Yellow: Being a Story of Blood and a Yellow Streak.* This book, which Democrats considered the most damaging critique of Wilson's Mexican policies, included transcriptions of signed and notarized affidavits from those who witnessed the persecutions inflicted upon prelates, priests, nuns, and laymen who remained faithful to the Church. Kelley insisted that Wilson refused to look to the Catholic heritage of Mexico, which Kelley considered the basis, the foundation, of Mexican society and which he believed was the only source of long-lasting and stable government worthy of recognition by the United States. Instead, Wilson had granted recognition to a shaky tyrannical structure that merely encouraged the revolutionaries to pursue further persecutions, with the Unites States government's apparent approval.[52]

Wilson was not, however, exclusively responsible for the persecution. Kelley also implicated the anti-Catholic Protestants in helping Carranza rise to power and work to destroy the Church. According to Kelley, Carranza had surrounded himself with former Protestant ministers in the revolutionary government, including the governors of two states, military leaders, and even Eulalio Guiterrez, the head of the provisional government.[53] The wife of Carranza's brother Jesus was a minister's daughter, who in 1920 donated some land and a building to the Methodist Church. Benjamin Velaseo, who later became a member of the Chamber of Deputies, observed in 1916 that "the Lord ha[d] given the protestants in Mexico the greatest opportunity to rebuild the country, in cooperation with the government, to uplift the people and show them what the Gospel life can do for the people through Christian education."[54]

Kelley's book pricked the sensibilities of the Wilson administration, and the secretary of state tried to assure Kelley that the administration was sensitive to the situation in Mexico. While the Wilson government had no intention to interfere in the internal affairs of our neighbor to the south, Bryan assured Kelley that the administration held as a high priority "the full flower of democracy, religious freedom, the principle which the builders of our own Republic made the crown of the whole structure" and to which political freedom was but a "handmaiden and servant." Bryan tried to correct Kelley's perception that the Wilson administration suffered from a deaf ear when it encountered stories of persecutions. The secretary of state maintained that whenever the government received evidence of persecution, it cautioned the Mexican government about the "fatal effect any . . . attack upon liberty of conscience or of worship would have upon the opinion of the people of the United States and of the world."[55] Kelley appreciated Bryan's position, yet he felt compelled to point out that Villa's representative in Washington claimed that the elimination of religious orders in Mexico was a fundamental goal of the revolution. Clearly, the ideal of religious liberty as conceived by Bryan and Villa differed considerably; Kelley noted that Villa's certainly were at odds with most Americans' ideas of freedom of religion.[56]

Kelley maintained his contrarian attitude toward the Wilson administration through the summer of 1915, but following Wilson's recognition of Carranza's government in October, Kelley shifted into high gear. He presented the exiled Mexican prelates in San Antonio with a proposal for a three-pronged attack on the Wilson White House. First, Kelley would approach both administration and *carrancista* officials in Washington to begin discussing the religious issue. As part of this effort, Kelley tried to get Wilson's perspectives down in black and white in the pages of *Extension*. Kelley maintained that he had no "political axe to grind" by inviting Wilson to pen an article for *Extension*. Wilson, after receiving the invitation, wrote instead a memorandum to his secretary, Joseph Tumulty: "I would be very much obliged if you would intimate to the Secretary of State the real character and activities of Father Kelley and say that, . . . I hope that [his] request for a personal message will simply be overlooked, not only as far as I am concerned, but so far as the members of the Cabinet are concerned."[57] Second, Kelley proposed that the Extension Society flex a bit of its muscle in an effort to influence Chicago's bankers. Kelley reasoned that Catholics, who comprised one-sixth of the American public, could exert pressure to block loans to the Carranza government, much as had German Americans with the sale of Anglo-French war bonds in the Midwest. Finally, Kelley proposed an election-year push to remove Wilson from the White House. Evidently, Kelley found little backing for these proposals, for this is the last we hear of them. While Kelley backed the Republican candidate for the presidency in 1916, he later recognized that this bout with partisan politics crippled his efforts to appeal to liberal leaders in the United States who could help mold public opinion on Mexico. He had also made himself "a persona non grata at the White House."[58] These failed initiatives are nonetheless important because they demonstrate a beginning of group awareness among American Catholics. They would be a force to be reckoned with if united in action.

Kelley's advocacy of the persecuted Mexican Catholics propelled him into the halls of power in Washington and further. Shortly before the peace talks began in Paris in 1917, Kelley decided to try to use the international forum to "alert the victors of the importance of world-wide religious freedom."[59] After he arrived in Paris, Kelley met with anti-Carranza exiles, including Porfirio Díaz's widow, Carmen, and a former Mexican ambassador and international lawyer, Francisco León de la Barra. He also received assistance from Edward L. Doheny, the industrialist and oil magnate, who feared that Carranza's confiscatory decrees threatened his vast holdings in Mexico.[60] By the time Kelley had arrived at the Versailles Conference, the conferees had already exchanged heated debate over the issue of religious freedom in Wilson's Article 19 of the League of Nations covenant, and had allowed it to die without a vote. While it appeared that Kelley would strike out in Paris, he managed to salvage one initiative. He successfully worked to get Section 5 of Article 22 passed, in which the signatories agreed to provide "freedom of conscience and religion" to the natives of former Turkish and German colonies. Kelley and de la Barra believed they had accomplished what Kelley had set out to do.[61]

The fires that Kelley had tended so diligently died down to a smolder during the relatively laissez-faire Carranza and Obregón administrations of the late 1910s and early 1920s, but burst again into full flame when Plutarco Calles began his assault on the Church.

Throughout the 1920s, the attitudes that Kelley fleshed out in *The Book of Red and Yellow* continued to direct his efforts. In 1929, in a confidential memorandum to Senator William Borah, chair of the Senate Foreign Relations Committee, Kelley returned to a well-honed message: "the United States ha[d] intervened in Mexico, with arms if not with men, and ha[d] taken, more than ever before, a sort of implied protectorate over the present Mexican administration. . . . [I]n the minds of the Mexican people we are to blame for their sufferings."[62]

Kelley's ordination as bishop of Oklahoma City and Tulsa in 1924 afforded him yet another venue for continuing his attacks on the Mexican Revolution. The major element of Kelley's activism in the 1920s, the American hierarchy's 1926 pastoral letter on the Mexican situation, of which he was the chief architect, avoided the issue of placing blame on the United States government. This was clearly a result of the divided nature of the hierarchy—the pastoral could only be expressed in the terms of the lowest common denominator, an expression of dedication to general principles. The letter did, however, pose the implicit question of the basis for American recognition of Mexico in light of the fact that religious freedom was a founding principle in the United States.[63] But the largest part of the pastoral was intended to establish the countless benefits showered upon Mexico from its long connection to the Catholic Church. It is in this section that Kelley's voice rings through. Kelley had long believed that Mexico was richer for its Catholic history. For instance, in the education of the Mexican people, the Catholic Church had established schools and colleges, many of which were intended for females as well as males, which were celebrating their golden anniversaries long before Harvard was established in 1639.[64] This firm belief in the extensive benefits heaped upon the Mexican people is an unmistakable element of the 1926 pastoral. Kelley speaks on behalf of the Church: "You may thrust me out, exile my bishops, murder my priests, and desecrate my sanctuary, but you cannot blot out history, you cannot erase the mark I made on you—not in a century of centuries."[65]

The last major period of Kelley's active participation in the United States' response to the Mexican persecution was punctuated with the publication of *Blood-Drenched Altars* in 1935.[66] This history of Mexico, in which Kelley again addressed the Catholic Church as an element of uplift, was intended as an educational campaign designed to evoke a change in the United States–Mexican policy by engendering a sympathetic public opinion. When the Catholic Book Club named it Book-of-the-Month for February 1935, mass distribution of the work was assured. It was largely due to this exposure that the first printing of four thousand copies sold out in less than two weeks.[67]

The book received an enthusiastic response. The Catholic press lauded it as a standard history that established a high mark to which other books would be measured. The supreme knight of the Knights of Columbus proclaimed before the order's 1935 annual convention that the book was "one of the outstanding works of all time with reference to Mexico."[68] Even H. L. Mencken was positive about the book's impact—he credited the work with opening his eyes to the situation in Mexico: "Hitherto I have had only a slight interest in the Mexico business, but now I begin to realize that it ought to be taken seriously." Secular presses generally, however, were much less laudatory. The liberal reviewer from *The New Republic* considered the book "badly written and historically unsound . . . with a narrowness reminiscent of the worst abuses of the Mexican hierarchy in the heyday of its power."[69] Luckily for Kelley, this review did not dampen the book's impact in the Catholic community. Curley appreciated Kelley's educational effort, and recognized that it was just the book to help lift the president out of his oblivion and ignorance.[70]

Kelley sought to make the fullest use of the educational potential of the book by trying to see that influential people were exposed to it. He solicited each of the prelates of the United States and Canada to purchase ten copies of the book for circulation on Capitol Hill. By late 1935, all of the members of Congress had a copy in their hands.[71] It was in this body that Kelley hoped the book's conclusion would have the greatest impact. Kelley claimed that the persecution of the Church in Mexico was objectionable in its own right, but that it portended far more danger for the United States than was clearly visible. The Communist Third International, as represented by Mexico's National Revolutionary Party (PNR), was the basis for the persecution: "Christ is on his way out of Mexico, and behind Him on this new Via Dolorosa [i.e., Christ's journey to His crucifixion on Calvary] the whips are swung by the Communists who, when they have finished below the Rio Grande, will not wait long before crossing—if they can."[72] Kelley repeated this warning in a *Baltimore Catholic Review* article in late 1935, in which he indicated that Mexico was but one country on a list of those whose religious rights had been attacked, with more to follow.[73] The high praise for Kelley's book did not equate with success in evoking protest sufficient to change the United States' Mexican policies, chiefly because Roosevelt could look to other influential Catholics for sympathetic support for his policies, especially from Burke and Archbishop George Cardinal Mundelein of Chicago.

Kelley's final salvo in his war against the Mexican persecution was his membership on the Catholic Bishops' Commission, Inc., for Mexican Relief. Kelley served as secretary-treasurer for the corporation and became a driving force behind this effort to support Mexican refugees in the United States. After Archbishop Curley, the commission's chair, resigned due to complications from high blood pressure, Kelley took up the slack until a new chairman, Bishop John Mark Gannon of Erie, Pennsylvania, took the helm. As treasurer of the commission, Kelley proved instrumental in promoting a nationwide, single-Sunday collection to pay for a seminary for the education of Mexican students. Under his leadership, the collection netted $384,886, more than enough for the purchase price and renovation of a former Baptist College located in a resort outside of Las Vegas, New Mexico.[74]

Kelley's relief work extended beyond his efforts to establish a seminary. He was instrumental in raising funds for the support of Catholic exiles and refugees in the United States who fled the persecution in Mexico. One diocese, El Paso, neared bankruptcy and general insolvency because of the immense strain of feeding and housing Mexican exiles. By 1929, the budget deficit for El Paso had reached $30,000, while that in Kelley's own diocese stood at $21,167.[75] Kelley's appeals to his fellow prelates for collections in the parishes garnered great support, but not quite enough to retire the considerable debts incurred. Kelley paid the $507 difference to retire El Paso's debt out of his own pocket, while his own diocese's debt fell to a more manageable $4,158. Under Kelley's leadership, the Extension Society became the single greatest source of relief monies for the care of Mexican refugees and exiles.[76]

Kelley, as a shepherd of the Church, saw it as his obligation to provide for the care of Catholic refugees. But at the same time, he worked to force a change in United States foreign policy. His most formidable asset in this effort was his voluminous prose. From the Wilson-bashing *Book of Red and Yellow* in 1915, through the appeals for fundamental principles of the hierarchy's 1926 pastoral letter, to the publication of *Blood-Drenched Altars* in 1935, Kelley's pen amounted to a powerful sword with which he battled the dragons of persecution and governmental inertia. While he managed to help mold American Catholic public opinion, he suffered from a lack of political influence because he had become too deeply entrenched in partisan politics in the mid-1910s, and because other Catholics closer to Roosevelt held the president's ear. Bishop Francis C. Kelley still looms large in the pantheon of prelates who fought for the religious freedom of the Mexican people, and his work undoubtedly contributed to the increasing official interest of the United States government in the Mexican situation. Without a doubt, Kelley's work accomplished far more for Mexican Catholics than did the best efforts of a more powerful and respected prelate, Archbishop O'Connell of Boston.

William H. Cardinal O'Connell, Archbishop of Boston

Archbishop O'Connell's involvement in the Mexican crisis was typical of most prelates in the United States—he believed in the power of prayer to bring change, and he delved into the matter of political influence hesitantly, and only when conditions required it. It was not the Mexican situation, but rather an ongoing battle with the NCWC that consumed the lion's share of his energies in the 1920s and 1930s. O'Connell was one of the most outspoken opponents of the organization.

That O'Connell was dead-set against the NCWC from its inception was clear in his correspondence with Apostolic Delegate John Bonzano. O'Connell accused the NCWC leadership of continually trying to turn the faithful against the prelates by having "disregarded episcopal authority and deliberately instructed both lay men and women to pay no attention to their Bishops but to do as the agents of the National Catholic Welfare Council bade them." There is no basis for the charge that the NCWC sought to undermine the authority of the bishops, although some may have perceived the activities of the NCWC as accomplishing just this. O'Connell also accused the NCWC in general and Burke in particular of fiscal impropriety and personal ineptitude. O'Connell provided an epitaph for the organization: "the experiment was novel and dangerous from the beginning, and ha[d] failed" because it was "too bulky, too [un]manageable and too separated to carry on so complicated and expensive a scheme."[77]

The supporters of the NCWC, in their efforts to establish it as a permanent organization in the United States, fought hard to gain the backing of the hierarchy. In an article in the *Boston Globe,* the Administrative Committee of the NCWC published a long list of prelates who supported the organization, and included a list of those who had not yet expressed their support. O'Connell was one of the latter, and in another blistering letter to Apostolic Delegate Bonzano, he launched an attack on the NCWC which jeopardized its future. O'Connell claimed that sympathetic editors intended the lists in the paper to praise the NCWC's supporters, but naming the opponents of the organization amounted to an effort to slam them for harboring sincere criticisms of the organization.[78] O'Connell wanted Bonzano to use his significant influence to see that the activities of "the same clique that have caused all our troubles in America—the Sulpician-Paulist Coterie [be] stopped and stopped at once."[79]

O'Connell was convinced that the NCWC was a megalomaniacal body out to eliminate the authority of the bishops even after the organization had received the support and sanction of the Vatican. When some members of the NCWC Administrative Committee protested after Rome recommended that the NCWC change its name from "Council" to "Conference," O'Connell interpreted the resistance as evidence that the Administrative Committee actually was engaged in an ongoing effort to wrest power away from the American hierarchy. According to O'Connell, the change would go far towards making it clear that the NCWC had only those powers a few bishops were willing to delegate to it, and no more.[80]

But O'Connell was a good and loyal foot soldier for the pope. After the papacy granted the NCWC its official sanction to carry on the work of the Church in the United States, he came to accept the organization, and provided regular financial support for its work. Apostolic Delegate Pietro Fumasoni-Biondi, in the depths of the Depression, asked that O'Connell continue his high level of support, even though some other "lesser work" might need to be discontinued in the archdiocese, because it was "inconceivable" in his estimation that the "vital work of the National Catholic Welfare Conference be jeopardized because of a lack of funds."[81]

In his effort to help the Catholics of Mexico, O'Connell made effective use of the pulpit in his exhortations to prayer. He used the sermon of the first Sunday of August 1926, the Feast of St.-Peter-in-Chains, to call on his people to pray for those Christians in Mexico who were being persecuted for their faith. Not only were the tyrants depriving the people of Mexico of their most basic civil rights, they intended to "strangle the very soul of the nation by crushing out its religion." O'Connell's sermon included a subtle challenge to the faithful for prayerful action by focusing honor on the Mexican Catholics engaged in a glorious struggle: "Can any Christian, nay, can any honest human being witness that battle with indifference? Is there anyone with a spark of honor in his soul who does not feel a sense of pride in the courage which . . . calmly bids [the Mexican government henchmen to] do their worst with their bodies and their possessions, but their souls they will never conquer?"[82]

Throughout the years of the persecution, O'Connell periodically called on the faithful in the Boston archdiocese to resort to prayer to end the hardships and restore peace and religious freedom to Mexico. In all cases, O'Connell made the call from the cathedral pulpit, or he sent letters to each parish to be read on a given Sunday. In most cases, O'Connell made it clear that since governments could be slow to act, people of faith had to turn to God for aid and succor.[83]

Archbishop O'Connell clearly saw the utility of simultaneously appealing for divine intervention and cajoling the faithful toward more direct action. In 1914, in a speech before the Boston Archdiocesan Federation, O'Connell praised the group for bringing before Washington the harshness of the persecution. He held up the federation as a model for other groups.

In the political arena, O'Connell proved himself ready and willing to approach the White House directly. O'Connell claimed to understand how to reach Calvin Coolidge on the Mexican issue. O'Connell recommended that the best way to handle Coolidge was not to approach him personally, but instead to use "an intimate friend" of the president, meaning several of O'Connell's own acquaintances.[84] O'Connell's willingness to take such an active role in working for the resolution of the crisis in Mexico demonstrates that he recognized the influence he had at his command as a cardinal and an archbishop.

Archbishop O'Connell clearly saw a distinction between religious activism on a personal and communal level and involvement in politics. His advice to the Knights of Columbus indicates that he opposed Catholics becoming involved in politics except when higher religious ends were involved. In an address to the Knights in 1926, he advised them to assiduously refrain from intervention in political matters. In light of this admonition, however, he encouraged action "whenever . . . a question is not merely a matter of politics as such, but aims at the destruction of the home, the freedom of religion and of education. . . ." Action in this context, he proclaimed, was "the highest kind of patriotism."[85] Although this advice may have presented a mixed message, it clearly laid out the prioritization of concerns in O'Connell's mind. Politics was to be carefully avoided when action was for political ends only, but when those political ends touched on religion, Catholics were not only encouraged, they were obliged to act.

Judging from these criteria, the events of 1927 provided an opportunity for Catholics to spring into action. O'Connell himself issued the call for protest and the condemnation of silence in the face of persecution. He pointed out that, as a proud American, he could not but "deplore this riotous, blasphemous communism at the very doors of our country," and expressed his anxiety that Mexicans had to face this scourge "without . . . a single protest from anyone in high position whose voice would carry across the Rio Grande and influence someone to cease his wolfish hunting down of perfectly innocent Mexicans whose only crime [was] their determination to serve God." O'Connell offered an explanation for this silence on the part of Washington: "there are influences not entirely imbued with the highest motives" in the capital.[86]

Cardinal O'Connell maintained throughout the years of the persecution that Catholics were to avoid politics. He was a firebrand of rhetoric, however, when religious rights were the issue at hand. As a leader of the Catholic Church in the United States, he was jealous of his power, and fought any challenges to it, particularly by the NCWC. He clearly recognized the value of his power, and that available to other clergymen. This power was not to be used for temporal matters, and well into the 1930s, O'Connell maintained his vigilance against clergy involvement in politics. His advice to Fr. Charles Coughlin, who was becoming one of Roosevelt's chief critics, is equally applicable to O'Connell's attitude toward involvement in the Mexican crisis from a political point of view: "Experience has taught me that in general, clergymen, no matter of what creed, are treading on hazardous ground when they try directly to solve political . . . problems."[87] Clearly, not all of his fellow prelates took O'Connell's words to heart.

Arthur J. Drossaerts, Archbishop of San Antonio

Archbishop Arthur Drossaerts was extremely active in the effort to mold United States policies toward Mexico during the Coolidge administration.[88] Most of his attacks on the persecution and on the response thereto by the United States government included language heavily laced with the fear of Communism and Bolshevism. The tenor of his argument is clear in the foreword to Father Michael Kenny's book, *No God Next Door,* in which he claimed that

> One must be blind not to detect the intense menace to our own free
> institutions, to our democracy and liberty in the Calles and Cárdenas

policies. Moscow has its laboratory, its efficient workshop in Mexico. And it is not so much a distracted Mexico they want to conquer; they are after bigger game: the Colossus, our own United States is what they wish to bag in their relentless war against God and Christian civilization. . . . Already the infection is spreading amongst us.[89]

For Drossaerts, correlations between Mexico and the Soviet Union involved no great leap of the imagination. Because of this clear connection, one issue that concerned him over and again was the contradiction inherent in the recognition of Mexico but not of Russia. Since he steadfastly opposed American recognition of the home of Bolshevism, he challenged the rationality of the recognition of Mexico. Drossaerts used the Communist power as a weapon with which he could attack the Coolidge administration's Mexican policies. In a *Baltimore Catholic Review* editorial, he pondered the question of "why Uncle Sam, refusing to recognize Soviet Russia, can logically keep a United States Ambassador in Soviet Mexico," especially since "the leaders of Mexico get their cue from Leningrad. . . ."[90]

In addition to the *Baltimore Catholic Review*, Drossaerts preferred to disseminate his ideas from the pulpit. The archbishop frequently used his sermons to forge the chain linking Mexico with Russian Communism: "See what the enemies of God and Christian civilization attempt in their war against Heaven. What did they do in France during their godless Revolution: the first step was to attack the churches of the land. The same occurred in Russia in our days—and no need to point out Mexico where Calles & his henchmen are following in the footsteps of the Russian Bolsheviki."[91]

Drossaerts recognized that America's Catholics had little hope for a protest from Washington. Indeed, if Washington would protest against the "orgy of crime" in Mexico, "it would be a real blessing for Mexico and a glorious victory for civilization. . . ." There was but one hope that Washington would act— that hope lay in the power of the people. Drossaerts was confident that if

but one hundredth part of the horrors in Mexico be known by our generous-hearted American people, there would be raised such a cry of indignation . . . that Washington, in spite of Mr. J. P. Morgan and Big Business, would be forced to send out a ringing, manly protest against these unbelievable atrocities; and lift the embargo of arms, which is the only thing which keeps up the power of Calles against the wishes of 98% of the Mexican people.[92]

Since the exiled Mexican hierarchy established itself in San Antonio, Drossaerts enjoyed a more intimate connection with the Mexican prelates than other members of the American hierarchy. He had the honor of celebrating the lives of two of those bishops, Archbishop José Mora y del Río of Mexico City, and Bishop Ignacio Valdespino of Aguascalientes, through honoring their deaths. Archbishop Drossaerts took advantage of the opportunities provided by the funerals of two Mexican prelates who died in exile to publicize the concern of the American Catholics for the plight of the Mexican clergy, and to attack the Coolidge administration. The funeral of Valdespino provided the forum for Drossaerts's most blistering attack on Washington. Drossaerts's eulogy of Valdespino conveys a sense of the emotion behind the words, which harkened the listeners to the basic ideal shared by all Americans:

> The saddest feature of the Mexican situation is doubtless the universal apathy of the civilized world: Mexico is bleeding from a thousand wounds, and no one seems to care; Mexico is being drowned in the tears and the blood of its best sons and daughters and the nations of the world remain cold and unconcerned. . . . Liberty is being crucified at our very door and the United States looks on with perfect indifference. Not a voice is raised in protest; yea, despotism seems to have become popular amongst us: are we not sending endless "good-will" parties to Mexico? Are we not courting the friendship and favor of the very men whose hands are dripping with the blood of their countless innocent victims?
>
> If we ratify the solemn judgment of the great American President Abraham Lincoln: "those who deny freedom to others, deserve it not for themselves and under a just God cannot long retain it", there cannot exist a bond of friendship between the liberty-loving American people and the so-called Government across the Rio Grande which is torturing, killing and outraging men and women who dare to invoke the name of God or dare to raise up their voice in defense of the most elementary liberty.
>
> In the final analysis, we are largely responsible for the present Mexican tragedy. If the blood of the innocent Abel cried for vengeance against Cain the murderer, will not the innocent blood poured out in Mexico, be crying against us for our help and friendship we have so lavishly bestowed on the men responsible for that horrible carnival of crime across our Southern boundary?

No one wants war with Mexico. Yet, would not decency, would not humanity, would not love of liberty demand a manly protest from the civilized nations of the world and in the foremost place, on account of our Monroe Doctrine, from Washington, against the brutal, barbarous policy of a Government trampling under foot all freedom . . . ? The internal government of a country is of no concern of any other nation. But violent, brutal persecution is the concern of humanity. What noble contribution to Civilization; what blessing to poor Mexico would be a ringing protest against this shameful disgrace of our 20th Century![93]

Despite San Antonio's propinquity with Mexico, and the familiarity that proximity afforded Archbishop Drossaerts, he nonetheless reflected a patriarchal racism toward Mexico common in the United States of the time. In an appeal for money to support the Mexicans in his archdiocese, Drossaerts made clear his attitude toward them: "The Mexican is a big child, with all the good and the bad qualities of a child. He is warm-hearted and affectionate; humble, patient and long suffering; charitable and hospitable. But also he is fickle and inconsistent, improvident, squandering away for baubles and mere trifles the hard-earned wages of a week or a month."[94]

Later, the archbishop reflected the same prejudices in an appeal to the readers of *Extension* magazine. He despaired that the typical Mexican, "like our American Indian, . . . Is totally improvident." Mexicans have no savings, nor prepare for the future. Rather, the average Mexican in exile in San Antonio prefers "big, foolish" displays and "mere toys and trifles," and his "dream and greatest ambition [is] to have a string-band at his wedding or to have the most expensive coffin for the burial of a child or wife. . . ."[95] Drossaerts grounded his paternalism in an attitude of true concern for the welfare of the Mexican exiles.

San Antonio's proximity to the crisis in Mexico, and Archbishop Drossaerts's witness of the effects of the persecution on the scores of Mexican Catholics who fled to San Antonio for exile or refuge clearly had a tremendous effect on his attitudes toward the Coolidge administration's inactivity in the face of hardship in Mexico.

There were two salient features of the activity of the hierarchy of the United States in their effort to mold United States–Mexican foreign policy, the first of which was the general attempt to stimulate and guide public opinion. The methods employed by different prelates to mold public opinion varied greatly in their immediate incarnation. The common goal of these efforts was to bring some kind of pressure to bear on the United States government. Most of the attempts to initiate this pressure fall into two categories. The first, including the hierarchy's December 1926 pastoral letter, the advocacy by both Curley and the NCWC of organized meetings to protest violations of ideals, the NCWC's publication of educational pamphlets, and the calls to prayer by the prelates, had less tangible and more idealistic goals than the second category. The second group of efforts ranged from relatively benign activities including Gibbons's and Kelley's requests for "one word" and "respectful resolutions," to Curley's more visceral electoral threats which were intended to ignite more immediate responses from the public and the government. Although these attempts to mold public opinion among the receptive audiences of each of these churchmen and groups were largely successful (as evidenced by the mass participation in protest meetings and the volume of protest correspondence which flooded the White House), the larger goals of evoking immediate shifts in policy remained mostly unfulfilled. This is not to say that these efforts were abject failures. The Coolidge and Roosevelt administrations exhibited increased official interest in the plight of the persecuted Catholics of Mexico, as demonstrated in the attention dedicated to the settlement of the *modus vivendi* in 1929 and the expressions of concern by Roosevelt and his advisors to the Mexican ambassador in Washington.

The second striking characteristic of the prelates' response to the Mexican persecution is a corollary to the variety of efforts to mold opinion. Notable among the various prelates' responses to the persecution in Mexico was a high degree of internal divisiveness among prelates who might be expected to follow a "company line." As axes that indicate the polar differences among the prelates, Curley and Chicago's Archbishop George Cardinal Mundelein serve nicely. Curley represents one extreme, in that his attacks on the United States government devolved to blatant political-electoral threats. He not only laid into the Coolidge and Roosevelt administrations; he also focused his venomous strikes on some of his fellow prelates. For instance, following the NCWC Administrative Committee's decision to refrain from supporting the Borah resolution, Curley sought to undermine completely the credibility of the committee by attacking the personalities involved in the organization.

Sitting at the opposite pole vis-à-vis the Roosevelt administration was Archbishop George Cardinal Mundelein of Chicago. Archbishop Mundelein stood out in the crowd of prelates in that he was Franklin Roosevelt's greatest advocate among the hierarchy. Mundelein proved to be a valuable ally for Roosevelt, and demonstrated great affinity for political gamesmanship in that alliance. He had contacts with government at a variety of different levels, including David Shanahan, the Speaker of the Illinois House, who effectively buried bills in committee which violated Catholic, or at least Mundelein's, sensitivities. On the federal level, Mundelein enjoyed other close personal contacts. His personal lawyer, William Campbell, was a confidante of Thomas Corcoran, a prominent member of Roosevelt's brain trust.[96]

In 1935, Mundelein performed an act that outraged Archbishop Curley and others who opposed Roosevelt's Mexican policy. On December 9, 1935, Mundelein presided at a ceremony at the University of Notre Dame in which Roosevelt was awarded the honorary degree of Doctor of Laws. During the ceremony, Mundelein criticized the condemnations of Roosevelt by Curley and the Knights of Columbus by claiming that neither Curley nor Mundelein nor anyone else could rightfully claim to bear the standard for American Catholic political allegiance.[97] During his acceptance speech, Roosevelt outlined a number of rights necessary for "true national life." He made it clear that he believed that "supreme among these rights, we . . . hold to be the rights of freedom of education and freedom of religious worship."[98] Clearly, that Roosevelt was willing to voice his praise for these universal ideals was sufficient to convince Mundelein that the president recognized their value for Mexico as well.

Josephus Daniels believed that Roosevelt owed Cardinal Mundelein for his support in Roosevelt's successful re-election bid in 1936. Daniels suggested that Roosevelt select Mundelein to offer a prayer before Roosevelt's January 20, 1937, inauguration, since the cardinal's loyalty to principles helped cause "the large body of Catholic voters to turn a deaf ear to the pleas of Mr. Carmody of the Knights of Columbus, Bishop Kelley of Oklahoma, Father Coughlin, and Al Smith to oppose your reelection."[99]

Curley's harsh criticism of the honors bestowed upon Roosevelt by Mundelein rang in the ears of other prelates and prominent Catholics who supported the president, including Burke. Just as Curley typified the extreme animosity among the prelates for Roosevelt and his Latin American policy, Mundelein stood at the opposite end of the spectrum through his enthusiastic support for the president. Clearly, bishops such as O'Connell, with his appeals for prayer and his hesitance to call for more direct action, represented the majority of prelates.

These divisions made some of the prelates self-conscious. Bishop Kelley, for example, blamed the failure of the Roosevelt administration to act on the mixed signals from the hierarchy as to the degree of the Church's support for his policies. While some bishops had little to say on subjects other than Mexico, others, including Hanna and the officials of the NCWC, favored silence on the whole issue when conferring with Roosevelt.[100] This lies at the root of the failure of the hierarchy to move the United States government toward a policy line more attentive to the plight of the Catholics in Mexico. Kelley's frustration over Roosevelt's apparent refusal to keep his promise to issue a protest expresses not only an awareness of the difficulty of influencing the United States–Mexican policy, but also the understanding of the source of that difficulty: "I do not understand the President. I had heard that he made a promise [to issue a protest]. Surely he had enough visits from ecclesiastical dignitaries to understand the situation. I am afraid that some of those who went to see him, by avoiding the subject of Mexico, gave him the idea that we are divided about it."[101]

The failure of the hierarchy to achieve their ultimate intention of improving the lot of Mexico's Catholics lies firmly rooted in the mixed signals that resulted from the divisiveness alluded to in Kelley's lament. Even to speak of "goals" of the "hierarchy" designed to reach this ideal is difficult, for the bishops could not agree on the various mediary goals, including lifting the arms embargo and severing diplomatic recognition in the Coolidge years and recalling Daniels, passage of the Borah resolution, and a strong protest from Roosevelt in the Mexican crisis. Divided as it was, the Roman Catholic hierarchy represents one of the primary difficulties of private interest groups attempting to influence or manipulate public policy: the need to present a united front. Clearly, as indicated in Bishop Kelley's comments above, this divisiveness was a sensitive issue for those activist prelates who sought a bold policy with Mexico. In the end, the hierarchy could agree on one thing. The lowest common denominator was in reality the loftiest ideal: the right of Mexicans to fully enjoy the benefits of religious freedom.

chapter 4

JOHN J. BURKE, CSP

The most important Roman Catholic in this country . . . a man of great
power and authority, very sure of himself, very adroit and clever. . . .
[John J. Burke] seems rather the type of the great ecclesiastic of two or
three hundred years ago who ran the political affairs of the Church,
adaptable outwardly but steel underneath.

—Assistant Secretary of State William Castle on Burke[1]

REVEREND JOHN J. BURKE, CSP, WAS A TREMENDOUS MOVING FORCE
behind many of the efforts of the Catholic Church in the United States to
influence United States–Mexican relations in the 1920s and 1930s. His activism brought him into contact with, and intimately involved him in, some
of the most profound movements within the Church in the period. He almost single-handedly forged a scheme of organization within the American
hierarchy through his work to establish the National Catholic War Council
and its successor organization, the National Catholic Welfare Conference
(NCWC). As general secretary of these organizations, he kept his finger on
the pulse of Catholic activism in the United States. His position also allowed
him to direct and refocus this energy, which placed an immense amount of

responsibility on his shoulders. Some bishops and archbishops disapproved of his activities, but for the most part, he acted with the support and on behalf of the American hierarchy and Rome. His efforts on behalf of the Catholics of Mexico began after the end of World War I, and stretched through the turbulent 1920s and into the mid-1930s. Foremost among these efforts were his attempts to stir up protest against the persecution of Mexican Catholics, his cooperation with Ambassador Dwight Whitney Morrow and Mexican President Plutarco Elías Calles to arrive at a *modus vivendi* between the Mexican government and the Mexican Church, and his work to get President Franklin D. Roosevelt to publicly denounce the continued persecution of Catholics in Mexico.

Burke wielded tremendous influence within the Catholic Church. Before being named general secretary of the NCWC, Burke served as editor of an influential Catholic journal, *The Catholic World*. When he became the NCWC's general secretary, many Catholics believed, incorrectly, that he spoke or wrote on behalf of the Catholic hierarchy of the United States. This misinterpretation of Burke's power was at the center of most of the animosity directed against him. Michael J. Curley, archbishop of Baltimore, was perhaps the most influential of Burke's critics. He chafed at the thought of a simple Paulist priest assuming the mantle of spokesman for the whole of the Catholic hierarchy of the United States.

These critics, however, clearly embraced a minority opinion. Burke worked hard as NCWC general secretary, and he earned the respect of the hierarchy and those both in and out of government. He earned a place for American Catholics as a group not to be taken lightly. Although the authority through which he worked was ambiguous to the point of frustration (especially during the *modus vivendi* negotiations), he remained dedicated to securing the rights of his co-religionists in Mexico. His efforts helped forge a new relationship between the Church and the Mexican government. These accomplishments, however, do not convey the fullness of Father Burke's importance to the Catholic Church in the United States. He was largely responsible for coalescing and charting the course of Catholic public affairs in the United States during the 1920s and 1930s.

Burke and the NCWC

John J. Burke recognized that Catholics needed to have an organization to spearhead the Church's answer to the Protestants' Federal Council of Churches' war effort. With the permission and authority of Baltimore Archbishop James Cardinal Gibbons behind him, Burke called the American hierarchy to Washington, D.C., in August 1917 to plan for and create the National Catholic War Council. Burke assented to the assembled prelates' recommendation that he assume the position of general secretary of the War Council. As general secretary, Burke served as the spokesman for the NCWC Administrative Committee, which carried on the work of the entire NCWC while the membership was not meeting in general session.[2]

At the end of the war, Administrative Committee member Bishop Peter J. Muldoon (Rockford, Illinois) lobbied to secure a permanent organization to continue to provide leadership for the Church. Gibbons supported Muldoon's efforts. Even before this permanent incarnation of the bishops' organization was established, Burke recognized that he would have to play a part, albeit reluctantly. Early in 1919, he confided to his friend Fr. William J. Kirby his reservations: "I have done my share and played my part. The motive of immediate service to my country [so keen during the world war] has gone. The motive of service to the Church would win my consent to further service if I were asked. But it wouldn't be what I liked."[3] In September 1919, 92 of America's 101 prelates founded the National Catholic Welfare Council (in 1923 changed to "Conference"). Burke's prediction proved accurate, as his effective service as the secretary of the War Council convinced the assembled hierarchy to choose him to serve as general secretary of the NCWC. He was most anxious about their selection and did not look forward to accepting such great responsibility:

I don't want the Welfare Council work. I'm not fitted for it. I never went into the priesthood for it. I don't think I'm called in any way to direct the national work of the Catholic Church in the United States. It's a pain and just now little short of agony to accept it. . . . The honors come thick: people consult me: I've looked forward to this and that—but all that doesn't give my soul a bit of comfort. . . . My days have been cut off from those I love most. I miss my home: my days have been cut off from those—yourself [Grace Murray, Burke's secretary at *The Catholic World*], Gertrude, Mary [other *Catholic World* staffers], the men in the [Paulist community] house to whom I was devotedly attached, whom I love, with whom I worked and loved to work just as one of themselves. They loved me and were devoted to me. It is not so nor can it be in the new work. . . . I wept when the invitation [to the NCWC post] was given to me. . . . I see the big things

I ought to do and my soul is not going to quake or go back. . . . But I do want you to know—or rather, my heart wants to tell you that it is all costing me a great deal; for my mission is to lead others. . . .[4]

With resignation to what he believed was his higher "mission," Burke accepted the position and the massive responsibility it entailed.

If Burke had done nothing more than provide the Catholics of the United States, through the NCWC, a centralized body through which the Church could express its official voice, he would deserve the praise and admiration of his co-religionists. However, he did much more. He became intimately involved in seeking for Catholics in Mexico the freedom of worship that Catholics in the United States enjoyed.

Early Protests

As we have seen, President Alvaro Obregón chose to show relative tolerance to the Church in the interest of minimizing unrest that threatened to fracture Mexico and jeopardize the official recognition of Mexico by the United States. When Plutarco Elías Calles assumed the presidency in December 1926, however, he felt no such constraints. Following Archbishop Mora y del Río's 1926 open challenge and condemnation of the Constitution of 1917, Calles proceeded against the Catholic Church in Mexico with revolutionary fervor.

Burke believed the situation in Mexico would have direct repercussions in the Catholic Church of the United States: "The behavior of the Church in Mexico in the present crisis is forcefully related in an intimate and important way with the position, the intelligence, and well-being of the church in our country. Between both there is a very real solidarity of interests."[5] Therefore, he recognized that the Mexican situation was one that Catholics in the United States would have to address. He was behind the NCWC Administrative Committee's decision to send Charles Phillips to Mexico in 1926. Phillips's report to the committee outlined the unease with which the Mexican hierarchy noticed the calls from north of the Río Bravo for force and American intervention, and called on American Catholics to fully educate themselves about conditions in Mexico.

Archbishop Michael Curley ignored Phillips's recommendations of cautious, measured actions in response to the volatile Mexican situation. Rather than caution, Curley exploited his position as nominal head of the American hierarchy to call for and organize a massive interdenominational protest meeting in Washington, D.C., for March 7, 1926. Burke questioned Curley's motives for disregarding Phillips's report by calling for public protests. He speculated, privately, that it was part of a Vatican scheme to drive Calles from power. What would be Curley's reward for his efforts? Burke believed that Curley would "journey to Rome and receive the red hat."[6] Nonetheless, once Curley had broken the ice with his public demand for protest, Burke recognized the need to capitalize on whatever momentum Curley's call might produce. He decided to use his position in the NCWC to foment a broad-based protest against Calles's persecution of Mexican Catholics.

As Calles intensified his movement against the Catholic Church in mid-1926, Burke also stepped up his activities. He presented Secretary of State Frank Kellogg a copy of a letter of protest aimed at President Calvin Coolidge for his inaction on behalf of persecuted Mexicans. Burke considered Coolidge's consideration of the letter vital, because Catholics in the United States needed reassurance that the Catholic hierarchy was providing the leadership they needed by pressing the issue with Washington. Burke confided to Kellogg that "the bishops could not leave the Catholic body with the impression that nothing could be done by them." Undersecretary of State Franklin Mott Gunther, head of Mexican affairs in the State Department, had specific problems with the letter. He believed the letter would only anger the Mexican government, which would not help the Mexican Catholics.[7] Burke and the Administrative Committee, however, believed that the letter was too important to allow it to wither on the vine, so they published it in spite of Gunther's objections in a press release dated May 18, 1926. Clearly frustrated with Burke's actions, Gunther noted to Kellogg that Burke's attitude "so far has been governed by the feeling that the Catholics of the United States are so important politically that more action should be taken on their behalf than in behalf of others."[8]

Gunther's attitude is understandable, but clearly Burke faced an uphill battle himself. One of the most effective weapons in the Mexican government's arsenal was a tremendous propaganda effort carried on through the Mexican embassy and consulates throughout the United States. Burke formally protested the fact that the Mexican government was publishing and distributing anti-Catholic propaganda under the guise of real news stories, and that the embassy's free access to the United States postal system made this distribution possible. In July 1926, Burke demanded an official protest from the United States Department of State. To bolster his protest against this propaganda effort, Burke cited the case of Reverend E. Kunkel in Santa Fe, New Mexico, who received in the mail a pamphlet titled "The Church Problem in Mexico," printed and distributed by the Mexican Consul General in New York. William M. Karsunky of Washington, D.C., received five copies of another Mexican government pamphlet, titled "Benificencia Privada," ("Private Beneficence"), from the Mexican consul in Chicago, and James C. Burrow received a copy from the consul in Norfolk, Virginia.[9] Kellogg promised that he would discuss the matter with Manuel Tellez, the Mexican ambassador to the United States.

Much more than the bishops' protest letter and the Mexican propaganda occupied Burke in mid-1926. George Caruana, the archbishop of Puerto Rico, had journeyed to Mexico to serve as the apostolic delegate. He entered the country quietly, and claimed to have followed all rules of declaration of occupation and intent. Nonetheless, Calles considered him a disruptive presence in Mexico and accused him of entering Mexico under false pretenses. The Mexican administration claimed that Caruana had claimed to be a native-born, Protestant professor upon entering the country, none of which was true.[10] Based on these claims, the government initiated deportation proceedings. Burke urged Kellogg to authorize Ambassador James Sheffield to fight the deportation order as a violation of the rights of an American citizen. William Montavon, chief legal counsel for the NCWC, confided to Secretary of Labor James J. Davis that if the State Department acted swiftly, Caruana might not face expulsion. Davis, however, remained convinced that Kellogg was doing everything that he could on Caruana's behalf. Clearly, these efforts were not sufficient, as Calles forced Caruana out of Mexico on May 16, 1926.

Burke was outraged at the Mexican government. During a visit to the Mexican embassy in Washington, he told Tellez that "this damn program of persecution has got to stop!" The Mexican ambassador angrily replied that if Burke insisted on swearing, he "could go somewhere else."[11] He did just that by initiating an effort to flood the White House with protests of the violation of the rights of an American citizen. He wired instructions for protests to numerous Catholic organizations, including the National Councils of Catholic Men and Catholic Women (the lay units of the NCWC), the Knights of Columbus, the National Catholic Alumni Federation, the Ancient Order of Hibernians, and the Catholic Order of Foresters, along with wires to members of the American hierarchy. Most of those solicited complied with Burke's request for protests, and copies of the statements fill his files. Bishop Francis Kelley's (Oklahoma City/Tulsa) was typical. He protested "the virtual protection extended by the Government of the United States to the present Government of Mexico through the continuance of a recognition granted only on an understanding that the rights of American citizens would be respected and that the Mexican Government would be conducted along lines plainly marked out by civilized society."[12]

Assistant Secretary of State Robert Olds was responsible for answering this mountain of protests. Burke's files contain numerous copies of Olds's formulaic replies, most of which state that "the Department has taken a deep interest in this case," or that it "feels everything has been done that this Government could consistently do in the circumstances."[13]

As protests such as these began to make their way to the White House and the State Department, Kellogg began to recognize the widespread opposition in the United States to the Mexican persecution. In a memo of a meeting with Kellogg, Burke noted that the secretary seemed to be "seriously contemplating lifting the embargo against the importation of arms into Mexico and setting Mexico adrift." Kellogg also indicated that he planned to write Ambassador Sheffield a confidential letter to have him privately inquire if the Mexican government was "willing to receive an Apostolic Delegate in Mexico and treat him with the courtesy and respect that his position demands." Burke took the tenor of the interview as a direct indication of "the continued and deepening effect that the protests and expression of American opinion have secured."[14]

Burke believed that for this protest to have a still more profound effect, it needed to be broadened and extended to a larger portion of the American public. In a *Wall Street Journal* editorial, Burke attempted to inflame loyal Americans against the threat looming to the south. He maintained that just as the issue of Bolshevism's spread in Russia became a concern for the United States, the Mexican government's violations of basic human rights would ultimately undermine free institutions in this country. This real threat to American values and ideals made the issue of religious persecution in Mexico more than a Catholic or a Mexican question. It had become a pan-American issue as well.[15]

William Green, president of the American Federation of Labor (AFL), responded to Burke's appeal. He claimed that religious freedom remained a basic ideal of the AFL, so clearly the persecution in Mexico was an issue of concern for all those associated with the AFL as well as all Americans. However, Green went on to state that although the Mexican Federation of Labor (MFL) had chosen to support the Mexican government, the AFL had no right to interfere with the decisions of the Mexican labor council.[16] As soon as Burke read Green's statement, he protested that the AFL had not only a right, but in fact, an obligation to condemn anyone, including the MFL, who supported the Mexican government's persecution of Catholics. In Burke's eyes, Green's refusal to denounce the MFL indicated, by omission, the AFL's support for MFL backing of the Mexican government.[17] Green was just as rapid in his response to Burke. He was confident that in the several conversations between Burke and himself, Green understood Burke's desire that the AFL distance itself from the MFL. Green believed that a more constructive tactic would be to criticize the MFL's politics rather than the organization itself. An August 8 statement he released from the AFL offices accomplished just that. As far as influencing the MFL to call for religious freedom, Green maintained that he had made a very forceful statement concerning the MFL and religious freedom when he claimed that the AFL had "endeavored to instill in the hearts and minds of the Mexican working people the principles and philosophy of the American Federation of Labor."[18] Clearly, Burke had little patience for anyone either unwilling or politically unable to make the strong, overt condemnations he sought.

Burke labored on many fronts to seek, for Catholics in Mexico, the right to worship freely. In his efforts to evoke from the Coolidge administration an official protest, to bring to the public's attention the Mexican government's mistreatment of Archbishop Caruana, and in his work to focus American Catholic outrage against the Mexican persecution, he served an invaluable purpose. He hoped an organized protest would win for his Catholic brothers and sisters in Mexico their basic human rights. Yet, he refused to stop there. He was determined to end the persecution.

The National Committee for the Protection of Religious Rights in Mexico

Burke feared that while the Coolidge administration had made some initial movement against the persecution, it had not fully grasped the importance of forceful action, as evidenced by the president's preoccupation with Mexican oil and land laws to the exclusion of the religious persecution. The Coolidge administration's advice that the NCWC demonstrate their loyalty as Americans by silencing their dissent would, in Burke's estimation, prove fatal for their cause. Although Burke recognized that earlier efforts to force the United States government into action had failed, he nevertheless remained steadfast in his belief that "it is even more than ever obligatory upon us to arouse and inform our fellow-citizens and to help create a moral sentiment that will make impossible the continuation of the Calles regime in Mexico."[19]

Following the call in early 1926 by Archbishop José Mora y del Río of Mexico City for active American protests, Burke and the NCWC Administrative Committee endeavored to form a national committee of laypersons to help create that moral sentiment. Burke directed the National Council of Catholic Men (NCCM) and the National Council of Catholic Women (NCCW) to form a committee dedicated to a program of education for the American people in order to foment a public opinion sympathetic to the plight of Mexico's Catholics.[20] Prominent Catholic Judge Morgan J. O'Brien had agreed to chair the National Committee for the Protection of Religious Rights in Mexico (NCPRRM). Burke solicited participation in the committee's work by sending form letters to prominent Catholics throughout the United States seeking members. Besides the publishing and distribution of pamphlets explaining the situation in Mexico, the committee planned and promoted public meetings throughout the nation where the persecution would be discussed by well-informed panels.

The response to Burke's appeals was by no means unanimous. While Burke's files contain long lists of members, most of whom were corporate chairs, judges, and attorneys, his files also contain refusals in the form of angry letters protesting the committee's goals and even its very existence. John K. Mullen, a wealthy Catholic businessman, believed that American Catholics had no business getting involved in the political movements of another nation. Moreover, he doubted that American Catholics were even getting the whole story. If Catholics should do anything, he thought they should discern the root causes of the crisis. Mullen wondered how, since Mexico was 90 percent Catholic, the revolutionary 10 percent were able to put through laws that jeopardized the liberty of the vast majority of Mexicans. He claimed that it was too much like the "tail wagging the dog" to be believed on face value.[21] Colonel Patrick H. Callahan, president of the Louisville Varnish Company and former high-ranking official of the Knights of Columbus, flatly refused Burke's invitation with a caustic note in which he blamed interference by Burke himself and the NCWC Administrative Committee for the crisis facing the Catholic Church in Mexico.[22]

Many of those who did accept Burke's invitations harbored reservations about the committee's goals and tactics. William M. Mumm, president of Mumm-Romer-Jaycox Company Advertising, was also reluctant to serve on the committee. In fact he believed the whole idea of such an organization, which he and others interpreted as an effort to force the United States government to intervene in Mexico, was a mistake. Repugnant though it may have been, the Mexican persecution was still an internal affair, and the American Catholics had no business in asking the United States government to take a stand on such an issue that did not directly concern this country. Mumm believed that a better course of action would be for the United States Catholics to champion all Christian denominations against the Mexican government. Catholics should base all requests for action on the basis of violations of the rights of Americans, and should "protest against this quite as vigorously in behalf of other Christian denominations as we do for our own."[23] Burke thanked Mumm for his acceptance, and took great pains to assure him that the NCWC had no intention of either demanding physical intervention or any move that might threaten to lead to war.[24]

Judge Martin T. Manton of the Second Judicial Circuit, United States Circuit Court of Appeals, also offered tepid support for the committee. While he was willing to become a member, he pointed out to Burke that at least three times in the past, American secretaries of state refused to act on behalf of persecuted religious groups, in spite of petitions from American citizens. These instances, during the administrations of Andrew Jackson, Benjamin Harrison, and Grover Cleveland, might "constitute sufficient basis for the present attitude of the Secretary of State." Manton believed that the only successful way to achieve change in Mexico was to cast the issue into the international spotlight, and that American Catholics should strive to convince the United States government to appeal to the International Court and to the League of Nations to declare Mexico an outlaw nation on the basis of the deprivations of human rights contained in the Constitution of 1917.[25] Burke, after consulting with the NCWC Administrative Committee, asserted that such proposals went far beyond the NCWC's responsibilities.[26]

As the NCPRRM struggled to gain momentum throughout 1927, a crisis in November peaked Burke's sense of emergency over the Mexican persecution. Following a failed attempt on the life of former president Alvaro Obregón, government authorities arrested Jesuit Father Miguel Pro Juarez, his brother Humberto, and two other alleged co-conspirators. Regardless of the fact that there was no evidence linking the Pro brothers to the assassination attempt, the four were nonetheless executed without trial on the personal orders of Calles on November 23.[27] Official photographs of the moment of Father Pro's execution, which show that Pro stretched out his arms as had Christ on the cross, did not achieve the desired effect. Instead of providing a warning to activist Catholics, the photographs actually provided the Mexican Catholics with a genuine martyr. Following the publication of the photos,

American Catholics railed against what they considered a gross miscarriage of justice. Catholic demands for a formal protest from the American government reached a fever pitch. Burke asked Coolidge and Kellogg to send an official note of protest to Calles, but the president refused. While Coolidge expressed his personal revulsion for Calles's violations of basic human rights, he maintained that Pro's execution was a Mexican internal affair. Moreover, Coolidge feared a curt reply from Calles, which would make further steps, such as deploying troops or withdrawing the United States ambassador from Mexico, necessary. He wanted, above all, to avoid any steps that could lead to war.[28]

Kellogg continued to insist that the State Department was doing everything it could. He had already spoken with Mexican Ambassador Tellez and had explained, unofficially, how seriously American Catholics felt about the persecution of their co-religionists in Mexico. He also handed Tellez a copy of the NCWC's protest of May 18, 1926, and asked that he transmit it to his government. Unaccountably, however, when Burke sought Kellogg's help in transmitting to the Mexican government a protest from a group of American citizens, the secretary of state refused, since such a letter would carry with it the apparent United States government stamp of approval as much as if it were a product of the State Department.[29] In response, Burke presented Kellogg with a forty-three-page report of Calles's anti-religious activities from February 12, 1926, to November 22, 1927. Graphic accounts of federal forces arresting and shooting priests, burning churches, closing schools, and of civilian torture at the hands of federal troops filled the pages of the report. Typical of the atrocities Burke cited was the story of one priest from Tamazula, whose hands were cut off to keep him from being able to say Mass.[30]

In spite of the power of this material, Burke's efforts to establish a central lay organization for the purpose of coordinating American protest against the Mexican persecution bore sparse fruit. He could not coordinate, for example, the NCPRRM, the Knights of Columbus, and other groups that had their own agendas for protest. Following the execution of Father Pro and the deafening silence from Washington, D.C., on the matter, he recognized that he needed to take a personal hand in the matter. This, however, was the last thing he wanted to do.

Burke and Morrow

One of the few things that went right for the Catholics of Mexico was the appointment of Dwight Whitney Morrow, formerly a partner in the J. P. Morgan

Company, as United States ambassador to Mexico on October 29, 1927. Morrow contrasted clearly with his predecessor, James Sheffield. Kellogg came to believe that Sheffield saw war as the only way to resolve the Mexico–United States tensions and Mexico's internal turmoil.[31] Morrow, on the other hand, firmly believed that if the religious issue were resolved, the other crises, such as those over oil concessions and land expropriation laws, would subside considerably. He earnestly maintained that peace could never last until peace prevailed between the Church and the state.[32] Burke found a great deal of hope for Mexico in Morrow's appointment. Burke, in fact, believed that Morrow's attitude towards the Mexican church-state crisis was most opportune.

Before Morrow left the United States to take up his post in Mexico City, he met with Burke, New York Archbishop Patrick Cardinal Hayes, and prominent Catholic Judge Morgan O'Brien. Burke hoped this meeting would convey to the new ambassador the attitudes of Catholics of the United States. Burke recognized that the pressure of public opinion that Catholics had placed on the United States government had accomplished little for the Catholics of Mexico. Consequently, they wanted to smooth the rift between American Catholics and both the Mexican government and the United States State Department. Moreover, they expressed the opinion that Morrow was in a truly advantageous position to offer help in achieving these ends.

Once Morrow arrived in Mexico, his reading of the diplomatic landscape led him to the realization that he would be able to catch more Mexican flies with honey than with Sheffield's saber-rattling vinegar. Many American Catholics criticized Morrow for pursuing friendly relations with Calles upon his arrival in Mexico. Judge O'Brien attempted to quiet some of this growing protest by claiming that critics "probably thought that Mr. Morrow should have taken a whip with him and immediately upon arrival should have attacked Calles so as to let him know that the new Ambassador did not desire to have anything to do with him." Many American Catholics believed that Morrow's acceptance of official invitations from Calles demonstrated a woeful insensitivity to their feelings about the persecution. In particular, an invitation to an official luncheon on November 23 for the Mexican Foreign Office brought the ambassador under fire. Unbeknownst to Morrow, at the same time that Calles was raising toasts to Ambassador Morrow, Mexican government agents had executed Father Miguel Pro and his brother for their alleged complicity in the Obregón assassination attempt.

Morrow accepted Calles's invitation to join him on a train trip through northern Mexico, which magnified American Catholic fears that the ambassa-

dor was oblivious to the persecutions. Morrow, however, recognized his difficult political position: accepting the invitation would surely anger Catholics in
the United States, yet if he were to protest the executions by refusing Calles's
invitation, he risked insulting the president and thereby jeopardizing all future
talks. Morrow decided that agreeing to go on the trip would potentially allow
him to appeal to Calles on behalf of Mexico's Catholics. Kellogg assured Morrow that he had made the right choice. On the trip, Morrow addressed the religious situation whenever Calles himself broached the subject. On one of
these occasions, Morrow suggested that Calles not overlook the influence
Catholics, particularly Catholics in the United States, could wield.[33]

Morrow held tremendous faith in the possibility for a church-state settlement. He believed that if Calles were to meet with representatives of the
Church, a mutually acceptable *modus vivendi* was possible. Morrow opined
that someone like Burke, who had counseled Morrow before he took up his
station in Mexico City, would be a logical choice to work with Calles to bring
about a settlement. In a conversation with Calles, Morrow broached the subject of a possible meeting. He indicated that someone like Burke, who "enjoyed
the full confidence of the leaders of the Church in America," might be willing
to discuss the matter. Calles responded that he was always open to meet anyone who could calmly and rationally discuss the Church issue.[34]

When Assistant Secretary of State Robert Olds met with Burke on December 20, 1927, Olds passed on Morrow's plan for Burke to negotiate with
Calles. Burke flatly exclaimed that his playing such a role was simply impossible. A second meeting several days later also ended abruptly when Olds asked
if Burke would be willing to travel to Mexico.[35] In a letter to San Francisco
Archbishop Edward J. Hanna, the chairman of the NCWC Administrative
Committee, Burke discounted such plans as "little short of the ridiculous."[36]

Clearly, Hanna did not see it the same way. The Administrative Committee decided that it needed to pursue every option, including the proposed
Burke-Calles meeting. Burke informed Olds of the Administrative Committee's decision on January 4, 1928. Olds made immediate plans for Burke
to link up with Morrow at the Pan-American Conference in Havana later in
January. Both Burke and Olds agreed that any meeting involving Burke, Morrow, and Calles would necessarily be wholly unofficial, and that any work done
was not on behalf of the State Department, but was due to Morrow's personal
efforts.[37]

Before departing for Havana, Burke met with Apostolic Delegate Pietro
Fumasoni-Biondi and Monsignor Filippo Bernardini, the nephew of the papal

secretary of state. They briefed Burke on the Vatican's stand, namely that the Mexican government must allow the exiled bishops to return to their dioceses. Burke tried to temper Fumasoni-Biondi's expectations by assuring the apostolic delegate that any work he did was but "the beginnings of a beginning of a possible reconciliation of the Church with the Mexican Government." Further, Burke told the apostolic delegate how displeased he was with his assignment: "Well, Your Excellency, you have got me into a very unpleasant task and one that is entirely against my taste and the tenor of my life. I never expected anything like this and it has upset me a great deal." The apostolic delegate assured Burke that he had full confidence in him; that he was "deliberate and just," and simply the best person suited for such a mission.[38]

Father Burke met Ambassador Morrow in the ambassador's room at the Sevilla Biltmore in Havana on January 17, 1928. Morrow warned Burke of the difficulties that lay ahead: Calles was "an obstinate, pig-headed, self-confident fanatic" in his belief that "the Catholic hierarchy and priests were always opposed to the real progress of the Mexican people and nation."[39] Morrow recommended that a committee of Mexican bishops approach Calles, but Burke countered that the only solution lay in Calles recognizing the Holy See, his accepting an apostolic delegate for Mexico, and his allowing the bishops to return from exile. When the four-hour meeting ended, Morrow despaired about the mission's success, and Burke left feeling "disappointed and depressed."[40]

The ambassador and the priest met a second time in Havana on the following day. At this meeting, Morrow continued to favor a commission of the Mexican bishops meeting with Calles, but Burke remained steadfast in his opinion that Calles first needed to recognize an apostolic delegate. Besides, claimed Burke, such a high-level meeting would make public statements necessary, which both sides would need to endorse. As yet, there was no common ground for such statements. Morrow realized that he would need to meet with Calles on the matter, and Burke acknowledged his own need to meet with Calles as well. While he found the matter personally odious, his ecclesiastical superiors had already determined the necessity of the meeting.[41] Morrow and Burke did not meet again until Burke traveled to Mexico in April.

Before Burke left Cuba for the United States, he met with the archbishop of Mexico, José Mora y del Río. After two years of American Catholic activism and a deepening persecution of the Mexican Catholics under President Calles, Mora had moderated his stand significantly. He remained completely convinced that the United States government had it in its power to end the religious crisis almost at will. He confided with Burke that if the

United States government made its desire for a church-state settlement clear, and would press the issue with Calles, the crisis would quickly pass. Burke was much more skeptical in his estimation of the latitude with which the United States government could act. The United States needed to move carefully to avoid a possible conflict. Mora agreed that a United States–Mexico war was out of the question, but posited that "all the United States would have to do would be to permit the Catholics to obtain arms and supplies and they would quickly overcome the opposition of Calles."[42]

Morrow remained busy while in Havana. In early February, he met secretly with a delegation of Mexican prelates and with Walter Lippmann, whose visit to Havana to report on the Pan-American Conference for the *New York World* was but a cover for a secret diplomatic mission. After the conference ended, Morrow, Lippmann, and Lippmann's family sailed to Mexico City with a rough compromise in hand. Although Lippmann was in Mexico on "vacation," he got little rest. For the next month, Morrow and Lippmann shuttled between the Mexican hierarchy and the presidential palace with letters they themselves had drafted in the names of both the prelates and the president. With each letter, from Calles to the hierarchy and back, the finer points of the settlement came into focus. Together, they outlined the statements for exchange upon which the settlement would rest.[43]

When Morrow and Lippmann determined that all was ready, the ambassador met with Calles and set up a meeting with Burke. Calles quickly canceled this meeting, however, because of a leak to the press, which he believed would make him look weak and as if he were requesting negotiations with the Church—tantamount to capitulation to the Church.[44] Burke believed that the *New York Herald-Tribune* story by Jack Starr-Hunt, which exposed the secret meeting, was proof that opponents of a church-state settlement were hard at work to spoil all plans. Olds, however, believed that the leak must have come from a group of Catholics opposed to the settlement within Calles's own office. Burke confided in frustration to Hanna, "that there is an organized effort to prevent a settlement, that certain Catholics are bound up with that effort, together with American lawyers of the oil interests, is beyond question."[45]

At an early March meeting, Olds briefed Burke on a conference between Morrow and Calles. Calles made it clear that while he still welcomed a meeting with Burke, the Church continued to oppose him with arms (a reference to the Cristero Rebellion) and was still, by extension, involved in politics. Eliminating the Church's political power remained Calles's first priority.

Morrow saw a solution to the church-state crisis in an exchange of state-ments—the same statements he and Walter Lippmann had drafted earlier. Morrow held great confidence in the statements. Not only had he and Lipp-mann drafted those messages in language they believed both sides would ac-cept, but Calles also admired Lippmann both personally and professionally. Moreover, Morrow and Lippmann remained confident that the statements would be acceptable to the Church, since the core of the messages had come directly from the Mexican hierarchy's 1926 statement. Morrow, Burke, and Olds decided that Burke should take the initiative by asking Calles if an ex-change of notes would smooth the way to the resumption of worship and an easing of tensions. According to Morrow's draft statements, the Mexican bish-ops would agree to return to their churches if Calles would declare the law re-quiring all priests to register an administrative and statistical measure, and not intended as a means by which the government hoped to dictate to the Church by determining who could be priests. In the exchange, as Morrow and Lipp-mann had planned it, Calles would respond with a letter assuring the bishops that the Mexican government had no plan or desire to eliminate the integrity of the Church, and that he had always intended the registration law to be ad-ministrative in nature. Finally, Calles would welcome a discussion of changes in the constitutional laws once worship had resumed and tensions had eased.[46]

In spite of the great hopes for these statements, Burke cautioned against unreasonable expectations. He reiterated the difficulty of a settlement, since it required consensus among the Mexican bishops, who in fact were badly di-vided. Burke noted in his notes that Olds was "beginning to see more clearly the difficulty, if not the impossibility," of the task which lay ahead.[47]

To help him prepare for his meeting with Calles, Burke met with Walter Lippmann. At this meeting, Burke first learned of the extent to which Lipp-mann was already involved. Lippmann apprised Burke of the shifting atti-tudes in the Mexican government, away from those of the framers of the Con-stitution of 1917. Lippmann quoted Louis Montes de Oca, Mexican finance minister and close friend of Calles: "We realize the framers of the 1917 Con-stitution intended it should crush the Church entirely, but we are not of that mind today. We would wish to see the Church live so long as it does not in-terfere with politics." Moreover, Lippmann determined from interviews with various cabinet officials that, except for Minister of War General Amaro, all the ministers believed that the Church issue was not the only one in which the framers did not represent the current attitudes of Mexico. Calles had as-sured Lippmann, at one of the two meetings they had in February 1928 at which they discussed the church-state issue, that he had no intention of destroying the Church. Instead, he only wanted priests to refrain from interfering in politics.[48] Lippmann suggested that Burke strike while the iron was hot, as Calles was to leave office in December 1928, and Obregón, his successor, was frequently unreliable, and held the Church in general, and priests in particular, in low disdain.[49]

Olds and Burke discussed final plans for the Burke-Calles meeting as Morrow's final draft of the statements arrived.[50] On the next day, March 29, Burke signed Morrow's letter to Calles, and Olds confirmed Morrow's latest plan: Burke and one companion, William Montavon, would meet Calles in Veracruz.

Once Ambassador Morrow had conceived of the idea of having Father Burke meet with Mexican President Calles as a method of arriving at a church-state accord in Mexico, and once Burke had accepted this great responsibility, a diplomatic ball had started rolling that would take more than two years to reach its goal. Without the close cooperation between these three men—Morrow, Burke, and Calles—few believed that an end to the clerical strike and the Cristero Rebellion would come soon. In this partnership, Morrow provided the letters for Calles and Burke to exchange, Burke provided the personal representation of the corporate entity of the Church (due to his assignment to the matter by the apostolic delegate), and Calles provided the official voice of a Mexican government weary of war and unrest. Little did they know both how tangled the lines of communication and how confusing the official status of the negotiators would become.

The Modus Vivendi *of 1929*

Father John J. Burke's meeting with Plutarco Elías Calles, where they discussed the Morrow-Lippmann statements for exchange, laid the groundwork for the 1929 *modus vivendi* between church and state. Burke and Montavon joined Morrow in conferring with Calles and brothers Albert and James Smithers (Americans who worked as Calles's representatives and interpreters) at the Veracruz castle of San Juan de Ullua on April 4, 1928.

Burke began the meeting by outlining the hopes of the Church and the pope: the Vatican's ultimate goals were peace and freedom of worship. To achieve these ends, the return of the bishops and the resumption of worship were the immediate priorities. Although Burke acknowledged that he had come to the meeting entirely without authority to either accept or reject any proposal, he sought assurances that the Church could accept and still retain its dignity.[51] Calles responded brusquely: "Father Burke, you are all wrong with regard to the facts. I will tell you the facts."[52]

The constitution, according to Calles, had no provisions for penalizing violations, and the government sought none. Nonetheless, Archbishop Mora pronounced on February 4, 1926, that the Church could not, would not accept the provisions of the constitution, and he called for a national boycott that threatened to deepen the economic turmoil that wracked Mexico in the 1920s. Then, the bishops closed the churches in an effort to prove that they and the wealthy class that aligned with them were the true rulers of Mexico. Calles, on the other hand, had done all that he had done for the good of the masses while the Church and the wealthy had opposed him at every turn. These threats to Mexican stability forced the Calles government to detain any priests then in prison not because they were priests, but because they were rebels plotting the overthrow of the Mexican government. Finally, he expressed the hope that the priests would return to Mexico to work for the good of the people, for the good of Mexico.

Daniels later recounted the following exchange, which indicates the tensions through which the conversation proceeded. When Burke remarked to Morrow that Calles ought to recall that it was a priest—Fr. Miguel Hidalgo—who had issued the first call for Mexican independence, the president chose to take issue with the priest:

> *Calles:* "Yes, I know but the Catholic Church excommunicated him."
>
> *Burke:* "He was excommunicated because, contrary to his vows of celibacy, Hidalgo was the father of children."
>
> *Calles:* "If all priests of that day who were the fathers of children had been excommunicated, there would not have been enough left to carry on the work of the church."[53]

Such was the atmosphere within which Burke had to work. He hoped to salvage the meeting by shifting the focus of discussion to safer ground—the Church's hope that an apostolic delegate could return to Mexico. As the meeting was drawing to a close, Burke and Calles signed the letters for exchange drafted by Morrow. When Burke ended the meeting by claiming that he had to brief the apostolic delegate, Calles expressed the hope that Burke's "visit means a new era for the life and people of Mexico."[54]

Upon returning to the United States from Mexico, Burke consulted Fumasoni-Biondi on the next step in the settlement process and recommended that Ruiz exchange notes with Calles based on those exchanged by Burke and Calles. After the apostolic delegate received the report, he decided that it would be best to delay transmittal of the statements to Rome until the Mexican hierarchy had a chance to consider them during their meeting in San Antonio. The Mexican hierarchy was under the leadership of Archbishop Leopoldo Ruiz y Flores, who ascended to the leadership upon the death of Archbishop José Mora y del Río on April 3, 1928. At their San Antonio conference, they voted to accept Rome's guidance in the matter, but asked that the Holy Father not approve of the notes until Calles agreed to return all ecclesiastical lands and properties necessary for worship and to grant a blanket amnesty for the exiled Mexican bishops.[55] Morrow recognized that it was impossible to expect Calles to accept these demands without another meeting. The ambassador was so interested in settling the crisis that he bought train tickets for Burke, Montavon, and Ruiz so that they could meet with Calles in Mexico City. Obregón would be at the meeting, and had committed himself to endorsing anything that Calles had decided.[56] Ruiz, Montavon, and Burke left Washington, D.C., by train on May 12, and since the apostolic delegate recommended that Burke and Ruiz not be seen together, they traveled apart and took meals separately.[57]

Two incidents during the journey must have left Burke filled with doubt as to the success of the trip. During a stopover in Laredo, Texas, Burke wrote a letter in jest from Calles to Ruiz. The archbishop did not take the note as a joke and insisted that Rome would demand much more than Calles (Burke) had offered in the note. When further pressed, Ruiz claimed that Calles should sign a note to the Vatican guaranteeing that the constitution would be changed in the Church's favor. Burke quickly dropped the subject, as he recognized that Ruiz's inflexibility and Calles's convictions could well doom hopes for a flourishing negotiation. Then, in a conversation with Albert Smithers, Calles's American interpreter, Burke learned that Calles was opposed to Ruiz's presence at the meeting. Calles feared Ruiz would only stir up trouble, but had agreed to letting him come because Burke wanted him there. Burke, however, believed that everyone at the meeting, including Calles and Obregón, accepted Ruiz's role in the talks. Burke had understood Calles's acceptance of Ruiz as a sign of Calles's goodwill. This new information about Ruiz's status darkened Burke's sense of foreboding about a successful meeting.

At the second conference, convened at Chapultepec Castle outside of Mexico City on May 17, 1928, Burke presented Calles with the main points of the San Antonio meeting. First, the bishops demanded that only they be able to name priests for registration by the government. Calles accepted this provision immediately, repeating his desire not to interfere in internal Church matters. Second, the Mexican bishops wanted to discuss the possibility of holding religious education classes in school buildings after hours. Calles held that this was a violation of the constitution, and was, therefore, unacceptable. Finally, the bishops asked for the return of church buildings transferred to the revolutionary government. On this demand, Calles claimed no responsibility by maintaining that any seizures were the result of "the imprudence of some of the Bishops." Return of buildings would be difficult, because most had been sold to private interests. However, Calles assured Burke that for "any request for a return, when public worship was resumed, the Government would hear and consider the evidence."[58]

These were not the responses Ruiz had been looking for, but he sought to continue the negotiations. He offered to write Calles a letter on behalf of the Mexican hierarchy, based on Burke's letter of March 29. That Calles was willing to proceed along these lines, knowing that Ruiz needed Rome's approval, demonstrated significant openness on Calles's part. Once Rome had assented to the notes, Ruiz and Calles agreed that both sides would publish the correspondence, clearing the way for the Mexican clergy to resume worship in the churches. Burke cabled Fumasoni-Biondi that the meeting had concluded to the overall satisfaction of those involved. He also sent a synopsis of the proposed letters for exchange between Ruiz and Calles. Ruiz requested fast action, so that the priests could return to the churches in time for Pentecost, May 27. A reply did come quickly, though it was not the one Burke and Ruiz sought. On May 19, Father James Ryan, in contact with the apostolic delegate, cabled Burke that he and Ruiz were to travel to Rome immediately to facilitate a settlement.[59] The trip was necessary, according to Ryan, because Fumasoni-Biondi doubted that the Vatican would act on another telegram. When Morrow learned that both Ruiz and Burke would have to sail to Rome before the matter was to be settled, his despair over the success of the mission deepened. Burke noted that the ambassador "was losing faith and hope and interest."[60]

After Morrow, Ruiz, and Burke arrived in Washington by train, the apostolic delegate expressed Rome's interest in dealing with a Mexican prelate. In an apparent attempt to avoid an insult to Mexican national pride, Fumasoni-Biondi decided that Ruiz would go to Rome alone. European crowds greeted Ruiz with much fanfare and publicity. One news report quoted Ruiz as having declared that any settlement in the Mexican church-state conflict hinged upon a repeal of the anti-religious provisions of the Constitution of 1917. Whether or not this quote was accurate is less important than the fact that Ruiz had obviously leaked news of the Calles-Burke-Morrow negotiations, thereby placing Calles in a difficult position vis-à-vis the Mexican revolutionaries. Ruiz denied the claim, but the Mexican newspapers were quick to publish the original story. Morrow feared Calles would cease all talks and publish the Burke correspondence to prove that the Mexican government did not appear to be selling out to the Church. When the ambassador warned that publishing the correspondence would not be in Mexico's best interests, Calles reconsidered his response. He did so not out of any obligation to Rome or to the Mexican hierarchy, but to avoid anything that could embarrass Burke, whom he held in high regard.[61]

Even after Ruiz arrived in Rome, the Vatican chose to wait before commenting on the talks thus far. As days stretched into weeks and weeks into months, the prospect for a settlement appeared increasingly dim. The Vatican clearly wanted to negotiate with Obregón, presumably because during his first presidency (1920–1924), he more or less left the Church alone. However, the longer the Vatican delayed, the less willing Calles became to bend on further proposals. While the Vatican sat on the Burke-Calles-Ruiz statements without action, Morrow grew more despondent about the settlement.

As President-elect Alvaro Obregón's inauguration neared, he became more interested in the proposed settlement. He made an appointment to meet with Morrow for the afternoon of July 17, 1928, to discuss the future of peace between the Church and state. This meeting never took place, however, as at a luncheon on that day, Catholic radical José de Leon Toral assassinated Obregón. In reaction, Calles linked the assassin to the Church and blamed "religious fanaticism" and "clerical action" for the killing, thus sounding the death knell for the proposed settlement.[62] Burke sprung into action to mitigate the damage done to the settlement talks. He implored Calles to clarify his comments, noting that his accusation jeopardized all hopes for a fair settlement.[63]

Burke worked to convince Ruiz not to seek a caustic note from the Vatican. *Osservatore Romano* responded to Calles's charges with a harsh series of articles, but Burke proceeded to secure a Vatican statement for Calles to the effect that the semi-official journal was the pope's spokesman only for pronouncements generated by the Vatican. The articles that criticized Calles were the journal's opinion, not the Holy See's.[64] Calles, upon the urging of Ruiz and NCWC Administrative Committee Chair Edward Hanna, and in view of Burke's efforts to protect the settlement talks, reversed himself, claiming that the assassination was the result of individual priests, not the Church as a whole.[65]

The near death of the peace process apparently spurred the Vatican into action on the Calles-Morrow-Burke negotiations. On November 14, Ruiz sent a telegram to Morrow from Washington relaying Rome's willingness to allow the bishops to return to Mexico, "provided (1) that the Government indicate its assent to their return and to their resuming their normal functions and (2) that the Government would indicate a willingness to discuss with an appropriate representative such changes in the Constitution or laws which might appear feasible."[66] A week later, Morrow informed Burke that Calles was ready to allow the bishops to return quietly from exile. Both Morrow and Burke urged Fumasoni-Biondi to take advantage of this attitude before Calles's successor, former Tamaulipas Governor Emilio Portes Gil, took office in December. Instead, the apostolic delegate once again chose to push for a better deal than the government was willing to offer, demanding that the Mexican government officially welcome the bishops back.

On December 1, 1928, Emilio Portes Gil became responsible, as the new president, for the church-state crisis. He first proved intractable to change, and unwilling to negotiate on the issue of changes in the constitution. Three days later, on December 4, Morrow returned to the United States for a long-needed vacation. When Morrow later returned to Mexico, he was surprised to find a different Portes Gil waiting for him. A failed attempt on his life, new victories for the Cristero rebels, and a new anti-government rebellion led by General José Gonzalo Escobar all combined to make Portes Gil interested in settling one of the crises which rocked his ship of state.

Portes Gil did what he could to smooth the way to a resolution of these crises. He made it clear that he recognized that the Church as a whole was not responsible for the rebellions, and that the bishops were welcome back to Mexico at any time, provided they were willing to obey the law. Ruiz, while continuing to hold a strong Vatican line, responded to this opening by claiming that all the Church sought was "the liberty indispensable for the well-being and happiness of the nation."[67] Portes Gil expressed his willingness to fall back on the Burke-Calles exchanges as the basis for negotiations with Ruiz. Morrow proved willing to cooperate, so long as the Vatican stood by the Calles-Burke-Ruiz statements of 1928. If the Vatican, however, tried to force the issue of immediate constitutional changes Morrow vowed to quit his efforts. He believed that if the Church's demands were to be based on a prerequisite of constitutional change, his efforts to use his good offices would only compromise his credibility in the future.[68] Before long, both sides began to soften their positions. The Mexican government was at least willing to discuss constitutional change. The Vatican dropped its former demands that the talks be carried out in Rome.

Just as relations appeared to be gearing up for a settlement in early 1929, the lines of authority became nearly fatally entangled. Portes Gil invited Burke to Mexico to renew the negotiations, but Burke, unfortunately, had already committed to traveling to Rome to discuss the negotiations with the Vatican. He declined Portes Gil's invitation since postponing his arrival in Rome would inevitably "give too much weight to his visit to Mexico."[69] This refusal by Burke may have helped open the door to a new influence, Father Edmund Walsh, SJ. Walsh, vice president of Georgetown University and the founder of Georgetown's School of Foreign Service, introduced himself to Morrow as Pope Pius XI's personal envoy. A longtime personal friend of Pius XI, Walsh had been in contact with Manuel Cruchága, former Chilean ambassador to the United States, then resident in Mexico. Cruchága, in turn, had been in correspondence with an unnamed Mexican bishop since the spring of 1928 concerning new proposals for a settlement. Cruchága then brought Walsh into the picture. In June 1928, Walsh went to Rome to brief the pope, who evidently approved of the Walsh-Cruchága plans.[70] According to Walsh, Pius XI favored a rapid resolution to the crisis, and commissioned Walsh to report directly to the Vatican. Morrow, however, had assumed that Burke—and not this new player—had been the pope's representative. Burke appeared inexplicably frozen out at the end of the negotiations. Morrow made it clear that he was frustrated over the fact that "the authorities at Rome seem to have paid no attention whatever to the steps heretofore taken by Father Burke and Archbishop Ruiz."[71]

Frustrated though he was, Morrow nonetheless recognized that Walsh presented a new opportunity to bring peace to Mexico. Morrow convinced Walsh to abandon any attempt to force Portes Gil to adopt changes in the constitution and to accept Burke's terms as the basis for discussions. Upon the urging of Augustin Legoretta, a powerful Mexican financier close to the Vatican, Rome named Ruiz as acting apostolic delegate, thus granting him full authority to carry on the negotiations. Thus buoyed by the prospect, at long last, for success, Morrow set up a June 12 conference between Ruiz and Portes Gil in Mexico City. This meeting was a cordial affair where Portes Gil and Ruiz agreed to exchange signed statements. Portes Gil stood by Calles's letter to Burke, and Ruiz accepted the president's pledge. They also agreed to draft statements, essentially based on the Burke-Calles talks, for exchange the following day. Upon Vatican approval, Portes Gil and Ruiz decided that the statements were to be published together.[72]

By June 21, the major stumbling blocks had been cleared and the long-anticipated settlement finally came to fruition. At a ceremony in Mexico City, the two Mexican prelates and the Mexican president signed statements for exchange and released them to the press.[73] These statements remained essentially the same as those Burke and Calles had exchanged in March and April 1928. Additionally, Portes Gil added a provision that Cristeros who would lay down their arms would receive amnesty.[74] The celebration of Mass in the Cathedral of Mexico City on June 30, 1929, ended the clerical strike begun in 1926 in reaction to Calles's crackdown on the Church.

In the final analysis, the *modus vivendi* did little to re-establish formally the Catholic Church in Mexico. While the archbishops, bishops, and priests were allowed back into the churches, the wording of the agreement did little more than end the clerical strike and force the surrender of the Cristeros. It was this surrender that made the *modus vivendi* a particularly bitter pill for many Mexicans to swallow. In fact, the leaders of the Liga Nacional de Defensora de la Libertad Religiosa claimed that their Cristero rebels had been fighting for the same rights for which the American revolutionaries yearned:

> Our rebel movement is . . . not fighting for loot but for an ideal and even with the powerful United States against us we shall keep the field until our wrongs are redressed. It must be fully understood that we are fighting for most elemental principles, we are fighting for the same things that you fought for in 1776, only that we are fighting a harder and crueler tyrant. Is it possible that honest Mexicans keep on rightly saying: "We are groaning under those monsters just because the United States of America, which claim to be the most civilized and humane nation in the world, chose to keep us in this shameful bondage?"[75]

Among the other pieces of evidence that the *modus vivendi* did little to re-establish the Church's position in Mexico is the fact that the anticlerical provisions of the constitution were still in effect, although there had been an informal agreement that the Mexican government would be open to future discussions with the Church about formal changes. For this reason in particular, the *modus vivendi* has been considered "essentially a defeat for the

Church."[76] Many Mexican states ignored the settlement and banned all religious ceremonies, in spite of Portes Gil's wishes. Most damaging of all, hundreds of the Cristeros, who listened to the Mexican hierarchy's pledge that they would be granted amnesty if they but laid down their guns, were shot as they tried to surrender to the Mexican federal forces.

Regardless of the official contents of the *modus vivendi,* the perception that it was a settlement of the church-state conflict sparked celebrations among Catholics in the United States and in Mexico. Many Catholics in the United States praised the settlement and Walsh and Morrow for their efforts. Walsh issued a statement full of hope for the future of the Church in Mexico. He viewed the Ruiz and Portes Gil declarations as "a welcome harbinger of eventual peace and domestic harmony" for Mexico.[77] Although the efforts of Burke, Morrow, and Walsh stood in the way of their own agenda, the Knights of Columbus heaped adulation on all those who worked for the settlement "by the terms of which all Roman Catholics may again partake of the blessings and comforts of their faith."[78] Supreme Knight Martin Carmody heartily endorsed Morrow and dedication to the settlement.[79]

Since Burke's efforts were known only to a select few, those at the center of the negotiations recognized him as the architect of the Ruiz–Portes Gil agreement. Archbishop Ruiz credited Burke and the NCWC for beginning the movement that culminated in the settlement. Morrow noted Burke's "courage, patience and faith" as hallmarks of his work in the long negotiations.[80] On June 24, 1929, Undersecretary of State Olds lauded Burke's efforts:

> The re-establishment of public worship in a country of fifteen million inhabitants is, indeed, an historic accomplishment and I can well understand your own deep satisfaction. No doubt you consider the result itself as reward enough for all that you have been through, but I shall never feel quite right about it all until I learn that the great institution which you serve with so much ability and devotion has given adequate and substantial recognition of the splendid thing which you have contributed so largely to bring about. Perhaps nobody can appreciate as I do that the result would have been quite impossible without your understanding personality and tireless effort. Your superiors owe you more than they will ever realize or can ever repay. . . .[81]

Not everyone in the United States or Mexico was as sanguine over the settlement. After analyzing the terms of the *modus vivendi,* Michael Williams, the editor of *The Commonweal,* claimed that major issues remained unresolved.[82] Throughout the year, *The Commonweal* remained cautious in its outlook on the settlement. In fact, early in 1930, the editor expressed his opinion that while "the religious situation in Mexico [is] precisely where it was three years ago [except that] open and lawless hostility has given way to legalized opposition," the editor had to agree that "the position of the Catholic Church in Mexico has improved."[83] Even before the peace was arranged, Bishop Leopoldo Lara y Torres of Tacámbaro claimed that Burke's interference demonstrated most clearly the hubris of the Americans and that this "triumph of egotism" would diminish the sacrifices of thousands of faithful victims, whose deaths would be made moot if this peace were to be arranged with the revolutionary government.[84] After the settlement was finalized, and the Cristeros were forced to lay down their arms, Lara y Torres opined that the *modus vivendi* ought more accurately be called the "*Modus Moriendi*" for the Catholic people killed "not standing proudly before Nero, but [dying] peacefully in the tomb of gold and marble [the *modus vivendi*] that is the work of the hollow Yankees."[85]

Signs of the weakness of the *modus vivendi* erupted quickly in late 1929. Archbishop Orozco y Jiminez (Guadalajara), an alleged supporter of the Cristeros, was sent out of the country, in Portes Gil's effort to secure the support of radicals in his party.[86]

Burke, however, retained confidence that his efforts had not been in vain. Following the establishment of the *modus vivendi,* Burke pressed the Mexican government to meet its commitment to begin discussing a change in the constitution. On December 28, 1929, while President-elect Pascual Ortiz Rubio was visiting Washington, Burke, Morrow, Montavon, and Lane met with him to discuss the future of the settlement. Burke conveyed the hope that under the new administration, the Mexican government might discuss changes in the constitution. Ortiz Rubio expressed his personal desire to see the laws changed, but recognized that radicals in his own party who opposed the move had effectively bound his hands. He did hold out hope, however: "If the Catholics will for the time being be patient and wait quietly, I will be able, after two years, to secure such changes. I think they ought to be made."[87] By early 1931, Burke recognized that the situation was nearing a flash point. Events such as the exile of Orozco y Jiminez had proved to Burke that the Mexican government had no intention of living up to what he believed were its obligations under the *modus vivendi.* According to Burke, "the eyes of the civilized world" were trained on Mexico.[88]

When it became clear that elements within the Mexican hierarchy, radical Bishop Manriquez of Huejutla in particular, were unwilling to wait for the Mexican government to live up to its obligations, Archbishop Ruiz requested that Burke return to Mexico. Burke's health made him unable to make the journey, so he sent Montavon as his emissary. Ruiz and Montavon recognized that the Vatican, which had sanctioned the *modus vivendi*, had a mistaken impression of the Mexican government. Clearly, Rome was unaware of the factionalization that rendered powerless those elements that favored constitutional change. The settlement was clearly not as solid as the Church had hoped.

Burke's faith in the future of the *modus vivendi* flagged as he became aware of developments in Mexico. It appeared to him that both sides—the government and the Mexican hierarchy—had lost faith in the settlement. On June 18, 1931, Ambassador J. Reuben Clark telephoned Burke to inform him that Veracruz had closed all churches in the state and limited the number of priests to one for every one-hundred thousand Catholics.[89] After the *modus vivendi*, Archbishop Díaz had established Accion Catolica Mexicana ("Catholic Action") to draw Mexican Catholics away from armed insurrection by uniting them behind peaceful action. Burke supported this move, since Catholic Action dissociated itself from the Liga Nacional de Defensora de la Libertad Religiosa or "Liga," which had provided the Cristeros with much of their leadership during the rebellion. Burke recognized that for the Catholic Church to forge ahead in Mexico, it must prove itself detached from Mexican politics. After Díaz appointed Luis G. Bustos (a Liga agent) to head Catholic Action, however, Burke feared that the organization was headed for clashes with the government.[90] Having such an inflammatory figure at the head of Catholic Action was a clear sign, according to Burke, that the Mexican hierarchy was not living up to the *modus vivendi* by abstaining from politics. Burke and Montavon feared that Catholic Action was in the hands of warmongering radicals.[91]

The *modus vivendi*'s tenuous nature became ultimately clear when the Mexican government abrogated the settlement and initiated a crackdown on the Church following the December 1931 celebration in recognition of the four hundredth anniversary of the apparition of Our Lady of Guadalupe to Mexican peasant Juan Diego. As part of this renewed effort to strip the Church of power, the government slashed priest quotas and sent Archbishop Ruiz once again into exile. Calles masterminded this crackdown, and Burke interpreted it as a political ploy by Calles to regain the support of those who began to believe that the strongman was becoming soft on the Church.[92] He also believed that as more states passed anticlerical legislation, the Mexican government clearly demonstrated that it had no desire to abide by its pledges.

Burke and the Roosevelt Administration: Josephus Daniels

In spite of the fact that the Church languished under the failing *modus vivendi*, it appears that the worsening economic condition in the depths of the global Depression distracted American Catholics from conditions in Mexico. It was not until Franklin Roosevelt named his old boss from the Navy Department, Josephus Daniels, as ambassador to Mexico in 1933 that Catholics in the United States became actively interested in the Mexican situation once again.

In early April 1933, before Daniels departed to occupy his new post in Mexico City, he met with Burke in Washington, D.C., Daniels and Burke enjoyed a long association, dating back to when Daniels was secretary of the navy during World War I and Burke served on the special war commission. In spite of their long acquaintance, the meeting left Burke with the impression that Daniels knew little of United States–Mexican relations or the importance of the religious situation to that relationship. Regardless, Burke assured Daniels that if he was a man of goodwill, the work he would do in Mexico would only help the persecuted Catholics there.[93] Burke's impression of the new ambassador was that while he demonstrated goodwill toward the Church, he was woefully ill informed, and could not be counted on to take the initiative in any situation.[94] Following an interview Daniels gave with the *New York Times* in early 1935, Burke observed that Daniels's tone indicated that he viewed the Church crisis as a trivial issue and that the interview was "another index that Mr. Daniels did not appreciate [the gravity of] the situation, nor was he a big enough man to be our Ambassador in Mexico."[95]

Daniels fell under Catholic microscopes when he first entered Mexico. His first blunder, in the eyes of the United States Catholics, was when he occupied the American embassy and presented his credentials to President Abelardo Rodriguez. Daniels praised his new host for the Mexican people's social and educational reforms.[96] Further, the ambassador committed a grave error, from American Catholics' perspective, in his July 26, 1934, American Seminar speech. While Daniels simply intended to uphold the American system of free public education as a goal for Mexico, the result, as we know, was altogether different in the United States. Daniels later assured Hull that he "had not read the full text of the address by General Calles and did not know it contained any reference to the church or the clergy" when he quoted the former Mexican president.[97] However, not only had Daniels praised Calles, but also Benito Juarez, president during one of the most strident anticlerical eras in the nineteenth century. Although Daniels had spoken only to Americans, and his speech represented values supporting public education in the United States, American Catholics saw this as a blow to Mexican Catholic education from which they feared it would never recover. The explosion of reaction among American Catholics was sudden and harsh. Demands for Daniels's recall began to pour into the White House and the State Department. Although Burke considered Daniels a friend, he claimed during a meeting with Roosevelt that "whether he intended to or not, our Ambassador had given the impression that our Government supported the ["socialistic"] educational programme as outlined by the National Revolutionary Party in the Six-Year Plan" and had "given a blanket approval to Calles's speech."[98]

American Catholics' claims that Daniels had no respect for religion stung the ambassador. For years, he taught weekly Sunday school classes to North Carolina's youth. He railed against the Ku Klux Klan, and was an energetic supporter of Catholic Alfred E. Smith in the 1928 presidential race. During his years as secretary of the navy under Woodrow Wilson, Daniels authorized more Catholic naval chaplains than any other denomination. He also promoted Catholic Captain William S. Benson to the position of chief of naval operations.[99] In spite of Daniels's defense of the speech as praising only universal education, and a press release in which Daniels affirmed his faith in "the principles of our country with reference to public schools, the freedom of religion and the freedom of the press,"[100] American Catholics almost immediately demanded Daniels's recall from Mexico.

In the midst of this storm of protest, Roosevelt turned to Burke for advice. He asked Burke what he would have the president do, to which Burke responded that he favored a statement to the effect that the United States "in no way supported education which was atheistic or anti-religious in nature."[101] Burke offered a suggestion for an explanation the ambassador might deliver: "It would be unwarranted to use my speech as a support of defense or encouragement of a denial of liberty in education or the full right of citizens to religious education. It must be clear to all that I stand unflinchingly for the principles and institutions of my own country where popular education is zealously promoted and full liberty of education and of schools is granted."[102]

While Roosevelt refused to take that step, the fact that the president accepted Burke's impressions of the situation is a clear indication of the respect with which Roosevelt regarded Burke. The president assured Burke that he would make the United States' position clear to the Mexican ambassador, namely that if the Mexican government continued to exile priests and bishops, and if it forced upon the Mexican people an atheistic educational program, "Mexico would make of itself a spectacle before the civilized world."[103] Roosevelt convinced Burke to refrain from publicizing their meeting. Later, after the president conferred with his secretary of state, he thought better of his pledge to Burke and decided that another position paper to Mexico would only confuse the issue. By October, Roosevelt, Hull, and Undersecretary Phillips had decided that a public statement would prove wholly counterproductive for long-term religious peace in Mexico.[104] Roosevelt's decision to break his promises angered and dismayed Burke.

Burke, while abiding by his promise to keep his meeting with Roosevelt a secret, did not avoid fostering protest wherever he could. In a letter to Burke, Thomas J. Pinkman, president of the Federation of College Catholic Clubs, claimed that while his organization felt the need to make an official protest against the secretary of state's Mexican policy, he had heard that the Mexican bishops asked that American protests be withheld, for fear of inflaming anti-Catholic sentiments in Mexico.[105] Burke replied that he believed that any American organization should feel free to express itself as it saw fit. Moreover, he had no recollection of such a request on the part of the Mexican bishops, and commented that he, as both the chief negotiator of the *modus vivendi* and the general secretary of the NCWC, would most likely be aware of any such requests. Burke went on to offer some recommendations for the protests: (1) Catholics should be careful what they ask for—requesting United States intervention, or a lifting of the arms embargo, or Daniels's recall would be futile at best or even counterproductive at worst; and (2) Catholics should protest Daniels's speech itself, since the ambassador "knowingly or unknowingly exceeded his privileges as our Ambassador in that speech. . . . He had no warrant whatsoever in throwing the weight of the prestige of the United States in favor of the present policies of the Mexican Government. Therein lies the justification and the obligation of every American citizen—and of the Catholic body in particular—to protest."[106] In time, however, it became clear that Roosevelt intended to stand behind Daniels, his longtime friend. Burke backed off on protests against the ambassador's speech as a new issue, the Borah resolution, occupied his attention.

Burke and the Roosevelt Administration: The Borah Resolution

Burke had been aware of the plans for a Senate resolution demanding an offi-cial investigation into the conditions of the Mexican persecution since they were formulated in early January 1935. When Burke caught wind of the meet-ing between Catholic senators and Colonel Patrick Callahan, formerly a high-ranking official in the Knights of Columbus, Burke warned that such a meet-ing was unwise since it invited the wrath and suspicion of the rest of the Senate, "and indeed would be misinterpreted by the majority of American citizens." Callahan assured Burke that as the meeting was secret, no one would ever know about it.[107] By the end of January, these senators had convinced Senator William Borah of Idaho to sponsor the resolution. Borah was a logi-cal choice, since he had long been interested in Mexican affairs.

When the Mexican government issued a statement denying the charges that it was carrying out religious persecution in Mexico,[108] Burke responded in his official capacity as general secretary of the NCWC that "the statement issued yesterday by the Mexican Embassy at Washington is absolutely con-trary to fact [and was] purposely worded to mislead the people of the United States and of other nations."[109]

Regardless of his attack on the Mexican embassy's statement, Burke sup-ported Roosevelt in his opposition to the Borah resolution. According to Burke, such an open, official investigation would only serve to increase the persecution of Catholics in Mexico because a formal protest from the United States government would place the Mexican government in a delicate posi-tion, forcing it to react. When Burke made this clear to Senator David Walsh, one of the original instigators of the resolution, Walsh informed Burke that the resolution was never intended to pass, but rather its authors designed it to publicize the persecution. Walsh maintained that it was intended for "show."[110]

Burke had a number of reasons for withholding support for the resolu-tion. In a conversation with Patrick Callahan, who spearheaded the Knights of Columbus effort to find a senator willing to adopt the resolution, Burke claimed that he could not announce NCWC support for the resolution be-cause the Administrative Committee had not had a chance to study the leg-islation before it was introduced. Moreover, he maintained that the NCWC had evidence that would support some of the allegations pointed to in the resolution, but not all of the charges. Burke added that if he was subpoenaed to appear before the committee, and asked whether the NCWC supported the resolution, he would be forced to answer in the negative. Callahan protested that that news would kill the measure. Burke assured Callahan that he "had no orders to inform the Senate Committee and unless so ordered [he] would not."[111]

Roosevelt undoubtedly interpreted Burke's refusal to publicly back the resolution as an endorsement of his position. It was presumably because of this perceived support by Burke that Roosevelt turned to him in the spring of 1935 for his advice and guidance. In March, Roosevelt further demonstrated his respect for Burke when the president sent his personal friend, and former governor of the Philippines, Frank Murphy, to discuss the Mexican situation with Burke. Murphy intended to convey Roosevelt's plan to send a private message to former Mexican President Calles, but in the course of the conversation, he and Burke both came to the realization that conditions warranted a public statement. Murphy asked if Burke would be willing to draft such a public statement, to which the priest pledged that he would do whatever he could to help. Burke qualified his promise, however, by stipulating that he would not go to the White House or the State Department, but preferred to work out the details in a private location. He recognized the potential Protestant outcry against such an overt Catholic effort to sway the president.[112]

Murphy relayed the plan for a public statement to Roosevelt, but when Secretary of State Hull heard of the plan, he loudly protested. He believed that the only thing such a public note would accomplish would be to stir up Protestant opposition to the administration.[113] As he had done before, and would do again, Roosevelt compromised his secretary of state's authority by sending a personal envoy, Sumner Welles, to do his bidding. Welles worked closely with Burke in preparation for Roosevelt's public address of October 2, 1935, in San Diego. In fact, Burke was given the chance to comment on Roosevelt's San Diego address before the president delivered it. Assistant Secretary of State Sumner Welles forwarded to the president a draft of the address that included this margin note: "Father Burke says OK. Has no changes or suggestions to offer."[114]

Another sign of Roosevelt's respect for Burke's position in the country in general and the Church in particular was when he sought Burke's advice for suggestions on how to respond to attacks from other Catholic forces. For instance, when Roosevelt was faced with a delicate situation following the receipt of a letter from Bishop John Noll of Fort Wayne, the president sent his secretary, Marvin McIntyre, to ask Burke how the bishop's letter should be answered.[115] Another example was after Roosevelt received a letter from the Knights of Columbus, seeking intervention in Mexico. Roosevelt again sent

McIntyre to get Burke's advice on his response to the Knights' letter.[116] While Burke's response to this particular letter remains a mystery, his attitude towards the Knights was made clear a month later, when Roosevelt accepted Burke's advice to refrain from consulting with the Knights of Columbus instead of the hierarchy.[117] The high esteem with which Roosevelt regarded Burke is clear in the president's willingness to follow through on pledges he made during his May 2 meeting with Burke. In keeping with his promises, the president set up a May 15 meeting with Mexican Ambassador Francisco Castille Najera. Roosevelt conveyed Burke's desire that the Mexican government be made well aware of the American people's dedication to the ideal of religious liberty. The political fallout that resulted from Najera's report back to his government (the Calles-Cárdenas split) belies the impact of Roosevelt's comments.

Burke was sensitive to the delicate position in which the Mexican government found itself after the Calles-Cárdenas break. That government clearly could not acknowledge any influence of the United States government or the Catholic Church on the shake-up. Similarly, the Roosevelt administration was in an uneasy position in the United States. If it became clear that the United States Catholics had succeeded in pressuring the president into seeking an end to the persecution of the Catholics in Mexico, Protestants in the United States would gorge themselves on the public relations problems of the administration. Burke requested that the American hierarchy honor this position and recognize the help offered by the Roosevelt administration by refraining from any statements that could embarrass either the administration or the Mexican government.[118]

From the re-establishment of the Cárdenas administration onward, the Mexican government worked gradually to ease the church-state tensions in Mexico. Najera believed that this trend would continue. The Mexican president, according to Najera, was committed to "a course which would lead to religious liberty within the existing restrictions of the Constitution."[119]

By the spring of 1936, Catholic unrest in the United States over the conditions in Mexico was easing. Churches opened, the enforcement of anticlerical policies moderated (though the constitution remained intact), and Daniels continued to meet with Cárdenas to discuss restrictions on priests' duties. Daniels noted that the reopening of churches was not the result of an openly stated policy shift by the Cárdenas government, but because of the "natural course" of events as the religious tensions eased.[120] This general improvement in the Mexican situation encouraged the American hierarchy. While some prelates criticized Roosevelt for not acting sooner or with more force, Burke steadfastly defended the president's actions. In a report to the chairman of the NCWC Administrative Committee, he summarized the president's contributions to the present easing of tensions in Mexico:

> Your Administrative Committee has earnestly and diligently sought to have the President use his good offices that the Mexican Government would change its constitution and laws which beget persecution of the Church. . . . In answer, the President did use his good offices in this respect and personally expressed his mind to the Mexican Ambassador and asked the latter to convey that mind to his Government. The President specifically informed the Mexican Ambassador that he, the President, was speaking informally, but asked that the present Mexican Government take positive steps to allow full liberty of religious worship to all citizens of Mexico; that it cease its persecution of the Catholic Church. . . . Your Administrative Committee was informed, as a consequence of this conversation, indirectly by the Mexican Government that the Mexican Government would . . . take steps to have priests minister in states where they are now forbidden.[121]

When Burke became a monsignor on September 21, 1936, he recognized that the restrictions on religious liberty in Mexico were steadily loosening, yet one sticking point remained: the Vatican and the Mexican government could not agree on the naming of a permanent apostolic delegate. When Lázaro Cárdenas became president in 1934, Sumner Welles, on Burke's request, urged the Mexican ambassador to request that the Mexican government accept an apostolic delegate who was a non-Mexican. The Mexican government, however, remained steadfast behind the constitutional prohibitions against foreign-born clergy of any kind. The Vatican then refused to appoint an apostolic delegate unless there were assurances that he would not be exiled. Moreover, it refused to allow its decisions to be bound by an openly hostile Mexican government. This obstinacy on the part of Rome caused Roosevelt and Burke much dismay. Burke claimed that a reactionary faction within the Vatican, which opposed any compromise with the Mexican government, had prevented the Vatican from acting even though the Roosevelt administration had done all it could. In mid-1936, the issue of representation resolved somewhat as a result of the Roosevelt administration working closely with Ambassador Najera. The Mexican government agreed to accept an interim representative from the Vatican. The American apostolic delegate, Amleto Cicognani, expressed the Vatican's gratitude for Roosevelt's efforts. Assistant Secretary of State Sumner Welles noted that Burke's presence at his meetings with Najera provided a fortunate stabilizing influence.[122] Finally, in 1937, the Vatican and the Mexican government agreed to the appointment of Archbishop Ruiz as permanent apostolic delegate.

Monsignor Burke died on October 30, 1936, before he had the chance to see the practical results of much of his efforts. While he did see the beginning of a new church-state relationship in Mexico, he died before Archbishop Ruiz was officially welcomed back to Mexico as the apostolic delegate.

October 1936 witnessed the passing of an era. With the death of Reverend John J. Burke, CSP, the Catholic Church lost a man of action. President Roosevelt recognized the tragedy of Burke's passing. He claimed that "a powerful spiritual force has been lost to our national life in the passing of Monsignor Burke. As scholar, writer and pulpit orator he touched life at many angles while always as a humble follower of the Master. He was a beautiful exemplar of that Christian teaching of which he was such an eloquent advocate. I personally mourn the loss of a faithful friend of many years."[123]

Burke used his talents as a diplomat to work with Catholic leaders in the United States and with the Mexican government to achieve a more organized, more secure position for the Church in North America. By providing for the Church in the United States a unified corporate voice through the National Catholic Welfare Conference, he succeeded in laying out a direction for coordinated, focused Catholic action in this country. He also provided the United States government with a definitive source of official Catholic positions on issues that affected the nation. By working on behalf of the Church in negotiating with Mexico, he helped end the clerical strike that benefited no one in Mexico. Finally, it was largely due to his influence as general secretary of the NCWC that Roosevelt eventually won from the Mexican ambassador a promise to express to the Mexican government the displeasure of the American government. For all of these accomplishments, for which Burke sacrificed his own desires and career plans, he must rightly hold a high position in the history of the Catholic Church in the twentieth century.

chapter 5

INDIVIDUAL ACTIVIST CLERICS

Roman catholics in the united states emerged from the years of conflict that wracked the nation and the world in the late 1910s with a new self-awareness. Their wartime experiences, notably their extraordinary contributions in money and manpower, left them with a new self-confidence about their place in society. Although the Ku Klux Klan revival in the 1920s and the thrashing Al Smith received in the presidential election of 1928 left Catholics bruised, they were not beaten. This self-confidence and assuredness in the postwar years found ready expression in "Thomism," the predominant philosophical milieu of the Church in the United States. The philosophy of Thomas Aquinas (1225–1274) provided an answer to a national need for security in a changing world—security rooted in the "ideal of unity of religion and life, the natural and the divine. . . ."[1] American Catholics incorporated this philosophy into their experience in the changed world of the postwar years. This unity of the divine and the natural inspired Catholics to strive to integrate Catholicism and American culture. They believed that their Catholicism provided them with the tools necessary to make America the best it could be—to enable them to build this nation towards its full potential.

Catholic clergy were among the chief progenitors of Thomist thought in the 1920s and 1930s. In their effort to perfect what it was to be an American, it is easier to understand the height of emotion with which many Catholic priests met the challenge of responding to the Mexican crisis. In fighting for the rights of the Mexican Catholics to worship as they saw fit, Catholics in the United States were struggling to preserve and define what made them *American* Catholics. Priests comprised much of the fight on behalf of the Catholics of Mexico. This chapter will examine the activities of priests who tried to ameliorate the hardships of the Mexican Church as best they could. The efforts of Wilfrid Parsons, SJ; Michael Kenny, SJ; Edmund A. Walsh, SJ; John A. Ryan; and James H. Ryan took a variety of forms, from serving as activist editors of Catholic journals, to support for armed conflict, to personal diplomacy. In their many different ways, these priests all sought a common goal to defend what they believed to be the perfect blend of Americanism and Catholicism by fostering a foreign policy between the United States and Mexico that preserved the religious freedoms of Catholics south of the Rio Grande as well as of those north of it. These men were agents of change—imbued with the desire to influence United States–Mexican relations, and as such, joined lay men and women as the shock troops doing much of the work in this private interest group effort to mold public policy in the 1920s and 1930s.

Wilfrid Parsons, SJ

Wilfrid Parsons, editor of *America* from June 20, 1925, to 1936, recognized the power of the pen. He used his position as editor to try to form a strong public opinion about the persecution in Mexico. In fact, Parsons considered it the duty of every American Catholic to become informed of the situation in Mexico, that they may see to it that the Calles tyranny in Mexico evoked the same outrage in the United States as did that in Mussolini's Italy and in Communist Russia.[2]

Parsons recognized the value of a strong public opinion. He believed that while some Catholics demanded the lifting of the arms embargo, or a condemnation of Calles by Coolidge, or even that the very few radical Catholics demanded armed intervention, the only real chance for progress would result from Catholics pursuing three objectives. First, Catholics had to mold public opinion and eventually governmental opinion to the position that the Mexican government under Calles was "not worthy of our friendship." Parsons cited the Knights of Columbus pamphlet "Red Mexico: The Facts" as being particularly useful in this respect. Second, Catholics had to persuade powerful private interests to use their access to the government to convince the administration that the opposition factions in Mexico held the real hope for the restoration of long-lasting peace in Mexico. Finally, American Catholics had to fortify their co-religionists by seeing to their moral and economic needs, that they may be strengthened for the fight.[3]

Through the late 1920s and early 1930s, Parsons constantly worked to inflame that public opinion. He even claimed that public opinion in the United States was of extreme importance in Mexico as well, since "every Mexican politician pays more attention to it than to public opinion at home."[4] He used a number of methods to shock the American public into the right opinion. For instance, he proved his assertion that Calles viewed the United States with contempt by claiming that the Mexican president's effort to trap Archbishop Caruana was an example of how low Calles's estimation of American intelligence truly was.[5] The secular press's refusal to cover what Parsons considered "one of the biggest news stories of the day" and "one of the most savage and bloody butcheries of all time," tremendously frustrated the editor.[6] This refusal to print the truth about Mexico, Parsons believed, was responsible for the public attitude about Mexico: "a curious compound of utter indifference, vague disquiet, profound ignorance, impulsive sympathy, unveiled hostility and extreme cynicism." Parsons considered this inaction by the secular press "the root of the problem" in Mexico.[7]

Parsons believed various elements, including a reluctant press, conspired against his effort to foster a sympathetic public opinion. The Federal Council of Churches of Christ in America, which published a report by the council's Department of Research and Education, bore much of the responsibility for conditions in Mexico. This report advocated giving the Calles government more time to settle oil lands claims in favor of the United States. Parsons claimed that to hope for a supreme court built by Calles himself to decide against the president was to hope for the impossible.[8] Other elements threatened Parsons's plan. His contempt for those popular Americans who courted Calles's favor spilled over in the columns of *America*. Parsons regarded Ambassador Dwight Morrow, who (reluctantly) accepted an invitation to travel with Calles on a train tour of Mexico, and humorist Will Rogers, who agreed to go along and who submitted regular updates to the American press, as dangerous threats to the opinion he was trying to foster. Parsons was perplexed at why "the banker" and "the buffoon" were willing to warm up to "the savage." The great danger, in Parsons's mind, was that their antics might make it seem as if the United States government planned to deal with the problem in Mexico with kid gloves. Parsons feared that the friendship between Calles and America's most popular humorist would make it appear that the United States sought to "powder this Mexican cancer with perfumed talc and announce a cure."[9] Colonel Charles Lindbergh, Morrow's future son-in-law, executed the first ever nonstop flight from Washington, D.C., to Mexico City shortly after the train trip ended, which added fuel to Parsons's growing fears of the public perception of the Mexican situation. But Lindbergh, "the Lone Eagle," was far too popular for Parsons to heap on him the same type of criticism he applied to Rogers and Morrow. Instead, Parsons painted the hero as unscrupulously exploited by others to build a positive perception of Calles.[10]

In the 1930s, Parsons concentrated his energies on the issue of whether or not Catholics sought the United States' intervention in Mexican affairs. This reflects not a decision to turn away from his desire to mold public opinion, but an added dimension of it. He worked to defend that public opinion and the position of the Church in the United States as a whole against those who sought to make Catholics appear to be radical interventionists. Over and over again, throughout the mid-1930s, Parsons published denials that Catholics sought intervention. His point was that the United States had been intervening in Mexican affairs for decades, from the initial recognition of the Carranza regime to the policy of supplying millions of dollars in arms to the government to suppress revolts. Parsons made it as clear as he could: "What we want is not intervention in Mexico, but the release of our Government from a foreign entanglement that is as certain as it is disastrous to religion,"[11] and later: "What we demand is that the United States stop intervening in Mexico. When that is done, the decent people of Mexico will be able to put down anarchy in that unhappy country, and restore peace."[12] His tone in the later releases convey his frustration over dogged harassment from those who claimed the Catholics wanted to push the United States into war with Mexico.

Among the clearest targets for the demand that the United States cease intervening was Josephus Daniels. Like millions of other Catholics, Parsons believed that Daniels had aided and abetted the Mexican strongman through official friendliness to the president. Again, Parsons's refrain was similar: Daniels's support for Calles kept him in power, and perpetuated the persecution. Unlike most Catholics, however, Parsons had a national podium from which to speak. And he made good use of that forum. Following Daniels's July 1934 speech before Herring's American Seminar, Parsons claimed that the ambassador had done "nothing more or less than endorse the tyrannous designs of Calles upon the children of the nation." Consequently, Parsons demanded that the Roosevelt administration do its least duty and recall Daniels. Parsons vowed not to rest until Roosevelt called the ambassador back to the United States.[13] In a later article, Parsons offered some explanations for Daniels's actions, and the just consequences for them: "Either he knew what Calles meant, or he did not. If he did know, he was guilty of an unwarrantable interference in Mexican politics, on the side of the anti-Christians. If he did not know, then he should not be in Mexico as our Ambassador. In either case, he should resign."[14]

According to Parsons, Daniels's ill-chosen words in support of the Mexican educational ideal were no more than the tip of the iceberg. In mid-1935, Parsons laid into the ambassador with a laundry list of occasions when Daniels had extended unjustified and interventionist support for the Calles government. First, as Calles's grip on power slipped in 1934, Daniels visited him at home and afterward announced that the United States government still stood behind Calles.[15] Second, while the Mexican Congress prepared to vote to expel all priests and prelates from Mexico, Daniels and Senator Robert R. Reynolds of North Carolina entered the chamber and spoke glowingly of the ruling National Revolutionary Party. Parsons accused Daniels of throwing a congratulatory celebration for the governor of the state of Puebla, who had earlier been honored for closing down all the churches in the state. Finally, Parsons scored Daniels for praising Cárdenas's Red Shirt supporters, a leading anticlerical group.[16] In 1935, however, Parsons decided that the most effective strategy was to focus his spotlight on the White House.

Parsons staunchly supported the Borah resolution, which he considered justified in terms of domestic interests. Parsons based his domestic justification on the unrest the persecution caused among groups representing various denominations in the United States. Evidently, Parsons expected the investigation to end the persecution, thereby ending the agitation of those American groups.[17] Parsons challenged Roosevelt's opposition to the resolution, but quickly backed off when he perceived movement in the White House. In mid-July 1935, Representatives Clare Gerald Fenerty of Pennsylvania and John Higgins of New York approached Roosevelt with a petition of some 250 names from congressmen of all denominations, seeking some statement on behalf of the persecuted Christians in Mexico. Roosevelt responded with a written statement, in which he declared his support for the ideal of freedom of religious worship "not only in the United States, but in other nations."[18] Although the president refused to "name names," Parsons congratulated him on the move, claiming that within the context of the petition in protest of the conditions in Mexico, "the fact of his statement was itself a sufficient indication of the importance which he attached to a public opinion rapidly forming in the United States."[19]

By early 1936, Mexico had begun to fade from headlines in the United States, as Cárdenas relaxed the enforcement of the anti-Catholic provisions of the Constitution of 1917. At the same time, the Spanish Civil War loomed large, and Catholics in the United States rapidly shifted their focus to that new conflict. Parsons continued his attacks on Cárdenas's Mexico, but did so obliquely. In covering the story of the Spanish conflict, he linked Mexico, Madrid, and Moscow. Cárdenas's government had sold twenty thousand rifles and 20 million cartridges to the anticlerical "Loyalist" forces in Spain. Parsons saw that as proof that "the tyranny in Mexico and the tyranny in Spain stem direct from Moscow. Any Government which adopts the policy of attacking religion, and begins by ordering or permitting the looting of churches and the slaughter of civilians, guilty of no offense except that of being Catholic, may look for the active support of Mexico and Moscow. Like loves like."[20]

Clearly, Parsons intended such loaded language to further inflame public opinion. He recognized the Spanish Civil War as the next front along which Catholics in the United States had to do battle with the forces of anticlericalism. His journal, *America*, was his chief weapon in this fight. In much the same way that Parsons used *America* as his mouthpiece, Fr. Michael Kenny, SJ, used the *Baltimore Catholic Review* to launch verbal broadsides against Roosevelt's White House.

Michael Kenny, SJ

Kenny steadfastly opposed the accommodationists who decided that making an enemy of the man in the White House would only hinder their efforts to aid the Mexican Catholics and make any real change in the situation impossible. From Kenny's perspective, Roosevelt and his crony Daniels were chiefly to blame for the dismal future facing the Mexican Catholics. From October 1934 until April 1935, the pages of the *Baltimore Catholic Review* blistered with the weekly attacks Kenny launched on the Roosevelt administration.[21]

Kenny used his articles as building blocks with which he constructed an elaborate argument that the United States government was traditionally anti-Catholic. He laid a foundation for his argument with a discussion of how the United States first emissary to Mexico, Joel Poinsett, incited the Scottish Rite Masons in Mexico to rebel against the first leader of independent Mexico, Iturbide, to try to eliminate Catholic power in Mexico.[22] His articles continued on through history, stopping here and there on the way. Examples included articles titled "President Buchanan In Campaign To Take Over Lower California Opposed the Church in Mexico—Dark Chapter in Our History Is Revealed,"[23] and "President Wilson's Support of Carranza Is Condemned by Father Michael Kenny."[24] According to Kenny, Wilson, after refusing to support Huerta, who used "firmness and justice" to impose order on Mexico, "supported with army and navy the worst scoundrels that ever raped and pillaged Mexico; whence issued the orgy of anarchy and tyranny that culminated in Calles."[25]

In keeping with his pledge to "spare no official, no matter how high he may be" Kenny turned his sights on the clearest, and most popular, target for Catholics in the early 1930s, Ambassador Josephus Daniels. According to Kenny, Daniels was a major architect in the persecution, since his actions, or lack thereof, "align[ed] us with Calles and his gang and put the authority of our nation behind their communistic tyranny."[26] Kenny hoped to use Archbishop Ruiz's 1935 pastoral, in which he pledged that the Mexican hierarchy would neither promote nor prohibit Catholic armed resistance, to encourage Vincent de Paul Fitzpatrick, the editor of the *Baltimore Catholic Review*, to use the journal in a "determined action, along with prayer, and by protest and pressure" to force Roosevelt "to recall Daniels and leave the Mexican people a free hand."[27]

Kenny continued his assaults on Daniels, but as these bore no fruit, it became clear to him that the real responsibility lay farther up the diplomatic food chain. According to Kenny, although Secretary of State Cordell Hull knew that the Mexican government regularly and flagrantly violated basic human rights in general and the rights of Americans in particular, he did nothing. Hull's refusal to protest or recall Daniels, in Kenny's estimation, demonstrated that Daniels was but a tool in Hull's hands, and therefore, the administration bore ultimate responsibility for the ambassador.[28] Moreover, Kenny's radicalism pushed him so far as to maintain that the Roosevelt administration's inactivity on behalf of universal rights in Mexico fostered Mexico as a "Communist breeding ground."[29] For this reason, Kenny found a united American reaction to the crisis in Mexico justified. In fact, Kenny maintained that "it is no longer a Catholic or Christian question, nor merely a religious question. It is a fundamental American question. It is a question whether Soviet

Communism shall reign in Mexico, and whether, having driven out God and the human rights He implanted, it shall extend its liberty-killing tentacles across our own border."[30]

The exchange of correspondence between Kenny, Bishop John Noll of Fort Wayne, and John J. Burke of the NCWC clearly demonstrates that the hierarchy recognized the danger inherent in Kenny's radical attitudes. In response to Kenny's query about how he could help the movement to aid the Mexican Catholics, Noll advised him to consult with Burke on appropriate action on the situation in Mexico. Kenny rejected this advice, claiming that Burke and his backers in the NCWC "brought about the foolish and futile agreement of 1929, from which the present woes of Mexico arise."[31] According to Kenny, the time had come for united action, and the NCWC was not up to the task. He claimed that he had heard from "the highest authorities [Archbishop Curley] that Father Burke is not the Voice and does not represent the Mind of the American hierarchy," but rather, Mexican Catholic leaders consider him and his supporters in the NCWC "the worst enemies of their cause."[32]

In an effort to make Kenny feel more involved and invested in the activities of the NCWC, Noll informed him, in a letter on April 9, 1935, of the proposed meeting between Burke and Roosevelt, and that the president vowed to act on the NCWC recommendations as expressed by Burke.[33] In another letter that same day, Noll wrote to Bishop Thomas F. Lillis of Kansas City, apprising him of the Noll-Kenny correspondence, in the interest of drawing Kenny, as an influential Catholic writer, closer to the NCWC decision-making process. Lillis passed on the information to Burke, who then consulted Archbishop Amleto Giovanni Cicognani, the apostolic delegate. Cicognani was extremely anxious about such sensitive information as that concerning the Burke-Roosevelt meeting falling into the hands of "one of the temperament of Father Kenny." Burke conveyed to Noll the request by the apostolic delegate that Noll demand that Kenny return the letter of April 9.[34] This episode must have only increased Kenny's animosity for the hierarchy, Burke, and anyone who he believed to be more accommodationist than himself.

Kenny's radicalism clearly set him apart from the main body of the clergy of the United States. While most of his attitudes struck resonant chords among many priests in this country, he was in rarefied company when it came to his claims that Roosevelt was fostering and even encouraging Communism in Mexico. He was not alone, however. Some priests, in fact, took more direct steps to battle the scourge in Mexico, including helping work through diplomatic channels in Mexico itself.

Edmund A. Walsh, SJ

Father Edmund A. Walsh, SJ, played a vital, though largely misunderstood, role in the effort to win peace in Mexico. His apparent papal legitimacy proved instrumental for the settlement of the *modus vivendi* of 1929, yet the true nature of his involvement remains vague. Although there were conflicting claims as to the authority with which he spoke, that he was an integral element in the negotiations is without question.

Walsh's most significant involvement with the Mexican church-state crisis began in late 1928.[35] In mid-November, Manuel Cruchága, former Chilean ambassador to the United States and then the chief commissioner of the Mexican-German and Mexican-Spanish Claims Commissions, approached Ambassador Morrow with the news that several months earlier, "an influential member of the Mexican clergy" had shared with him a proposal for a settlement. Cruchága informed Morrow that he had also briefed Walsh on the proposal, who in turn consulted the Vatican. Pope Pius XI, Walsh's personal friend, authorized him to pursue the plan.[36] Walsh did not travel to Mexico until late April 1929, under instructions from Rome that he travel incognito as a lay professor from Georgetown University.[37] Upon arriving in Mexico City on May 1, he met with Morrow for the first time. At their May 4 meeting, Walsh informed the ambassador that he was in Mexico on a fact-finding mission for the Vatican. He had no authority to negotiate, and his mission had been made known to neither Burke nor Ruiz.[38]

Walsh's primary achievement during his mission to Mexico lay in his access to principles involved in the negotiations. In only four days between Walsh's May 4 and May 8, 1929, meetings with Morrow, he had managed to meet with representatives of the main factions among the Mexican hierarchy. Because he enjoyed this "close contact with strong elements of the Mexican Church which opposed the settlement," Walsh was able to reconcile "the church die-hards to the agreement."[39] As it became clear that Walsh was succeeding in convincing the prelates of Portes Gil's apparent willingness to negotiate with Catholics, Cruchága urged Rome to change Walsh's instructions to empower him to proceed with the negotiations. In reply to Cruchága's urging, Cardinal Gasparri, the papal secretary of state, sent the following instruction: "Please tell Father Walsh to cooperate with Mgr. Ruiz and thus assist the action eventually taken by the Holy See."[40]

Walsh's unique status in the negotiations positioned him to serve as a vital link between the prelates and the Mexican government. When Archbishop Ruiz and Bishop Díaz arrived in Mexico City in late May 1929, they secluded themselves in a private home and restricted visitors to eliminate the influence of those who opposed any settlement, particularly the members of the Liga. Ruiz and Díaz refused access by anyone, including their fellow Mexican prelates. Walsh, however, acting as their spokesman, was the sole exception. He kept Ruiz and Díaz in contact with Rome through the Chilean embassy's coded cable.[41]

After the talks ground down following the unsuccessful second meeting between Portes Gil, Ruiz, and Díaz on June 12, 1929, Morrow succeeded in convincing the prelates to abide by their earlier agreements.[42] The ambassador also drafted the final notes for exchange, basing his June 15 statements on the Calles-Burke letters, which he submitted to Calles, Portes Gil, Ruiz, and Díaz for approval. Walsh, assisting the Mexican bishops, forwarded these documents and a telegram signed by Ruiz, Díaz, and himself urging Rome for official approval.[43] When Morrow learned of this he was both confused and very anxious, because he considered the move one more opportunity for Rome to take a strong stand and thereby derail the talks.[44]

The Vatican neglected to answer Walsh's telegram for five days, which only deepened Morrow's fear of a dead end. When the Vatican did respond with a cable to Walsh, it had added new demands on the Mexican government: "(1) The Holy Father is most anxious for a peaceful and laic solution. (2) Full amnesty for Bishops, priests and faithful. (3) Restoration of property—Churches, Bishops' and Priests' houses and Seminaries. (4) Free relations between Vatican and Mexican Church. Only on these understandings you may close if you think proper before God."[45]

Morrow saw this cable, especially demands two, three, and four, as potentially fatal to the negotiations. Walsh conferred with Ruiz on the cable, and Ruiz surprised Morrow with a liberal interpretation of these orders. Ruiz considered all these provisions hinging on the first. A "laic" solution was one, according to Ruiz, based on Mexican law. Following this interpretation, "amnesty" would mean that the priests and bishops would return to their own churches, and the "restoration of property" meant that the clergy were to try to regain as much of its former property as they could under Mexican law.[46] Having been granted the "go ahead" from his superiors, Ruiz agreed to a final meeting, leading to the *modus vivendi* of 1929 in the exchange of notes between President Emilio Portes Gil and Archbishop Ruiz.

Morrow, uneasy over Walsh's telegram of June 15, nonetheless valued his contribution to the settlement. He considered Walsh "helpful, particularly in keeping some former intransigents from impeding the negotiations."[47] The ambassador expressed similar sentiments in a meeting with Burke, when he claimed that Walsh "did good work, helping to reconcile some of the irreconcilables." Edward Reed of the State Department's Division of Mexican Affairs credited Walsh with "keeping the negotiations off the rocks." Walsh, however, paid a price for his work. According to Reed, the Jesuit incurred "the jealousy of other Church representatives engaged in the negotiations." Clearly, Reed was referring to Burke.[48]

Burke had plenty of reason to be angry with Walsh. While Burke had clearly been given a mandate by Apostolic Delegate Fumasoni-Biondi to guide the negotiations, Walsh's official status remained ambiguous.[49] This ambiguity was doubtless the result of confusion as to Walsh's actual role in the *modus vivendi* negotiations, in part fostered by Walsh himself. On one hand, numerous sources placed him at the center of the official church negotiation effort. One such source was Walsh's own telegram to the American embassy in Chile in praise of Cruchága's contributions to the settlement. In the telegram, Walsh claimed to have spent two months in Mexico working toward a "successful termination [of the] religious conflict."[50] Other sources demonstrate the growing assumption that Walsh was the official negotiator. E. Gil Borges congratulated Walsh's superior, Father W. Coleman Nevils, president of Georgetown University, on Walsh's assignment: "It is a high honor for Georgetown University that one of the lights of this most famous of the Catholic Institutions of the New World has been chosen by His Holiness as his representative to settle the difficulties of the church in Mexico. It is a well deserve[d] honor for both the University, his President, and Father Walsh for which I am deeply gratified."[51] Once the *Washington Post* broke the story on June 10, detailing Walsh's six-week stay in Mexico working for a resolution, other papers picked up the story.[52] Before long, the media had established Walsh as the pope's official negotiator.[53]

While these sources placed Walsh in the center of the Church's effort to negotiate a settlement, others strenuously denied that Walsh was the pope's negotiator. Burke's files contain an undated telegram from the Vatican to the NCWC, stating that Walsh was never approved as the Vatican's representative.[54] Also, a June 30, 1929, editorial in the Jesuit journal *Revista Católica* claimed that false rumors had connected Walsh with the pope as his special envoy and identified him as a semi-official representative to the United States government. To these allegations, the editor stated: "We can state authoritatively that Father Walsh did not go to Mexico, nor is he in Mexico in connection with the religious question. As vice-president of Georgetown University he made the trip to Mexico to arrange summer courses for his students."[55] The *Indiana Catholic*, on June 14, and the *Washington Post* on June 15 carried an official denial by Walsh, dictated to Dr. Thomas H. Healey, Walsh's assistant at Georgetown's Foreign Service School:

> I have been informed of a report in American newspapers to the effect that I have been named to the official capacity of envoy in the present negotiations between Church and State in Mexico. May I request that you deny this as entirely inaccurate and unauthorized, the only person named for that purpose by the Holy See being Archbishop Leopoldo Ruiz y Flores, the Apostolic Delegate.
>
> As the existing differences lie entirely between the Mexican Government and the Catholic Church in Mexico, the Holy See has properly appointed a Mexican prelate of high standing to bring to a successful termination the negotiations which have resulted from the constructive and praiseworthy statement made by the President of the Republic on June 8.[56]

This statement helps explain the semantics with which Walsh clouded his own involvement in the negotiations. Ruiz and Díaz were, indeed, the *official* representatives of the Vatican, while Walsh himself was more of a *personal* representative of the pope. Regardless of whether or not he had formal instructions as the pope's personal representative, his personal relationship with Pius XI placed him in a position to influence the outcome of the negotiations, and his contributions to the negotiations remain considerable.

Walsh's efforts to help bring an end to the strife which wracked Mexico stand as an example of how American Catholics saw themselves as important tools to be wielded in the interest of establishing harmony in Mexico. For it was only when peace was restored that a new approach to Mexican-American relations could best be arranged. Walsh's contribution to peace in Mexico set him apart from the work of most clergymen involved with improving the conditions facing Mexican Catholics, who worked on the home front, in the trenches of the United States' public opinion battlefield. One of the most intrepid fighters in that theater of battle was Father John A. Ryan.

John A. Ryan

Father John A. Ryan, director of the NCWC's Social Action Department, and a leading liberal in the 1920s and 1930s, was certainly one of the most prolific Catholic writers of the early twentieth century. He contributed heavily to journals such as *America, The American Catholic Quarterly Review, The American Ecclesiastical Review, The Catholic World,* and various newspapers. His major books include his published dissertation, *A Living Wage* (1906), followed by *Distributive Justice* (1916), and *Social Doctrine in Action* (1941). Through all of his writings, his liberalism shines through, and it was this liberalism that was the basis for his attitude toward the Mexican persecution.

Ryan spent relatively little time or energy trying to liberalize the masses compared to his strenuous efforts to call various American liberals back to their roots. Most liberals based their support for Calles in his liberal economic reforms, and in doing so overlooked the Mexican president's violation of civil and religious liberties. Ryan began to get the idea that those who claimed to be liberals believed that religious and civil rights were not "matters of universal principle," but instead amounted to "merely matters of policy."[57] While "liberalism" clearly had a number of levels and facets of interpretation, for Ryan, the key elements were the principles of support for the ideal of religious worship, expression, assembly, and property. The violation of these ideals fueled the fires of his attacks on other liberals who were less concerned about the welfare of the Catholic Church.[58]

John Ryan focused his invective on two liberals as particularly guilty of silence in the face of injustice in Mexico: Norman Thomas, and *The Nation* editor, Oswald Garrison Villard, both of whom he battled through the mails and in the columns of various newspapers.[59] Ryan singled out Villard and *The Nation* as exemplary of the misguided nature of American liberalism. While Villard filled the columns of *The Nation* with condemnation of Mussolini's attacks on the freedoms of the Italians, he neglected to address the Mexican crisis, which Ryan considered far worse tyranny at the very door of the United States — and which *The Nation* considered a matter of "persistent clerical interference in state matters." After summarizing the anticlerical provisions of the Constitution of 1917, Ryan claimed that liberals' indifference to the oppression in Mexico had brought about the forfeiture of "their claim to the title of liberals."[60] Another of Ryan's criticisms of Villard was that the editor scored Calles for prohibiting priests from discussing religion and restrictions on the freedom of the press, but neglected the fact that Catholics could not worship freely. Villard worried that any strong action by the United States would result in war with Mexico. Ryan characterized this attitude as one of a "tory," favoring "liberty for himself and his friends and in their rights to order the lives of everyone else according to their conception of what is good for everyone else."[61] Moreover, Ryan did not fear war with Mexico, because he saw no possibility of it occurring. The most extreme scenario that Ryan could foresee was that if the United States withdrew diplomatic recognition (which Ryan endorsed wholeheartedly), civil war would probably erupt, and Calles would be overthrown. According to Ryan this was an attractive alternative, since "at worst the outcome could not be as bad for the Mexican Church and the Mexican people as the present intolerable situation."[62]

Bishop Francis C. Kelley and Colonel Patrick Callahan praised Ryan for his forthright portrayal of the attitude of American liberals who neglected the Mexican Catholics. Kelley claimed that Ryan's criticism of Villard was "right" and "frank," and noted that "one of the things which in my judgment has done a great deal of harm in the Mexican situation is the misunderstanding that has existed for years on the part of American 'liberals.'"[63] Callahan, for his part, supported Ryan's position and offered to forward copies of Ryan's correspondence to one thousand influential Catholics and non-Catholics, including some journal editors.[64]

John A. Ryan's work targeted the base of the philosophy that would most likely support the universal rights of man—at least the same universal rights that he felt were most important. The depth of frustration over the liberals' (at least Thomas's and Villard's) decisions to ignore what he saw as the most basic and important universal rights demonstrated Ryan's desire to call the liberals back to what he believed their base to be. By criticizing the liberals for endorsing strictly economic liberalism, Ryan challenged them to a deeper interpretation of liberalism, and to support the religious and civil rights that he considered inalienable. Ryan clearly understood the potential of having Thomas or Villard use the pages of their journals to aid in the battle of Catholics to win back their most basic rights. He tried to change public opinion by changing the attitudes of those who are commonly assumed to have major influences on that opinion. Father James H. Ryan, Burke's assistant and successor as general secretary of the National Catholic Welfare Conference, employed similar tactics, but limited his sights to debating one influential Catholic, William Franklin Sands, in the pages of one journal, *The Commonweal*.[65]

James H. Ryan

The James Ryan–William Sands debates of 1926 kept the readers of *The Commonweal* occupied in a game of philosophical ping-pong over the issue of the position of the United States in the affairs of another nation. The central issue of this debate was the recognition of the Carranza government by Woodrow Wilson and the infamous "Arredondo Pledge." Sands maintained, on May 5, that on the issue of the religious rights of Mexicans, the United States had "nothing whatever to do" with getting involved.[66] Ryan responded on May 19 that this assumption was "not only not safe but very false," based on "historical fact." The fact to which Ryan referred was the "most solemn assurances" of Carranza's representative, Eliseo Arredondo, "that Mexico would respect the freedom of religion and of education of all Mexican citizens." Since this pledge was the basis for the Wilson administration's de facto recognition of the Carranza government on October 19, 1915, and since Carranza "failed to keep his promises," the United States had very much with which to be interested. After all, the United States' "trust ha[d] been shamefully abused by a foreign nation and its faith in promises made put to a severe test."[67]

The debate continued off and on through the summer. It was not until September that Sands landed a crushing blow to the argument of those who maintained that the Arredondo Pledge was sufficient justification for active involvement in the Mexican crisis. In an article noting the publication of an article by Marie Regine Madden comparing the Mexican constitutions of 1857 and 1917 in the Jesuit journal, *Thought*, Sands carefully analyzed the pledge itself. He claimed that

> Religious liberty is, in fact, not recognized in the Mexican Constitution. In particular, the Catholic Church clashes completely, in its organization, with the Mexican concept of equality. The "Arredondo pledge" to the Wilson administration carefully guarantees religious liberty "subject to no limitation but that of the constitution," which gives it exactly no value at all; any administration would walk on very delicate ground in attempting to consider it a binding pledge.[68]

Ryan apparently conceded Sands's point, and when he offered no response, the debate faded from the pages of *The Commonweal.*

These five priests are examples of the type of leadership offered to the American Catholics as they struggled with the nature of their response to the crisis brewing in Mexico. Their tactics varied as widely as did their philosophies, from Walsh's efforts to work within the system to mollify the hardships facing Mexico's Catholics to Kenny's blistering attacks on the administration. Whether they were editors of Catholic journals, as was Parsons at *America,* or staffers in the NCWC, as were the two Ryans, they all worked to foster a public opinion conducive to support for their co-religionists in Mexico. John Ryan's challenge for the liberals in the United States to "put their money where their mouths are" is a clear example of how these Catholic clergymen were internalizing the prevailing philosophy of Thomism. Ryan and the others sought a Thomist unity between Americanism and Catholicism by developing an atmosphere conducive to the establishment of a foreign policy between the United States and Mexico—the nexus of the private interest group/public policy connection—that preserved the religious freedoms of Catholics in Mexico, which these priests enjoyed as Catholics in the United States.

chapter 6

THE KNIGHTS OF COLUMBUS

I N THE ATTEMPT OF THE ROMAN CATHOLIC CHURCH IN THE UNITED
States to combat what it believed to be a clear threat to the survival of the
Church in Mexico, Catholics sought to influence United States–Mexican relations along two independent fronts. The hierarchy and the National Catholic
Welfare Conference (NCWC) represented the "official" position of the Roman
Catholic Church in the United States. In concert with the clergy's pressure,
the Knights of Columbus and the secular arms of the NCWC constituted an
"unofficial" movement to influence public policy through a grassroots effort
that touched every corner of the country. This was not an orchestrated movement, but one that simply arose out of personal decisions of American Catholics to try to secure what they believed to be the natural, God-given right of all
people to worship as they saw fit.

The Knights of Columbus was by far the single largest nationally organized organization through which the Church attempted to influence United
States–Mexican diplomatic relations during the Mexican Revolution.[1] During the 1920s and 1930s, the Knights concentrated on four goals to aid their
co-religionists south of the Rio Grande. First, they used their vast numbers

to attempt to force the Coolidge administration to withdraw diplomatic recognition of Mexico and to lift the arms embargo on Mexico. Second, they initiated a movement intended to force the recall of Franklin Roosevelt's ambassador to Mexico, Josephus Daniels. Third, the Knights tried to use a Senate resolution to force the United States government to initiate an official Senate investigation of the Mexican persecution of the Catholic Church. Finally, the Knights appealed to Roosevelt to issue a clear and public condemnation of Mexico based on universal and fundamental American values. That the Knights of Columbus failed to achieve these ambitious stated goals is not really surprising; that they achieved the wider, unstated goals of increasing the United States government's interest in the persecution and inducing the government to formulate informal recommendations to the Mexican government is the focus of this chapter.

The Coolidge Administration

The first major salvo the Knights of Columbus fired in the war against Mexican religious persecution was a series of resolutions directed toward Calvin Coolidge's Mexican policy. One such resolution resulted from a 1926 interdenominational meeting on the Mexican situation sponsored by the Maryland State Knights. The resolution, which arose out of the meeting, condemned the Mexican government in general, and the anti-religious provisions of the Constitution of 1917 in particular.[2] State councils and local chapters of the Knights of Columbus also adopted resolutions and forwarded them to Washington. These resolutions lodged general protests against the Mexican persecution, and issued a call on the United States government for action.[3]

The most ardent of the Knights of Columbus pronouncements in 1926 was the unanimous August 5 resolution from the twenty-five thousand Knights attending the order's annual convention in Philadelphia.[4] In addition to acknowledging the Knights of Columbus's responsibility to provide aid to their Mexican co-religionists, the resolution made two demands of the Coolidge administration. First, the Knights addressed an issue to which they would return repeatedly in their involvement with Mexico when they called on the Coolidge administration to lift an arms embargo imposed against nongovernmental factions in Mexico. The Knights believed the embargo prevented the majority of people in Mexico from asserting their will on the government. In September 1926, the Supreme Board predicted that "as long as

Calles knows that the great majority of the people of Mexico are powerless in the matter of securing arms . . . the more tyrannical will he be in carrying out the policies of the Bolshevistic government now in control in Mexico."[5] Second, the Knights called on Coolidge to withdraw diplomatic recognition of Mexico. This, they believed, would be the strongest possible protest short of war. From their reading of past intervention by the United States government on behalf of religious groups, this demand seemed not too much to ask to preserve Catholicism in Mexico.[6]

Responses to the August 5 resolution were both swift and harsh. Most of the criticism pointed to the dangers of intervention in Mexican affairs. The *New York Times* asserted that the Knights of Columbus clearly did not have the Mexicans' best interests in mind when they passed the resolution. The Mexican episcopate itself condemned armed revolution, which would surely result from the lifted arms export ban.[7]

Coolidge and Secretary of State Frank Kellogg met over the resolution, and decided that no justification existed for a stiffer Mexican policy since no Americans in Mexico had been denied rights spelled out in the treaties of 1831, 1848, or 1853. They concurred in their determination that the United States had no basis for intervention in Mexico's church-state conflict, which was essentially an internal, domestic affair. Firm in his resolve that the Mexican affair was beyond the pale of official involvement by the United States government, Coolidge agreed to meet with the Knights' leaders on September 1, 1926, to discuss the resolution and his response to it. This meeting had an obvious cooling effect on the Knights' demands. Supreme Knight James Flaherty called a press conference immediately following the meeting to outline the Knights' position. According to the new interpretation of their position, the Knights *opposed* a lifting of the arms embargo, they favored continued recognition of the Calles government, and they emphasized that it was their belief that the Mexican situation was the direct result of the policies of the Wilson and Harding administrations, and, as such, could not be attributed to the Coolidge administration.[8] For a time, at least, it appeared that the Knights' righteous indignation had been tamed.

One of the main provisions of the 1926 resolution was a direct reply to appeals from the Mexican Knights of Columbus and became a matter of great controversy. In a letter to Flaherty, a leading Mexican Knight asked the Knights of Columbus of the United States to donate money to the Mexican Knights to ease the pain of Mexican Catholics. Not only would this directly aid the Mexican people, but also it would amount to "an important work of self-defense, [by] building a dam against the [B]olshevist wave which threatens America."[9]

The Knights believed that the single best way to combat the enemy they identified as Mexican Bolshevism was to create a proactive public sentiment in the United States. To accomplish this, they established a $1 million Mexican Fund. The Knights intended this fund to be available for donations from all Americans, regardless of their religious affiliation. To facilitate the collection of this amount from Catholics and non-Catholics alike, Knights were encouraged to publicize the conditions facing Mexican religion in general.[10] In establishing this fund for educating the American public about the conditions in Mexico, the Knights drew the praise of some leaders of the hierarchy. The Supreme Council's work, according to Dennis Cardinal Dougherty, archbishop of Philadelphia, was proof that "American Catholics may not, with impunity, be disregarded and slighted."[11]

After the Knights of Columbus established the fund, the Supreme Council received a great deal of unsolicited advice about how the money could best be used. For instance, William Franklin Sands, a career diplomat and Georgetown University professor of public relations, opposed the Knights' plan to use the fund for more protests and demands for government action, but instead sought to have the Knights re-create their World War I welfare efforts to help José Mora y del Río, archbishop of Mexico City and head of the Mexican hierarchy, to run schools in the Mexican capital.[12] He also foresaw the establishment of a Pan-American college at the Catholic University of America in Washington, D.C., to bring together the best minds of the Americas and to create a leading Latin American library.[13] Michael Williams, editor of the important Catholic journal *Commonweal,* recommended that a portion of the fund be used to finance a commission to investigate and report on the situation in Mexico and the historical background of the church-state struggle in Mexico.[14]

Senator Thomas Heflin of Alabama, habitually hostile to Catholic interests, was less interested in suggesting where the fund should be spent as he was in pointing out the dangers inherent in the fund itself. He leveled the charge, on the floor of Congress, that the $1 million fund was actually a Knights of Columbus effort to rush the United States into war with Mexico.[15] While most senators believed that the charge did not even merit comment, Senator Thomas Walsh of Montana came to the Knights' defense. He inserted into the *Congressional Record* the American hierarchy's 1926 pastoral letter, in which the prelates clearly stated that "Christian principles forbid the Church founded by the Prince of Peace to take up the sword," even in an effort to end the crisis in Mexico.[16]

While the Knights had previously paid little attention to attacks such as Heflin's (which they had, in fact, come to expect), Supreme Knight Flaherty chose to refute Heflin's charges since they were "made by men who have a voice in the affairs of the nation." Flaherty emphasized that the Knights' fund was strictly for education of Americans as to the actual events in Mexico, and reiterated that the Knights favored an end to all intervention in Mexico. Flaherty reaffirmed the Knights of Columbus's desire only to educate: "Our duty is done when, by telling the story, defending the truth and emphasizing the principles, we sound a warning to Christian civilization that its foundations are again being attacked and undermined."[17]

The Knights' fund was the target of misunderstanding and propaganda on both sides of the border, chiefly over the baseless charge that the fund would finance the Cristero Rebellion.[18] While Senator Heflin's spurious accusations flew around the Senate, Mexicans were deluged with anti-Knight propaganda such as the following warning, allegedly from the Knights to the Mexican people: "Face the Rio Grande and say to yourself: 'Senior Bolshevist, the Knights of Columbus have accepted your challenge and are coming one million dollars strong. And they are standing by 800,000 strong and will stand by until you and your so-called constitution are dead.'"[19]

Mexican official Gonzalo Santos claimed that the Knights conspired with oil interests to raise the fund to $4 million to outfit and support the Cristeros. Santos's suspicion was not completely unfounded. Indeed, Cristero supporters heavily solicited the Knights of Columbus through an anonymous Cristero report on the Constitution of 1917. According to the report, the Mexican people had never ratified the constitution. Instead, the military elite had rammed it down their throats. The Cristeros issued an urgent appeal for support necessary to continue their fight against the revolutionary government. While the American episcopate's 1926 pastoral letter and the Knights of Columbus efforts had helped mold a positive public opinion, the Cristero report claimed that "the time has come when propaganda is not any longer necessary. IT IS THE ACTUAL FINANCIAL HELP THAT WE NEED."[20] Flaherty flatly denied these appeals, again claiming that the $1 million fund was purely for domestic education and relief work.[21]

In fact, one cause on which the Knights judiciously refused to expend any of the fund was the Cristero Rebellion. Although rumors flew around the country that military aid to the rebels was an essential reason the Knights founded the fund, no evidence exists that the Knights of Columbus planned to provide such support. On the contrary, Father Michael Kenny, a staunch supporter of the Cristero cause, found it ironic that "out of the million dollar fund raised by the Knights of Columbus for the Mexican cause, there was no assignment available to the men who were fighting for it."[22] Although individuals within the Knights of Columbus, most notably Supreme Advocate Luke Hart, maintained sympathetic ties to the rebels, the organization itself cautiously avoided any official ties to the Cristeros. Since the Mexican Knights were the objects of much of the relief efforts of the Knights of Columbus in the United States, and since the Mexican Knights were so closely linked to the Cristero Rebellion, it is logical to assume that a certain amount of the relief monies provided by the Knights fell into the hands of the rebels. However, it was the expressed policy of the Knights' leadership to deny official connections, or even allusions to aid to the rebels. Supreme Knight Martin Carmody criticized the American press for contributing to anti-Catholic sentiment in the United States by allowing the Mexican government to correlate the Knights and the Church with "every happening in Mexico, whether it be a case of common banditry or military demonstration."[23]

Throughout the Coolidge administration, the Knights of Columbus in the United States waged a spirited campaign to convince the United States government to act, or from the Knights' perspective, to *cease* complicity in the Mexican persecution of the Catholic Church. According to the prevailing sentiment among the Knights in the late 1920s, if only the United States government would end its unjust "intervention" in Mexican affairs by lifting arms export bans, the Mexican people would be able to assert their will on the Mexican government and end the persecution of their Church. The Knights directed resolution after resolution toward the Capitol and the White House, and met with the president and his secretary of state to demand action. Coolidge and Kellogg's well-worn justification for inaction was that the Mexican affair was basically domestic in nature, and the United States had no business getting involved in it.

There were a number of factors behind the failure of the Knights to move the Coolidge administration towards a more activist position. A Mexican refugee in New York, Nemesio García Naranjo, former secretary of education under Victoriano Huerta, spelled out these factors most clearly. García Naranjo pointed to the primary reasons that the Knights of Columbus failed in their attempts to sway the Coolidge administration. First, the Knights publicly demanded that Coolidge withdraw recognition from Mexico, which the president refused to do since the church-state conflict was an internal matter for Mexico to handle. However, García Naranjo maintained that it was widely known that Coolidge wanted to call attention to the revolution and the violation of American property rights inherent in the 1917 Constitution. Coolidge was sensitive to American outrage over property seizures, particularly as it concerned the huge American investment in oil and railroad interests. Yet, at the same time, he was sensitive to the domestic political implications of appearing to bow to pressure from the Knights of Columbus. Therefore, since Coolidge did not want his defense of Americans' property rights to coincide with the Knights' call for the defense of religious freedom, the president postponed his comments for three months. Consequently, the Knights of Columbus ironically caused a postponement of Coolidge's criticism of Mexico. Second, the Knights used a large part of their $1 million fund to publish pamphlets designed to arouse public sentiment against the persecution. However, most of these articles had already appeared earlier in the major American dailies. García Naranjo further pointed out that when the Knights of Columbus collected and published these articles, the articles acquired a clearly partisan nature absent in their original publication.[24] Moreover, since Catholics were the primary consumers of this propaganda, and since the American hierarchy had already come out against the Calles regime, the Knights were essentially preaching to the choir, and all this worked only to arouse the suspicion of the Protestants. García Naranjo summarized the failures of the Knights of Columbus in blunt terms:

> If General Calles had sought to neutralize the undoubted force possessed by the Catholics of the United States, he would never have invented a procedure so efficacious as that which has been developed by his enemies, the Knights of Columbus. The petition which they addressed to Mr. Coolidge served only to postpone the storm for three months and then, with the disbursement of a million dollars for the printing of worthless pamphlets, they have inspired ninety millions of Protestants with the determination to defend the Government of Mexico.[25]

In spite of García Naranjo's critique of their efforts, the Knights of Columbus considered the Mexican Fund a success, even if it drew the suspicions and accusations of those unsympathetic to their cause. Because of this fund, the Knights were able to finance the publication and distribution of literature designed to educate the American public as to the conditions in Mexico. Consequently, this first phase of the Knights' action on behalf of Mexico met with mixed results.

Daniel(s) in the Lion's Den

By the late 1920s, the anticlericalism of the revolution had cooled somewhat, due primarily to the cessation of the Cristero Rebellion and to the tenuous Burke-Calles church-state *modus vivendi* of 1929. During 1930, Calles moderated his stand, temporarily, on economic and social issues. However, in an effort to reinforce his stance as a champion of the revolution, in 1931 Calles renewed his attacks on the Church, thereby causing the failure of the Burke-Calles *modus vivendi*. President-elect Lázaro Cárdenas's Partido Nacional Revolucionario turned the revolutionary spotlight on Mexican education by exerting new socialistic control over primary and secondary education, thereby totally displacing traditional Catholic education.[26] In the light of this resurgent anticlericalism, the Knights of Columbus again took up their banner and besieged the new Franklin Roosevelt administration in the name of Mexico's Catholics. One of the greatest concerns of the Knights was Roosevelt's appointment of his old boss from the Navy Department, Josephus Daniels, as ambassador to Mexico in 1933.

Daniels's ill-chosen words in his July 1934 American Seminar speech led Supreme Knight Carmody to observe that while the United States benignly looked on, Mexico was trying to "out-Russia Russia in making men chattels of the State."[27] The American Knights immediately demanded Daniels's recall from Mexico.

In a resolution proposed during the annual Knights of Columbus convention of 1935, the Knights demanded that Daniels be recalled to the United States and that he be replaced with someone who had strict instructions to "refrain from comment . . . on questions which are the concern of the Mexican people alone." In addition, as a sign of strict impartiality and in recognition of the value of self-determination, the Knights resurrected their demand that the United States government lift the arms embargo.[28]

The central issue around which Daniels's opponents rallied was that since Daniels was the official United States representative, his actions provided a green light to further persecutions. Moreover, it was but one more indication of the ways that the United States government was "intervening" in Mexican affairs. As one Mexican layman put it, "whether you will it or not, recognition, in the eyes of most Mexicans, means approval."[29]

Despite the vehemence of this reaction, Daniels counted influential Catholics among his supporters. Archbishop Mundelein of Chicago opposed the recall of Daniels as "a dubious redress, even for an aggravated wrong."[30] Colonel Patrick H. Callahan, a former Knights of Columbus executive and a close friend of the ambassador, remained in close contact with Daniels in the midst of these attacks. Callahan reiterated exiled Archbishop Pascual Díaz's claim that any United States Catholic meddling in the Mexican church-state crisis would be harmful for the Catholic people of Mexico. He believed that recalling Daniels would cause a serious backlash of Protestant repercussion against the Catholics' involvement in politics and influence with Roosevelt.[31] To Callahan, it was clear that "few things could be more injurious to Catholicism in America."[32]

Although leading American Catholics were among Daniels's most vocal supporters, the Knights were tenacious in their effort to see some action from the White House. The majority of Knights viewed Daniels as more than an inept envoy to Mexico. The Knights feared that his actions and attitudes in support of public, state-run education sounded the death knell for Catholic education in Mexico. The values which the vast majority of the American Knights of Columbus believed that Daniels stood for jeopardized not only the intellectual welfare of the Mexican Catholics, but more dangerously, their spiritual well-being as well.

The Knights also recognized that Daniels reflected the attitudes and opinions of the president. The Knights recognized that their greatest hindrance to active defense of the religious liberty of Mexican Catholics was the man in the White House. The Knights spilled much ink in efforts to convince Roosevelt that he needed to take clear action against the Mexican situation, and Daniels's recall would be an excellent sign of sympathy with the Mexican Catholics. Roosevelt, however, staunchly refused to consider Daniels's recall. That subject, as far as the man in the White House was concerned, was closed.

This effort to have Ambassador Josephus Daniels recalled was an intensive, yet ill-fated attempt of the American Knights to influence United States–Mexican relations. The Knights' failure to achieve the goal of Daniels's replacement with someone who would not aid the revolutionary anticlerical movement was in part an indication of the diversity of opinion among the Knights of Columbus. While the majority of Knights believed that Roosevelt needed to recall Daniels, many others rallied to support both Roosevelt and

Daniels. The attempt to get Daniels recalled highlighted the Knights' internal divisions, which in fact doomed this effort to failure. If these divisions among the Knights over the issue of Daniels's recall appeared formidable, the chasm between the Knights and different coalitions of American Catholics that developed over the Borah resolution proved insurmountable.

The Borah Resolution

The mid-thirties was a busy time for the Knights of Columbus in their effort to have some effect on United States–Mexican relations. Within the context of the failing effort to get Daniels recalled from the embassy in Mexico City, the Knights decided that they needed to take a more aggressive approach to get the Roosevelt administration to act on behalf of Mexico's Catholics. The greatest effort through which the Knights sought to help their Mexican co-religionists was an official United States Senate investigation introduced in what came to be known as the Borah resolution.

The idea for the Borah resolution found its roots in the recommendations for how the Knights should use their $1 million fund. As we recall, Michael Williams, editor of *The Commonweal,* had recommended that the Knights finance an investigation to discover the truth about the conditions in Mexico and their historical backgrounds. Williams's recommendation was in keeping with earlier calls for investigations so that "the people of this country may judge the responsibility of our government...."[33]

At the January 1935 meeting of the Supreme Board of Directors, Carmody referred to Father Michael Kenny's alarming book, *No God Next Door,* which included pictures of Catholics hanged on a string of telephone poles along a stretch of road, to prove that conditions were deteriorating. The Supreme Board decided that a more active effort needed to be made, besides another resolution, as "the files ... and the waste baskets in Washington have been filled with resolutions that have been adopted pertaining to outrages in Mexico."[34] Following this meeting, the Supreme Board arranged a January 21 meeting between officers of the Supreme Board and Secretary of State Cordell Hull. At this meeting, Carmody demanded that the United States threaten to withdraw diplomatic recognition of Mexico if the "persecution and murder" of Catholics was not stopped.[35] Hull assured Carmody of the State Department's "sympathy" for the Knights' "high purpose of promoting the principles of Jeffersonian liberty, opportunity and freedom to oppressed peoples

everywhere." However, beyond this statement of sympathy, and an assurance that the United States government would continue to look with interest on the situation in Mexico, Hull would go no further. Hull ended the
meeting with the request that the sentiments he had expressed remain strictly
confidential.[36]

The Knights followed their conference with Hull immediately with another meeting with a group of sympathetic senators at the Capitol, during
which the Supreme Board spelled out its plan for a special congressional investigation of the conditions in Mexico. Senator Robert Wagner (New York)
committed himself to help convince Senator William Borah of Idaho, the ranking minority member of the Senate Foreign Relations Committee, to sponsor
a Senate resolution. This resolution not only authorized the Senate to embark
on a full-scale investigation into the persecution in Mexico, but it went further
by including a provision condemning Mexico based on the anticipated results
of that investigation.[37]

The Roosevelt administration's opposition to the resolution was immediate. Secretary of State Cordell Hull, upon learning about the Borah resolution, announced that an investigation such as that proposed by Borah would
amount to no less than intervention in the affairs of another nation. Moreover, Hull asserted that such an indictment of a friendly government would
be highly damaging to the reputation of the United States in Latin America.[38]
The Knights responded that what they wanted was not interference, but some
sign of active interest, such as when Secretary of State James G. Blaine instructed Charles Emory Smith, the American minister to Russia in 1891, to express the United States government's concern over the plight of persecuted
Russian Jews:

> The Government of the United States does not assume to dictate the
> internal policy of other nations.... Nevertheless, the mutual duties of
> nations require that each should use its power with due regard for the
> results which exercise produces on the rest of the world. It is in this
> respect that the condition of the Jews in Russia is now brought to the
> attention of the United States, upon whose shores are cast daily evi-
> dences of suffering and destitution wrought by the enforcement of
> the edicts against these unhappy people. I am persuaded that his Im-
> perial Majesty the Emperor of Russia, and his councilors, can have no
> sympathy with measures which are forced on other nations by such
> deplorable consequences.[39]

Precedents such as these inspired the Knights to put the full force of their influence behind the Borah resolution. In a May 3, 1935, letter to Roosevelt, Carmody claimed to speak not only for the Knights of Columbus, but also for millions of American Catholics when he noted that in light of the long history of American defense of religious freedom everywhere, the Knights sought the United States government's agreement to demand no more and no less for the people of Mexico.

Influential members of the American Catholic hierarchy also supported the resolution. Archbishop Michael Curley of Baltimore backed the Borah resolution so adamantly that he criticized the Knights for not making a bigger fuss over the president's resistance to meet with them over the issue.[40] Bishop Francis Kelley of Tulsa/Oklahoma City, a Knight himself, and a very active bishop in the Mexican controversy, agreed with the Knights in general, but differed on strategy. He recommended that the Knights should manage their efforts for the resolution "in such a way as to not identify our Order with it, because of a feeling that our Order is tremendously powerful and influential and that, therefore, it has aroused such antagonisms in Mexico that it is more cordially disliked than is the Church itself."[41] Kelley clearly sought to insulate the Knights of Columbus from the public scourging that would surely result from a perceived exercise of influence over the Roosevelt administration's Mexican policy.

A formidable array of Catholics and others aligned themselves in opposition to the Borah resolution in both Mexico and in the United States. As we know, Mexican newspapers, and even Mexico's primate, Archbishop Pascual Díaz of Mexico City, asked that the United States Congress stay out of Mexico's business. Domestically, such powerful Catholic clergy leaders as the NCWC Administrative Committee and George Cardinal Mundelein, archbishop of Chicago, agreed with Roosevelt and Hull that such a public pronouncement as the Borah resolution would only cause an insulted Mexico to step up the persecutions. Later that year, Mundelein found another opportunity to thwart the efforts of the Knights, in the controversy surrounding the Knights' demand for a public statement.

Faced with this considerable body of opposition, the Knights pulled every political string at their disposal to influence the Senate Foreign Relations Committee to pass the resolution and discuss it on the Senate floor. In order to counterbalance the criticism of the resolution by Archbishop Díaz, the Supreme Council decided that an appeal to exiled Mexican Archbishop Leopoldo Ruiz was in order. Supreme Advocate Luke Hart wrote to Ruiz and asked him to send a pro-resolution letter to every member of the American hierarchy, trying to convince them to urge their senators and Roosevelt himself to support the measure. Hart assured Ruiz that his efforts would go far towards a successful adoption and implementation of the resolution in the Senate.[42]

The Supreme Council blamed Roosevelt himself as the ultimate reason that the resolution languished in committee. Supreme Advocate Hart recommended that the Knights, in effect, go over Roosevelt's head by appealing directly to the public. If the supreme knight were to issue a personal appeal to the head of every local Knights of Columbus chapter in the country, their letters and resolutions, along with those from the hierarchy, would "build up a campaign that the President is bound to give consideration to."[43] Carmody agreed with Hart, and issued a form letter, along with sample telegrams and resolutions, to each grand knight on March 25. Carmody encouraged all grand knights to participate in the liberation of Mexico by wiring messages to Roosevelt and their senators urging their support of the Borah resolution. Not only should all Knights write letters, but Carmody also urged them to convince as many citizens of their communities as possible to do so as well. According to Carmody, the order had never asked its members "to serve in a greater cause nor to contribute to one that should appeal more strongly to Catholic sentiment."[44] Carmody was confident about the fruits of his labor. Knights would respond to his call and flood Washington, D.C., with letters and telegrams.[45]

The response to Carmody's appeal was, indeed, impressive. Local and state councils deluged their senators' mailboxes with letters, telegrams, and resolutions.[46] Dozens of state chapters presented resolutions at the national conventions in 1935 and 1936, and the order forwarded unanimous resolutions passed by the convention as a whole to Roosevelt, Hull, and to key senators. Luke Hart wrote to Knight Thomas Pendergast, the Democratic boss in Kansas City, Missouri, seeking his influence on Senator Harry Truman. Truman wrote back, assuring Pendergast of his support: "I never did think the Mexican Government was a real government. It is a sort of Bolshevik organization just like Russia. It has always been my opinion ever since I was a school kid that James K. Pope [Polk] made a mistake when he didn't make the Panama Canal the southern boundary of the United States."[47]

One state council resolution in particular included veiled political threats. Michael F. Walsh, New York state deputy of the Knights of Columbus, called on Roosevelt to support the resolution in the name of "255 councils . . . comprising more than 65,000 members, who, with their families and friends aggregate more than one million adult citizens [i.e., *voters*] of this State."[48] Files filled with copies of telegrams favoring the Borah resolution indicate that Carmody cajoled state senators and representatives, local officials, including a New York police commissioner, industrial leaders, law firms, insurance companies, and other influential Catholics to exert the pressure of mass demand on the Roosevelt administration.[49] The appeal to Knights and other American Catholics to urge their senators to support the measure frequently resorted to visceral, emotional tactics. One poster designed to reach this level of appeal exhorted Catholics to act:

"Abel? Eh? Am I my brother's keeper?"—Cain.

"Christ? Eh? I wash my hands of this innocent man."—Pontius Pilate.

"Mexico? The Borah Resolution? Eh? What can I do?"—Mr. & Mrs. Francis X. American. . . .[50]

Sentiments such as Truman's and Archbishop Curley's notwithstanding, this effort by the Knights was not of sufficient size or weight to overcome the growing resistance to the resolution. In the end, Roosevelt's influence on Capitol Hill, the division among the American hierarchy, and the cooperation of Protestant and pro-administration Catholics combined to keep the resolution tabled.

The Knights suffered a profound defeat in their backing of the Borah resolution. The insurmountable forces aligned against the measure were a manifestation of the feeling of impending danger which surrounded the proposed investigation. It would have forced the hand of a reluctant president bent on maintaining the image of the Good Neighbor. That prominent Catholics, including members of the hierarchy, were numbered among the leading supporters of Roosevelt against the resolution is very significant. The division among Catholics in the United States over the resolution was fatal for the Knights' effort. The Knights mobilized and encouraged all Catholics to register their support of the resolution. In spite of these Herculean labors to mobilize Catholics at every level—from American and Mexican archbishops, to senators, on down to laymen—in support of the resolution, Roosevelt and Hull succeeded in avoiding taking direct action on behalf of the Knights of Columbus in the interest of Mexican Catholics. This effort differed significantly from the move to recall Daniels in that the Knights were unified behind the Borah resolution. The difficulty came when the Knights were opposed by other Catholics, particularly powerful prelates. These leading Catholics, especially the Administrative Committee of the National Catholic Welfare Conference, the organizational body of Catholic bishops, were attuned to the intricacies and delicacies of international diplomacy, and therefore, supported the Roosevelt administration and its Mexican policy.

The Public Remonstrance

Following the Knights' inability to get the Borah resolution reported out of committee, they decided to take their appeal directly to the president, and recast their message as an appeal based on their bedrock dedication to universal values. In order for the Knights and the president to gauge each other's positions, the Supreme Council believed that a direct, face-to-face meeting with the president would clear up many of their concerns. At such a meeting, the Knights would confront the president over his inaction on behalf of Catholics persecuted by a Bolshevistic regime that stood as a black menace at our southern border. The Knights of Columbus were careful to make the connection between the lack of religious freedom for Mexicans and the abrogation of the religious rights of Americans in Mexico. They sought a public condemnation of the Mexican government by the Roosevelt administration. To succeed in convincing the president to promise that he would make such a public statement, the Knights needed to meet with him.

Supreme Knight Martin Carmody wrote Roosevelt requesting a meeting to discuss the Knights' attitudes and opinions of Mexico within the context of the worsening conditions for Catholics there. Supreme Advocate Luke Hart was none too optimistic for the chances for such a meeting. Especially in light of Roosevelt and Hull's victory in the Borah resolution issue, Hart was convinced that Roosevelt would resist the order's efforts to meet with him, and that Daniels would convince the president to continue the policy line begun the year before. Hart foresaw that the only way to counterbalance this pro–status quo attitude was to forge a forceful public opinion against the conditions in Mexico, and to fight to emphasize the administration's responsibility for those conditions.[51]

When the president refused to reply to the Knights' request for a meeting, Carmody and the Supreme Board of Directors wrote a terse letter to

Roosevelt. The Knights of Columbus, according to the letter, had never been so resolutely neglected in their requests to visit the White House as they were in Roosevelt's refusal to answer their letter. They traditionally met with the president to express their views on "questions affecting the public welfare. . . ." Considering the abysmal conditions in Mexico, the Knights believed that they had a fundamental right to the opportunity to express themselves and urge that the United States government might take steps to withdraw diplomatic recognition of Mexico if it did not cease the merciless persecution.[52] Carmody made it clear that Roosevelt's negligence in answering the Knights of Columbus letter, combined with his efforts to keep the Borah resolution bottled up in the Senate Foreign Relations Committee, amounted to "keen disappointments" to the Knights.[53]

In particular, the Knights wished to inform Roosevelt that they knew that such a stand by the State Department was "at variance with the facts and ignores the policy of the Government of the United States as established by precedents extending over a period of a century, including that of [the Roosevelt] administration."[54] Such precedents for United States intervention on behalf of "oppressed peoples" date from 1840, and continued up into Roosevelt's own representations in November 1933 to the Russian envoy Litvinoff, in which the president expressed his desire that Americans living inside the U.S.S.R. "should enjoy freedom of conscience and religious liberty," that they should retain their right to have ministers of various denominations available to meet their spiritual needs, and that such ministers "not be denied entry into the . . . Soviet Union because of their ecclesiastical status." The Knights of Columbus claimed that they demanded no less than this for Mexico, and they "renew[ed their] protest against the silence of the Government of the United States and its tacit acquiescence in the persecution of the Mexican people in the name of Government. . . ."[55]

Roosevelt quickly responded to this latter letter and explained the lack of a speedy reply to the first letter by claiming that pressing public business had preoccupied him. Nonetheless, he was willing to meet with the Knights, which he did on July 8, 1935. When Roosevelt began the meeting by noting that conditions for Mexican Catholics had greatly improved, Carmody noted that this contradicted a telegram he had received that same morning.[56] Clearly, Carmody's main purpose for the meeting was to get the president to agree to publicly oppose the Mexican persecution. He reviewed various instances in which the United States government had become involved in foreign religious persecution, and explained the American Catholics' confusion over "the apparent indifference and unconcern" of the administration concerning the Mexican situation. Roosevelt defended the government's actions by citing changing relations in Latin America, particularly, increasing antipathy for the United States and the power plays of various states (especially Argentina) on the regional level. *Any* activity such as the Knights recommended would be met with a concerted outcry against the United States and could result in "the killing of one hundred priests and nuns in Mexico."[57] Roosevelt then referred to the list of precedents: "Take the precedents that are referred to in your letter, what did they amount to? Not a damned thing. Nothing ever came out of any of them and they amounted to nothing. Suppose that this government does all of these things that you are asking for and that Cárdenas takes no action, what then?"[58]

Carmody responded by asserting that the abuses in the Constitution of 1917 could be mitigated through "an aroused public sentiment in this country and the co-operation of our government." Roosevelt interjected: "What do you want? It is certain that we are not going to war with Mexico." Carmody denied that the Knights of Columbus were asking for war and observed that "neither did he go to war with England over Ireland, and yet it was nothing but aroused public sentiment in this country that brought about the freedom of Ireland. . . ."[59]

Roosevelt tried to end the meeting by assuring Carmody that he was in close contact with Rome, Apostolic Delegate Archbishop Amleto Cicognani, the NCWC, and Father John J. Burke. Carmody pointed out that Burke was responsible for the failed *modus vivendi* of 1929 and that any other of his settlements would surely be as unsatisfactory. The meeting ended with Carmody asking Roosevelt to make some kind of public statement about the attitude of the United States government on the Mexican situation. The president agreed to the request, and promised to make some comment in his next public speech. The Knights feared that in spite of the president's words, he was hesitant to take a stand against the persecution south of the Rio Grande.

To increase pressure on Roosevelt to get him to live up to his promise to make a public statement about the United States government's attitude toward the situation in Mexico, Carmody sent out a form letter to each Knight. Carmody wanted the Knights to urge Roosevelt to come forward with his statement. Included with the letter was an itinerary of the president's travel plans; the members of the order were asked to form into committees to present Roosevelt with resolutions calling for the statement at each stop along his trip.[60] Carmody sought to insure that the president heard the Knights on this issue. He called on all state deputies to act: "I believe that there should be held meetings throughout the country, all set up in a big way. In a number of cities meetings already have been held in condemnation of the persecutions in Mexico, at which strong resolutions were adopted that were forwarded to some members of the United States Senate with the request that they be presented to that body, and at least entered on the record."[61] Carmody clearly believed this pressure on Congress would force Roosevelt to act on his pledge.

The president intended to live up to the spirit of his promise to Carmody in a speech in San Diego, on October 2, 1935. Roosevelt used the occasion of his address to emphasize American ideals concerning religious liberty:

> In the United States we regard it as axiomatic that every person shall enjoy the free exercise of his religion according to the dictates of his conscience. Our flag for a century and a half has been the symbol of the principles of liberty of conscience, of religious freedom, and equality before the law, and these concepts are deeply ingrained in our national character.
>
> It is true that other nations may, as they do, enforce contrary rules of conscience and conduct. It is true that policies that may be pursued under flags other than our own are beyond our jurisdiction. Yet in our inner individual lives we can never be indifferent, and we assert for ourselves complete freedom to embrace, to profess and to observe the principles for which our flag has so long been the lofty symbol. As it was so well said by James Madison, "We hold it for a fundamental and inalienable truth that religion and the manner of discharging it can be directed only by reason and conviction, not by force or violence."[62]

The NCWC News Service report of the speech considered it a "notable" statement, but the Knights did not agree. Hart considered the NCWC report as but one more example of how the NCWC had become "a mere apologist for the president insofar as his attitude concerning the persecution of the Mexican people is concerned."[63] The Knights' main complaint was that Roosevelt, while standing within twenty miles of the border, never mentioned Mexico specifically. The Knights made note of this point in a letter to Roosevelt. They reminded the president of his pledge, and indicated that the San Diego speech did not fill the bill. The president had said nothing that would dissuade the Mexican government from continuing a policy line for which Roosevelt's actions implied consent and approval.

The Knights made it clear that Roosevelt, as demonstrated in his comments in San Diego, was not living up to the obligations and responsibilities of his office. According to the Knights, there was a long tradition of American presidents who had called attention to oppression in other lands. Roosevelt's predecessors, "Jackson, Van Buren, Fillmore, Pierce, Buchanan, Grant, Hayes, Arthur, Cleveland, Harrison, McKinley, Theodore Roosevelt, Taft and Wilson gave consolation to the down-trodden and oppressed minorities of other lands and deterred their governments from continuing such persecutions, by remonstrating against them in the name of humanity and in the name of religion."[64] Then the Knights hit the president hard:

> There can be no misunderstanding, on our part or on yours, of the simple facts involved. . . . You cannot escape responsibility for the endorsement given to the Mexican Government and its policies by your ambassador to that country. You cannot escape responsibility for failure and refusal to follow the long line of precedents founded upon established American principles. You cannot escape responsibility for non-action on behalf of bleeding and oppressed Mexico.[65]

Roosevelt responded to the letter from the Supreme Board of Directors with a firm hand. The policies of the United States government were justified by the fact that there had been *no* complaints by any Americans of their rights being abridged in Mexico. Within this context, he had no intention of changing his policy to intervene in Mexico. Further, he claimed that his San Diego speech clearly spelled out the United States' dedication to religious freedom, even though other countries may pursue "contrary rules of conscience and conduct." Finally, Roosevelt blasted the Knights for using Theodore Roosevelt to defend their position. The president quoted a speech by the earlier Roosevelt, in which he stated that

> Ordinarily it is very much wiser and more useful for us to concern ourselves with striving for our own moral and material betterment here at home than to concern ourselves with trying to better the condition of things in other nations. We have plenty of sins of our own to war against, and under ordinary circumstances we can do more for the general uplifting of humanity by striving with heart and soul to put a stop to . . . corruption, . . . lawlessness [and] . . . prejudices here at home than by passing resolutions about wrongdoing elsewhere.[66]

The Knights used this letter, which was on the surface a clear justification for inaction by Franklin Roosevelt, to their best advantage. They were able to turn each of his points into arguments for their own position. First, that Roosevelt had not heard of any complaints did not mean anything. He did not consider that in fourteen of thirty-two Mexican states ministers had been outlawed altogether, and when only 197 priests must meet the needs of 15 million, was it fair to say that Americans can "worship freely" in places where the law makes religion illegal or nearly impossible?[67]

Second, the Knights of Columbus asked "Who, may we ask, ever requested you to *intervene* in the concerns of the Mexican Government? Surely not the Knights of Columbus." The Knights claimed that in a review of all of the Knights of Columbus correspondence, not once did the order request an intervention. When the United States defended various Christian and Jewish groups in other nations, from 1833 to 1933, was that intervention? The Knights thought not.[68]

Finally, in the president's use of Theodore Roosevelt's December 6, 1904, annual address to Congress to justify his inaction, the Knights believed Roosevelt had opened a can of worms, and made "not a happy selection." That speech, according to the Supreme Board, did not justify inaction, but just the opposite; it called for justified action in the face of oppression. The passage Roosevelt quoted ended with "we can do more for the general uplifting of humanity by [working] . . . here at home than by passing resolutions about wrongdoing elsewhere," but in the original address, the earlier Roosevelt continued thus:

> Nevertheless, there are occasional crimes committed on so vast a scale and of such peculiar horror as to make us doubt whether it is not our manifest duty to endeavor at least to show our disapproval of the deed and our sympathy with those who have suffered by it. The cases must be extreme in which such a course is justifiable. . . . [I]n extreme cases action may be justifiable and proper. . . . Yet it is [is it?] not to be expected that a people like ours, which in spite of certain very obvious shortcomings, nevertheless as a whole shows by its consistent practice its belief in the principles of civil and religious liberty and of orderly freedom. . . ."[69]

If Theodore Roosevelt was to be an authority on inaction, as the president maintained, the Knights took great pleasure in quoting from *Fear God and Take Your Own Part,* Theodore Roosevelt's own 1916 book. Roosevelt summarized the brutality of "bandits masquerading as military or civil leaders of the Mexican people" and pinned responsibility for the outrages on the fact that "our Government has let these people procure ammunition with which to murder our own soldiers and their own peaceful citizens; and the president [Wilson] has actually proclaimed that they ought not to be interfered with in 'spilling blood.' . . . The effect of our inaction in Mexico has been unspeakably dreadful."[70]

After Roosevelt received this letter, he recognized that the two positions were irreconcilable and chose not to reply. James A. Farley, the Democratic National Committee chairman and postmaster general, who was also a Catholic, told the president that "this crowd in New Haven has been terribly discourteous and I wouldn't bother with them at all."[71]

The confusion, identified above, of whether or not the Knights of Columbus demanded intervention or not was one that plagued their efforts from the beginning. The order's 1935 resolution, written after the Supreme Board of Directors consulted Secretary of State Cordell Hull, condemned the Mexican persecution. The Knights claimed that "five hundred thousand patriotic liberty loving Christian men of America [and] the sentiments of God-fearing men and women everywhere" called on the United States government to "make representations to the Government of Mexico" such that if it did not stop its persecutions of Catholics, "further recognition of the Mexican Government will be withdrawn and diplomatic relations between the United States and the Mexican Government will be severed."[72] Knights of Columbus local and state councils from all over the country sent similar resolutions and requested that the Roosevelt administration exert its "moral influence" on behalf of the Mexican people.[73] Such calls were interpreted over and over again as demands for active intervention into Mexican affairs, but the Knights of Columbus continually reverted back to the justifications used during the Flaherty years. The Knights of Columbus demanded not intervention, but a remonstrance, or a public protestation. What the Knights really wanted was an end to all intervention by the United States government. As we have already seen, this was clearly designed to bring about an end to the long-standing arms embargo against rebel groups in Mexico, and an end to the support afforded the Mexican government through continued sympathetic diplomatic recognition, embodied in the Knights' eyes in the person of Josephus Daniels.

Roosevelt's unwillingness to enunciate what the Knights believed to be a very basic human right was unconscionable to more than just the Knights of Columbus. The president suffered the slings and arrows of a whole host of critics. When Roosevelt had refused the order's request for action, the editor of the *Baltimore Catholic Review* claimed that the president had clearly announced that he was unwilling to stand up to tyrants in defense of the oppressed. The editor continued, "In that respect, he stands before the world as a champion of a doctrine that in the minds of millions of human beings must be construed not only as selfish, but downright inhuman."[74] Wilfrid Parsons, editor of *America,* claimed that this refusal to act in the face of injustice provided nothing less than a "green light" to those who would oppress others, and it provided "comfort to the enemies of religion."[75]

Michael Williams, the editor of *The Commonweal,* agreed with the sentiments expressed by the Knights. According to Williams, it follows from Roosevelt's logic, in basing his inaction on the fact that there had been no complaints, that

> The government of any nation which has been officially recognized by the United States, and has become, officially, at any rate, "a good neighbor," may persecute its own subjects, or citizens, or slaves, because of their religious beliefs and practices and customs, as violently and as unjustly as that government chooses to do—even if such conduct is in flagrant contradiction of "the principles of liberty of conscience, of religious freedom and equality before the law," which were "concepts deeply ingrained in our national character."[76]

The Knights clearly had a difficult time rationalizing Roosevelt's resistance to defend something as basic to Americans as freedom of religion. One of the explanations they developed was that Roosevelt evidently did not embrace religious freedom as tightly as did they. Paul Bakewell, president of the National Committee for the Defense of American Rights in Mexico (NC-DARM), wrote to Hart with the belief that Roosevelt must be a Mason. This would explain the administration's unwillingness to cooperate with the Knights. Moreover, Bakewell guessed that Hull, Daniels, and vice president Garner were Masons as well.[77] Hart agreed with Bakewell, and opined that Roosevelt's secretary, Colonel Marvin McIntyre, was also a Mason. It was McIntyre, according to Hart, "who [had] probably done more than anyone else to keep us from having an interview with the president."[78] Hart and Bakewell found more evidence that supported their Masonic conspiracy theory when Bakewell discovered that the president had officiated at a ceremony inducting his sons into Free Masonry. Bakewell maintained that "it is not unreasonable to suppose that, as the president of the United States is such a prominent member of that Order, that fact alone may have at least something to do with the indifference which he has shown to the awful . . . persecution of the Catholic Church in Mexico."[79]

The Knights, in their request for a meeting with Roosevelt to express their concerns over his Mexican policy, and in their demand that the president publicly remonstrate against the persecution of Catholics, were acting in accordance with their belief that the future of Catholicism in Mexico hung in the balance. The Knights of Columbus remained genuinely confused by Roosevelt's reluctance to take a stand—a stand that they interpreted as a defense of something as basic to Americans as freedom of religion. Moreover, according to the Knights' list, such a position had numerous historical precedents dating from as far back as the 1830s. This confusion drove some Knights to rationalize Roosevelt's inaction; one such rationalization was the Masonic conspiracy that reached into the White House itself. The Knights firmly believed that in their calls for the Roosevelt administration to stand up for the defense of religious liberty, they were fighting for rights inalienable and God-given.

Divisions in the Ranks

One factor that helps explain the inability of the Knights of Columbus and others to move Franklin D. Roosevelt farther on the path of a full advocacy of Mexican Catholics was the fact that the president counted among his most ardent supporters a number of influential Catholics. Postmaster General James Farley, as we have already seen, was closely allied to his boss. Other Catholics, not so directly positioned under Roosevelt's thumb, regarded the president's policies as rational and sound. Father John J. Burke, general secretary of the NCWC, remained in close contact with the president. His counsel was one of the reasons Roosevelt hesitated to respond to Carmody's correspondence. When McIntyre, Roosevelt's secretary, informed Burke that Roosevelt wanted to inform Carmody of the efforts being made, Burke recommended patience. If the president bowed to the order's pressure, thus making the Knights of Columbus the "repository of . . . confidences" over the Catholic hierarchy, a grave injustice would be felt by the NCWC.[80] Father John F. O'Hara, president of the University of Notre Dame and an expert on Latin America, recognized that Roosevelt's policy was the only possible course, as any action such as that endorsed by the Knights would cause irreparable damage to the administration's goals in the region.[81]

The Knights included in their ranks some who actively supported and sympathized with Roosevelt's position and in turn, criticized the Knights' leadership. A. Reisweber, state deputy of the Wisconsin Knights, expressed the belief that many priests and laymen, including members of the Knights of Columbus, were opposed to the order's demands that Roosevelt intervene in Mexico. Such a demand will surely founder "the ship of Columbianism" on "the shoals of vicious Anti-Catholic attack and Catholic persecution." Reisweber warned that if the Supreme Council continued on its course, "it will cause an exodus of members from our Order."[82] In a similar vein, Paul J. Kilday, the Texas state deputy, forwarded to Roosevelt a telegram assuring the president of Texas Knights' "undying loyalty."[83] Former Knights of Columbus official Patrick H. Callahan, in a 1926 personal letter, claimed that "nearly every thoughtful member of the Knights of Columbus who writes or speaks to me on the subject [of the protests against the persecution and against the Coolidge administration] always starts out by saying 'Flaherty does not speak for me' or 'It was a great mistake to include me in that 800,000.'"[84] Later, he stood up for the president when he claimed that "If [Roosevelt] were the direct representative of the Holy Father and on the payroll of the Vatican he could hardly do all things that some of the Catholics [read: the Knights of Columbus] in this country want him to do in Mexico."[85]

Roosevelt had a powerful backer among the American hierarchy. As we found in chapter 3, Cardinal Mundelein of Chicago traditionally supported the president, and this case was no different. Cardinal Mundelein cautioned Catholics to stay out of politics, and declared that no group, including the Knights of Columbus, could speak for the Church on political matters. Mundelein was unreserved in his support for Roosevelt during the election of 1936. Other prelates were not so much backers of the president as they were detractors of the Knights of Columbus. In a letter to Papal Secretary of State Eugenio Cardinal Pacelli, Count Enrico P. Galeazzi noted that the Knights of Columbus's protest was significantly diminished by the actions of Archbishop John T. McNicholas of Cincinnati.[86] McNicholas, in a pastoral letter that was read in all parishes in his archdiocese on Sunday, November 3, 1935, dropped a bombshell on the efforts of the Knights of Columbus:

> We wish our priests and people to understand unmistakably that the Knights of Columbus in no sense speak for the priesthood nor for the Catholic laity of the Cincinnati Archdiocese on the persecution of religion in Mexico, or on any other subject having religious implications,

unless they have a commission from us. We do not make this statement in defense of the National Administration. We are convinced that much more could and should have been done by our Government to bring to an end the brutal persecution of the Catholics of Mexico.[87]

The Knights were dumbstruck by this attack on their efforts. Luke Hart called the statement a "totally unwarranted and volunteered affront" to the order, and as such, was "entirely gratuitous and tended to minimize the worth and effect" of the Roosevelt–Knights of Columbus correspondence.[88] Hart, however, understood that McNicholas did not represent the attitude of the whole hierarchy. Among the Knights' strongest backers were Archbishop Dennis Cardinal Dougherty (Philadelphia), Archbishop Arthur Drossaerts (San Antonio), Bishop Bernard Mahoney (Sioux Falls), and Archbishop Joseph F. Rummel (New Orleans).[89]

In spite of the assurances Roosevelt received from his Catholic backers, as a politician he began to worry about the potential influence the Knights of Columbus might hold in the upcoming election of 1936. He welcomed all positive news from Mexico, and used it to extol the justice of his policy. Daniels reported that the states of Zacatecas, Colima, Guana Juato, and Tabasco all were re-opening churches and allowing priests to return in later 1935.[90]

The Knights' efforts and the tone used in the Roosevelt correspondence inevitably led to suspicions that the order sought to jeopardize Roosevelt's political future. As the awareness of this possibility spread, Catholics flocked to the president's defense. Joseph Leib of South Bend, Indiana, wrote to Carmody concerned that the Knights' October 25, 1935, letter contained a veiled threat by saying that "the members of the Knights of Columbus will be requested to oppose Mr. Roosevelt's re-election in 1936." Carmody replied that "there was nothing partisan or personal in the letter," and noted that surely, Leib recognized United States citizens' rights to protest persecution and the propaganda flooding the nation.[91] Father Maurice Sheehy of Catholic University was most concerned that the Knights' attacks were intended to tarnish the president's reputation, thereby ruining his chances at the polls. Carmody again denied any such plans. According to Carmody, the Knights had no intention of placing the responsibility of the conditions in Mexico on either the president or the State Department.[92] This position changed radically over the next four months, as the Knights faced a president increasingly reluctant to bend to their wishes.

A number of Knights declared themselves opposed to the order's demands on the president. P. F. Dougherty, a Knight from Santa Monica, California, was vehement in his criticism of the Knights' policies. He blasted *Columbia*'s editor, John Donahue. The Knights of Columbus, in Dougherty's opinion, had no business whatsoever attacking "our Great President." If the Knights continued in this effort, Dougherty would be obliged to terminate his membership. Dougherty also quoted from the *Los Angeles Times,* which he considered a "very radical republican paper" that provided evidence of the Knights' political agenda: "The republicans are not asleep to the possibility of profiting. Supreme Knight, Martin H. Carmody of the Knights of Columbus is a loyal Republican and can be expected to make the most of the Presidential refusal to intervene in Mexico."[93] Carmody responded to all of these attacks with the insistence that the order was merely informing the administration of the precedents for action, and was meeting the call of the hierarchy of the United States to "pray that such a reign [of "anti-Christian tyranny"] may cease, and to do everything *in their power by word and by act* to make the fact of such tyranny known."[94]

As the election of 1936 neared, the Knights of Columbus were trying to arouse the "Catholic vote" against the president, but a series of conditions combined to circumvent this effort. Cárdenas shifted his efforts toward social and economic reforms, and eased off of the anticlerical movement, thereby eliminating the Knights' political ammunition. Rifts over the correct Mexican policy widened between factions within the American hierarchy. Also, American Catholics looked more to home, and the social and economic condition of the United States. To a large degree, American Catholics joined the landslide of voters rushing to return Roosevelt to office. In fact, according to an October 1936 Gallup poll, 78 percent of American Catholics were for Roosevelt's re-election.[95]

In early 1936, a member of the Supreme Board of Directors, Ray T. Miller, journeyed to Mexico and reported to Carmody that the Knights had made great strides for the people of Mexico. Miller made it clear that the Knights had not reached their ultimate goal of ending religious persecution by summarizing the deplorable conditions which continued to plague the Catholics of Mexico. Nevertheless, he also noted that

> most of the Americans in business in Mexico and many Mexicans told [him] that the only real power in all America creating public opinion favorable to better conditions in Mexico is the Knights of Columbus; that it was the propaganda of the Knights of Columbus that the officials of the Mexican Government were attempting to offset by their own propaganda to the tourist in Mexico. . . . The Knights of Columbus are

a real thorn in the side of the Mexican Government. It is very apparent that the Knights of Columbus' crusade against Mexican religious persecution is bringing about better conditions for the present-day Mexican Catholic.[96]

Supreme Knight Martin Carmody's 1937 annual address assessed the Knights' successes in their fight for religious freedom in Mexico. Once the order had answered the hierarchy's call for action, their efforts resulted in positive moves for the Mexican Church. Resolutions by the Knights brought the Mexican situation to the world's attention and encouraged the Mexican people to continue the struggle at home. Carmody believed that the Knights achieved results even in Washington: "there can be no uncertainty on this, our petitions and protests, in spite of a prevailing attitude to the contrary, were not without effect in arousing our government to a more serious consideration of the religious cause of the Mexican people than would otherwise have been the case." In light of the improving conditions for the Church in Mexico in 1936 and 1937, Carmody observed that "it may appear advisable that further action should not be taken."[97] Nonetheless, Carmody offered this warning: the Mexican government was still "hostile to God and religion. It is still dominated by atheistic Communism, and it is still the center for Communistic propaganda in America. The leopard does not change its spots. . . ."[98] The Supreme Council provided the last word in *Columbia* on the Mexican crisis. Although the persecutions had been easing for well over a year, Catholic schools remained closed and public education remained compulsory. Therefore, the council resolved to renew its protest "against the persecution of religion and the denial of human and divine rights to the Mexican people by the Government of Mexico." The council also took up the demand that it had made in the beginning of the Knights' involvement in the affair: that "the American Government remonstrate against those violations of civil and religious rights." Finally, the council assured the Mexican Catholics that the Knights' "interest in them and in their welfare remain[ed] steadfast and unabated," and that their dedication to the religious freedom of those south of the Rio Grande remained undiminished.[99] That the Knights did not achieve their stated goals was clear to all. Carmody, however, made it clear that that failure would, in no way, dissuade the order from taking similar action in the future, wherever it might be called for. With this assurance of continued interest, the Knights closed their active efforts on behalf of the Mexican Catholics.

The Knights had expended a massive amount of effort to achieve their stated goals designed to force the United States government to re-evaluate its relationship with the revolutionary government of Mexico. Supreme Knights Flaherty and Carmody mobilized their membership and buried Washington in an avalanche of paper. The Knights convinced important elements of the American Catholic hierarchy that their cause was right and just. Powerful members of the United States Congress heeded their call. Nonetheless, the Knights failed to reach their goals.

This is not to downplay the significant achievements of the Knights of Columbus. The Knights educated American Catholics through their Mexican Fund, they focused attention on the Mexican situation through their support of the Borah resolution, and they initiated letter-writing campaigns to force Congress and the Roosevelt administration to address their concerns. Perhaps the most important goal of these efforts was to create an informed public opinion that could be mobilized to influence public policy.

Work by the Knights and others to build this public opinion did bear fruit. During the Coolidge administration, Knights' letters of protest helped induce Secretary of State Frank Kellogg to meet with Mexican Ambassador Manuel Tellez to inform him that "the Mexican laws and regulations put out by President Calles [restricting the practice of religion were] creating a very unfortunate sentiment in this country not only among Catholics but among other classes of people." This demonstrated that not only was the State Department sensitive to the Catholic protests, but that those protests represented the "sentiment in this country."[100] Later, the Knights of Columbus's public opinion efforts provided impetus for Roosevelt's speech in San Diego in which he articulated the American desire for all peoples to enjoy the blessings of religious liberty. These achievements contributed to the formation of an atmosphere in the United States which helped to change the American approach to Mexican anticlericalism. The immense pressure exerted by the Knights did, in fact, result in renewed interest in the Mexican situation. Without a doubt, the Knights of Columbus's grassroots appeal certainly made Washington at least sit up and take notice. They were, clearly, the most successful agents of this private interest group effort to influence public policy.

The efforts of the Knights of Columbus on behalf of the Catholic Church in Mexico garnered the order the praises of William Cardinal O'Connell, archbishop of Boston and dean of the American hierarchy. The Knights had commended themselves through their devotion to their cause in the name of God and Country, and to "their conception of fundamental human needs and values." They had fought valiantly for "the preservation of our priceless heritage of religious and civil liberty."[101]

chapter 7

CATHOLIC LAY MEN AND WOMEN AND LAY ORGANIZATIONS

THE KNIGHTS OF COLUMBUS WAS FAR FROM BEING THE SOLE LAY voice of protest against the United States government's inactivity on the persecution of Catholics in Mexico. Millions of Catholics spoke out in loud protest against the policy line chosen by the Coolidge, Hoover, and Roosevelt administrations as it affected United States–Mexican relations and the church-state struggle.

Lay men and women's activities in dealing with the United States' response to the persecution fall into two rough categories: individual and group efforts. Hundreds of thousands of individuals worked in their own neighborhoods and towns on behalf of the Mexican Catholics. However, it was the work of a few key individuals close to the government and armed with considerable personal influence that accomplished the most in the effort towards engendering the official interest of the government. These key individuals include William Montavon, the National Catholic Welfare Conference (NCWC) Legal Department director; diplomat and writer William Franklin Sands; and former Knights of Columbus official Colonel Patrick Callahan. Other Catholics enjoyed a more intimate relationship with governmental power, since they worked within Congress to bring about American aid for the Mexican Catholics. Democratic Representatives John J. Boylan (New York) and James Gallivan (Massachusetts), Republican Clare Gerald Fenerty (Pennsylvania), and Democratic Senator David I. Walsh (Massachusetts) stand out among them in their work to author legislation and pass resolutions calling for a firm stand by the United States.

Besides these individual efforts, various groups concentrated on evoking from the government a protest of some kind; indeed, many organizations formed solely for this purpose. These include the National Committee for the Protection of Religious Rights in Mexico (NCPRRM), the Association for the Protection of Religious Rights in Mexico (APRRM), the National Committee for the Defense of American Rights in Mexico (NCDARM), and the Friends of Catholic Mexico. Other organizations which existed prior to the crisis in Mexico but which became actively involved include the Holy Name Society, the National Council of Catholic Women (NCCW), and the National Council of Catholic Men (NCCM).

Together, the activities of these individuals and organizations spoke eloquently to the issue of the need for the United States government to establish before the Mexican government their belief that religious freedoms were both universal and inalienable. These lay men and women hoped protests — both general and particular — would force the United States government to stand up for the ideals upon which it was founded. Their protests proved to be an important corollary to the activities of the clergy, the hierarchy, and their fellow laymen in the Knights of Columbus in their collective efforts to guide and mold United States–Mexican relations along their own lines.

Montavon, Sands, and Callahan

William Montavon proved invaluable to the American Catholic effort on behalf of the Catholics of Mexico. As NCWC Legal Department director, Montavon's fluency with the Spanish language was a tremendous resource — he provided the Administrative Committee with translations of news articles and public statements by the Mexican government and hierarchy. However, through his writing and speaking abilities, Montavon made his most important contributions to the effort to ease conditions that faced the Catholics of Mexico. He combated the Mexican government's propaganda campaign by writing numerous articles and statements, entering debates over the Mexican church-state crisis, and by delivering public addresses. Through all of his efforts, Montavon sought to hold up American ideals as applicable to Mexico to create a sympathetic public opinion.

Montavon frequently contributed to the *N.C.W.C. Bulletin*. In his articles and speeches, he effectively drew from his background as a lawyer to challenge the legality of the Mexican persecution.[1] Montavon used the argument about the validity of Mexican anticlerical laws effectively to advance the position of American Catholics. His appeals to his fellow Americans harkened to ideals that lay at the root of the American character. According to Montavon, "the American people have a solemn obligation. We must first be loyal to our own institutions, *practicing the democracy we inherited* and reflecting it in the sympathy that goes out from us to the struggling masses of Mexico who hunger and thirst not alone for justice, but for liberty to work out their own salvation."[2]

Montavon maintained that besides the rights of Mexicans and Americans in Mexico to worship freely, the very principles for which this county's founders fought were threatened by the Mexican government, which denounced those principles and stood to undermine them. He asserted that the American people rising up to "stay the hand which would set up on our continent a system and a law subversive" of the ideals most dear to Americans was the only valid response to this challenge.[3]

Montavon, in advocating Americanist ideals, sought to prove that the Mexican crisis was actually an American problem. He made a strong case. Financial issues became a primary concern. Not only did the Mexican Revolution endanger tens of millions of dollars of American investment and the labors of twenty-five thousand United States citizens working in Mexico, but also the staggering cost of care and maintenance of thousands of Mexican refugees stretched state and local aid budgets to the breaking point. More fundamentally, Montavon argued, the United States' position as standard-bearer of human liberty brought Mexican persecution to high relief in this country.[4]

In pursuit of his campaign to place the Mexican persecution in the light of American ideals, Montavon advocated the formation of a public opinion that would bring change in Mexico. Montavon was clear about the best way to foster that opinion. In order for it to be truly effective, it had to be well informed, and based on solid fact. Otherwise, this public mood would be partisan, inviting "only disaster."[5] In fact, Montavon maintained that *most* of the effort to inflame the public was of the latter sort, and would produce no more than an explosion which was all flash and smoke, without blasting away the fa-cade of misinformation the Mexican government had constructed, thereby ex-posing the ugliness of the persecution. He demonstrated his supreme faith in the efficacy of a well-informed public opinion in a speech before the Knights of Columbus of Baltimore. He assured the Knights that if they could work to get the daily press to begin printing the truth about conditions in Mexico, an educated public opinion would form, and the Mexican government would be forced to chart a new course other than that which it was following.[6]

Montavon took an active role in the effort to bring peace to Mexico. In fact, he proved to be a vital link in the settlement negotiations of 1928 be-tween Calles and the Mexican Church. He accompanied Burke on all of the trips to Mexico for talks with Calles, and maintained active connections with the United States Department of State. He reported to Clark and Kellogg on the attitude of the Mexican hierarchy during the negotiations, and acted as liaison between the Mexican prelates and the United States government. He also served as liaison between Morrow in Mexico City and Burke in Rome during the summer of 1928.[7] Montavon kept secret his contributions toward the settlement until July 1929, when he wrote his account of the trips to Vera-cruz and Mexico City with Burke.[8] For his part in bringing peace to Mexico, temporary though that peace may have been, the Vatican awarded Montavon its highest honor when a papal pronouncement designated him as a Knight of the Order of St. Gregory the Great.[9]

Montavon's direct activism in dealing with the Mexican crisis continued long after the 1929 *modus vivendi*. Montavon became involved with the im-broglio over the Josephus Daniels' speech of 1934. In Daniels's copious corre-spondence with Montavon, he continued to express his surprise over the bil-ious reaction that greeted the speech in the United States, especially since he was merely advocating an educated population as the basis of Mexico's fu-ture.[10] In later correspondence, he admitted that he had not read the full Calles speech from which he drew the much-maligned quote, but added that this should not lead Catholics to draw a conclusion on Daniels's philosophy that was at variance with his whole career. Daniels further assured Montavon that he believed that "freedom of religion is the dearest possession of our America. I have never done anything or said anything at any time or any-where not in keeping with this chart and compass of our American ship...."[11]

Montavon's correspondence with Josephus Daniels capped a career of involvement with the Mexican persecution that began in the mid-1920s. Dur-ing this period, his work saw him not only writing and speaking on behalf of the rights of Mexicans and Americans as well, but also witnessed him put his words into action by traveling to Mexico and participating in the search for a settlement in 1929. William Montavon's activism on behalf of the persecuted Mexican Catholics was unusual in the breadth of involvement among American laymen, but was typical of the depth of feeling among many lay Catholics.

William Franklin Sands, another lay American Catholic involved with the Mexican crisis, embraced sentiments radically different from those of William Montavon. Sands, a career diplomat with extensive experience in Latin America, stood opposed to the involvement of Americans in the spiritual affairs of another nation.[12] Sands maintained that throughout his years in the diplomatic corps, never was he aware that the United States government had shirked its responsibility when it came to protecting the rights of its citizens abroad. He believed that the government had done all it could to protect Americans in Mexico.[13]

Sands went still farther. Not only was the United States government not at fault, since it was doing all it could to aid Americans in Mexico, but he maintained that blame for the conditions in Mexico lay in part on the shoulders of American Catholics themselves. He claimed that divisions and factions among American Catholics had doomed any chance for real improvement in the conditions facing Mexican Catholics. Salvation could only come about if American Catholics "would stop fighting each other long enough to take the lead in studying, reasserting and re-establishing American principles."[14] Moreover, the tactics most Catholic activists in the United States used to draw attention to the crisis south of the Rio Grande—"agitation and invective and vituperation"—had no more than nuisance value and in fact, obscured the situation beyond all comprehension.[15] As a result, any measured response to the persecution became much more difficult because Catholic rhetoric had obscured the truth about Mexico.

It was in this context of accusations and recriminations that Sands stood up in support of the embattled Ambassador Daniels. Sands considered Daniels "most unjustly maligned," since he was accused of expressing undue friendliness toward the Mexican government. He noted that if American Catholics had their way, and a Catholic ambassador were to be appointed to the Mexico City post, that minister, in order to accomplish any good work as the representative of the United States government, would need to do the same as Daniels, by demonstrating "every outward appearance of cordiality with a government for which he could have no possible personal sympathy."[16] Sands also noted that American Catholic papers neglected to report that Mexican officials claimed that Daniels had "consistently and persistently" placed the religious crisis before the Mexican government as an issue needing rapid resolution. From his experience of serving in the diplomatic corps under three administrations, Sands observed that "the President could not have a better man in Mexico."[17]

Sands's considerable experience in Latin America qualified him for service on the American Committee of Religious Rights and Minorities, an independent interdenominational group—whose membership included former President Herbert Hoover—which sought to uncover the truth about the conditions in Mexico. This committee of prominent Protestants, Jews, and Catholics sent a three-man delegation to Mexico on a fact-finding tour. Sands occupied a position in the delegation along with Carl Sherman, Jewish former New York City district attorney, and Dr. Philip Marshall Brown, a Protestant professor at Princeton University. After their return to the United States, they wrote a report based not on the hyperbolic condemnations of the opponents of the revolution, but rather on the actions and attitudes of the Mexican government itself. The delegation's conclusion conveys a position in curiously stark contrast with Sands's earlier stances on the Mexican issue. The delegation found that the Mexican government's "deliberate purpose is not merely the correction of alleged abuses in any Church but the extirpation of all religion in the country." Moreover, the delegation's report seemed to support those whom Sands previously castigated, by justifying "the strong protest, not only of the Mexican churches and their members, but of the friends of religious liberty in other lands, irrespective of their church affiliations."[18] Sands himself, in an editorial in the Knights of Columbus journal, *Columbia,* asserted that "it must be clear that an apparent anti-clerical, anti-Catholic movement in Mexico, instead of being merely a domestic matter of the Catholic Church, is unquestionably an anti-religious movement, which is of positive and legitimate interest to all religious bodies."[19] Sands and the rest of the delegation noted that the best way to deal with this situation was "the operation of an informed and enlightened public opinion."[20]

In spite of his new attitude about the appropriateness of involvement by American Catholics in the Mexican persecution, Sands continued to defend Daniels. He shared this position with a prominent Catholic and former Knights of Columbus official, Patrick H. Callahan, president of the Louisville Varnish Company. In fact, Callahan was one of Daniels's most prominent and most faithful Catholic supporters, and he spared no quarter in defending the ambassador.

Callahan's friendship with Daniels dated from the World War I years, when Fr. John J. Burke appointed Callahan to head the National Catholic War Council's Committee on Resolutions. In this capacity, Callahan worked at times with Navy Secretary Josephus Daniels in establishing policies for the running of serviceman's corps. Callahan and Daniels were also of one mind on the issue of support for prohibition—a position that put Callahan squarely at odds with most of his fellow Catholics.[21] Their close friendship, born in a time of war and cultivated through years of collaboration, positioned Callahan to most effectively defend Daniels during his ambassadorship.

The Catholic press became intimately familiar with Callahan in 1934 and 1935. During these years, as Catholic outrage against Daniels peaked, Callahan rose to meet the challenge of defending his friend the ambassador in some of the leading Catholic journals in the country. Daniels's tireless defender carried on a correspondence with nearly fifteen hundred Catholic laymen and clergymen in his efforts on the ambassador's behalf.[22] In *The Michigan Catholic,* Callahan sparred with editor Anthony Beck over Beck's claim that Daniels harbored nascent anti-Catholic sentiments. Callahan asserted that the facts belied Beck's charges. During World War I, Daniels doubled the percentage of Catholic chaplains, and appointed a prominent Catholic, Admiral William Benson, chief of naval operations, to represent the navy's interests at the 1919 Versailles Conference.[23]

Moreover, it seemed to Callahan that many Catholics in the United States had lost sight of Daniels's true responsibilities. By advocating intervention into Mexican affairs—the real result of actions Beck and other proposed—it was becoming clear that they expected Daniels to act as envoy of the pope in the Vatican rather than as the representative of the United States.[24] As Callahan railed to one of his correspondents, the press's attitudes frustrated him to no end: "If [Daniels] were the direct representative of the Holy Father and on the payroll of the Vatican he could hardly do all the things that some of the Catholics in this country want him to do in Mexico."[25]

Patrick Scanlon, editor of *The Brooklyn Tablet,* castigated Daniels for "shaking hands and fraternizing with the 'enemies of the Church'" in Mexico. Callahan countered the charge by noting that if he were to be named ambassador to Mexico, the first thing he would do would be to cultivate the friendship of Calles, Cárdenas, and the editor of *El Universal,* as they were the only people with power sufficient to help the Catholics. Callahan observed that it would only be possible to advance the condition of the Mexican Catholics by having the United States ambassador work closely with those in power. Indeed, claimed Callahan, cordiality was integral to Daniels's job, because snubbing the Mexican government would surely result in failure in Mexico.[26]

In an effort to deflect Scanlon's and others' condemnations of Daniels, Callahan claimed that conditions in Mexico resulted from their own misguided efforts: "you may remember many features of the 1917 constitution were not enforced until after the appearance of the Charles Phillips Letters on Mexico . . . which [were] resented more by the Mexicans than the sending of the Pershing troops into their country in 1916. . . . The Catholics in this country, in my solemn opinion, for more than twenty years, owing to their mistaken tactics, have added to instead of reduced the troubles of their co-religionists in Mexico."[27]

In *The Catholic New World*, Callahan took up Daniels's cause when the editor, Msgr. Thomas Shannon, called for Daniels to be brought back in shame from the embassy in Mexico City. Callahan quoted one of the leading political pundits in the country at the time, H. L. Mencken, on the dangers of Daniels's recall: "It is not strange that these editors cannot realize that if a Southern Protestant like Josephus Daniels is recalled from Mexico upon the demand of the Catholics of this country, there would be started right away an anti-Catholic movement that would make the noise raised by the Ku Klux Klan seem like a pop-gun compared to the Big Berthas."[28]

It is important to note that Callahan, in his vigorous and energetic defense of Daniels, clearly did not ignore the need to address the brutal persecution Mexican Catholics faced. He was merely more interested than others in defending an honest representative of the United States. He was so committed to the cause, in fact, that he was willing to put his money where his mouth was. In most of the letters Callahan wrote to Daniels's assailants, Callahan made an offer of "a Hart, Shaffer & Marx suit of clothes as an honorarium" if any of his correspondents could prove that Daniels had ever endorsed pagan or atheistic education.[29]

This verbal sparring with Beck, Scanlon, and Shannon notwithstanding, no Catholic journal editor fought with Callahan as fiercely as Vincent de Paul Fitzpatrick, editor of the *Baltimore Catholic Review*. From December 1934 to January 1935, the high season of the blistering correspondence between the two, Callahan asserted that, from the perspective of his close association with Daniels, he could assure readers that he knew of no man who had *less* religious prejudice. Fitzpatrick countered that regardless of his lack of prejudice, nothing could justify Daniels's defense of "paganistic" education in Mexico. According to the editor, every "real Catholic" recognized the unpardonable nature of Daniels's offense and noted "anyone who calls him-self a Catholic and apologizes for Mr. Daniels must find himself in a very em-barrassing position."[30] Callahan responded to the attack by taking the higher ground. As a former supreme director of the Knights of Columbus who con-ferred high honors on Knights throughout the country, Callahan called on all to work always for justice, and to "speak out fearlessly always for the right."[31] Unfazed, Fitzpatrick published in the editorial section of the *Review* a call for Callahan to return the papal honors naming him a Knight of St. Gregory the Great, since the honor did not consider Callahan's "intellectual qualifications." The editor noted "even a papal decoration can not give intelligence and back-bone where intelligence and backbone are lacking."[32]

Callahan, Sands, and Montavon each worked to ease conditions in Mexico in his own way. Their efforts were essentially singular in nature and outside of the power structure through which direct action could be accomplished. Other Catholics, however, were in the thick of the Washington, D.C., power structure. As members of Congress, John J. Boylan, Clare Gerald Fenerty, James Gallivan, and David I. Walsh stand out among the Catholics on Capitol Hill who maintained an active and vigilant watch over the Mexican situation.

Representatives and Senators

New York Representative John J. Boylan was among the first congressmen to become actively interested in the Mexican persecution. He was a key participant in the mass protest rally held at Poli's Theater in Washington and sponsored by the Knights of Columbus and Archbishop Michael Cur-ley of Baltimore. Throughout his years of work on behalf of the Mexican Catholics—1926–1935—Boylan maintained a close correspondence with both the Knights and Curley.[33]

One of the central themes Boylan employed as he railed against the Mexi-can government was the issue of recognition of the revolutionary regime. Boylan's main concern was that although the United States had refused to recognize the Russian Bolshevik government, it granted recognition to the "Bolshevists of Mexico."[34] Boylan pressed this interpretation still further by introducing in the House of Representatives a resolution calling for the sus-pension of diplomatic relations with Mexico, because of its policy "destructive of all religion and education in duplication of that initiated and carried into effect by the Bolshevist regime of Russia [which had] ostentatiously declared its sympathy with the principles of that regime."[35] According to Boylan, the Coolidge administration faced two choices. First, it could finally break down and afford full diplomatic recognition to Soviet Russia. Second, if the United States government could not do this, it had to use "the same moral influence" by withdrawing recognition from Mexico.[36] Boylan based his demand on the basic understanding that through diplomatic recognition, the United States was associated with the persecution. American support for the Calles government enabled the strongman to use the army against rebel opponents, including the Catholics who opposed the Calles program. Boylan was thoroughly convinced that if the United States were to withdraw its recognition of the Mexican government, that government would surely collapse. Consequently, Boylan insisted that the diplomatic recognition of the United States made the Coolidge administration, in part, responsible for the persecution.[37]

Boylan intended his resolution to address another issue—the expulsion of American citizens without cause from Mexico. This issue gained a new immediacy following the expulsion of Archbishop George Caruana on trumped-up charges in May 1926. Boylan claimed that if the United States refused to act in the face of this controversy, it would result in "further submission to Mexico's anarchistic conduct [which would] announce to all the world that the American Government is so helpless and so deaf to the demands of justice that it no longer protects its citizens or its honor."[38] Boylan continued to push this issue, even into 1935. Finally, at least one of Boylan's colleagues in the House of Representatives had had enough. Representative Thomas Blanton of Texas finally rose to protest "this continual ding-dong here on this floor . . . against foreign countries and against the rulers of foreign nations, regarding their national policies."[39] Blanton clearly represented a silent majority, since Boylan's resolutions regularly fell to defeat.

In spite of his failure to get his legislation passed, Boylan remained convinced of the utility of raising the Mexican situation on the floor of the House. He was not alone in his extensive use of the floor of the House of Representatives as a forum for arguing against the persecution ravaging the Mexican people. Massachusetts Representative James Gallivan, in long, agonizing speeches, placed before his colleagues the harshness and brutality of the persecution. One address, titled "Liberty Dead in Mexico," included a listing of the violations of the principle of freedom of religion and religious persecution in Mexico City alone from February 12 to March 12, 1926. Gallivan noted that in that time, the Calles government committed more than one hundred violations of the ideal of religious liberty, ranging from school and orphanage closings and church seizures to the detainment of American citizens and the beating, torture, and even murder of Mexican Catholics.[40] Gallivan quoted the bishop of Huejutla, José de Jesus Manriquez y Zarate, who appealed for action, but who counseled nonviolence: "Our mother is in the claws of the wolves who are tearing [her] member from member—how shall we fly to her rescue—availing ourselves of our only weapon—the terrible sword of our voice?"[41] Gallivan took full advantage of these heartrending accounts to convince his fellow congressmen that the time for the United States to act on the crisis was passing.

In a January 25, 1927, address titled "America or Mexico, WHICH?" Gallivan once again called on the United States to forcefully notify Mexico that the right of religious freedom was universal and inalienable. To push his point, Gallivan cited another instance in which the United States chose to act: "America squandered 100,000 of the flower of her youth and thirty billions of treasure to save a European phantom called democracy; but it would not spend a dollar or fire a shot to-day to save American life and property at our very door." Gallivan tried to use strident language and sarcasm to demonstrate the irony of the situation:

> What do 600 robbed and murdered Americans, more or less, amount to anyhow? Why disturb the slumbers of our yellow friends of peace over a few dead Yankees, rotting by a Mexican roadside? They probably violated that sacred document, the Mexican constitution of 1917, written and promulgated by Carranza, Calles, Villa, Obregon, and the other patriotic gunmen when they had a day off from cutting throats and purses—a noble instrument to make homicide and grand larceny easy and legitimate—in liberty-loving Mexico.[42]

Gallivan noted that although his was not a universally held opinion in the United States, it was time for the nation to take a stand—to prove that the national bird was an "eagle" and not "an old hen."[43]

Much of Gallivan and Boylan's discourse continued in the House in the mid-1930s through the efforts of one of the Mexican Catholics' most active advocates in the United States Congress, Representative Clare Gerald Fenerty of Pennsylvania. Like Boylan, Fenerty authored a House resolution to demand that the religious rights of all Americans in Mexico be recognized, upon pain of a severance of diplomatic recognition of the Mexican government. In keeping with the rhetoric employed by Boylan, Fenerty saw a Russian Communist hiding in the shadow cast by every Mexican persecutor. In fact, he claimed that Calles strove to "out-Soviet" the Russians, and that following the "Russianization" of Mexico, the United States was next.[44] He later noted that it was vital for the American public to look seriously at the persecution to "ascertain whether or not the religious persecution is merely a blind to conceal a sinister oriental plot against our own nation."[45]

Fenerty maintained that this Communist threat stood at the southern door of the United States because earlier United States administrations had deemed it necessary to intervene in Mexico. He claimed that although there was plenty of precedence for intervention on behalf of the Mexican Catholics, American Catholics stood opposed to intervention that was "invariably against the best interests of the Mexican people." One of the earliest wrongful interventions was when Woodrow Wilson doomed the government of Victoriano Huerta, which resulted in "the orgy of anarchy and persecution that today is culminating in the sovietizing of Mexico" under Calles, the "Red Czar of the Montezumas."[46] Intervention in the Mexican crisis, including an arms embargo that supplied United States guns only to those Mexicans— supported by the Soviets—who used them against innocent Catholics in the churches, was responsible for bringing the confrontation between the United States and the Union of Soviet Socialist Republics to the American continent. Fenerty warned of an epic conflict mounting between Freedom and "the red czar of Mexico and the Russian Soviet in their mad endeavor to crucify Christian civilization upon the crimson cross of communism. . . . The forces of pagan darkness, of reversalism, of communist animalism are arrayed against reason, against America. The fight is not now on the blood-stained steppes of Siberia, it is at our own door—the fight to save America from the degradation of Russia."[47]

According to Fenerty, the only recourse was not intervention, but solid statesmanship. He cited the countless protests that flooded the State Department and the White House, none of which, according to Fenerty, amounted to a call for intervention. He maintained that the best remedy for the near-terminal illness that plagued Mexico was a combination of diplomacy, courage, sympathy, and understanding.[48] The person best suited for this duty was most certainly *not* Josephus Daniels.

Clare Fenerty ruthlessly attacked the ambassador. In fact, Fenerty maintained that Daniels was the worst possible representative for the United States in Mexico. He was "intellectually incapable of understanding Mexico," and his wholesale acceptance of the Mexican government's assertion that there was no religious persecution was a prime example of "Ambassadorial stupidity." Daniels had turned from a representative of the United States into nothing less than a "press agent for Mexican Communists."[49]

By maintaining Daniels in the Mexico City post, Franklin Roosevelt had refused to do what Fenerty claimed was necessary for a resolution. Therefore, Fenerty focused his attacks on the White House. Fenerty believed sincerely that if the president were willing to make the decision to do so, he could end the Mexican persecution once and for all. Roosevelt was well aware, according to Fenerty, that Americans had been murdered in Mexico, but he simply "smiles and plays Pollyanna while men and women die and little children suffer in body and soul."[50] For this negligence, Fenerty claimed that Roosevelt's political life would soon be in jeopardy: "If, as a statesman, he will not think of human rights, let him, as a politician, think of the next election."[51] Fenerty was unwilling to settle for an oblique political threat, however. Desperate times called for more direct action.

Fenerty worked very effectively in concert with Congregationalist Representative John P. Higgins from Massachusetts. In 1935, Higgins and Fenerty, with help from Boylan, and Emanuel Celler and Hamilton Fish of New York, drafted a petition, which they then circulated throughout the House. Celler was a vocal ally. In an article printed in the *Baltimore Catholic Review,* Celler listed precedents, dating from 1853, in which the United States involved itself in the affairs of other nations due to perceived threats to religious liberty.[52] The petition called on the president and the secretary of state to launch an inquiry into the religious situation in Mexico. By this time, July 1935, Catholics in Congress were able to read the handwriting on the wall, and recognized that the Borah resolution was doomed to failure. They hoped that this more innocuous statement of general interest in investigation would make a new resolution much more palatable than was the Borah resolution. Moreover, they offered an interesting argument for justification of this investigation:

> At the present time it is reported that there are 14 States in the Republic of Mexico where no minister of religion . . . is permitted to exercise his sacred functions. Taking cognizance of this condition, the British Secretary of State for Foreign Affairs, Sir John Simon, has promised the members of the House of Commons that he would interest the British Minister at Mexico City as well as the British consular officials throughout the aforesaid 14 States of Mexico to institute

an inquiry as to the facilities for Divine worship available to British citizens resident in or visiting these communities.

In view of the fact that there are more American citizens of all denominations than there are British citizens, both resident in and visiting the 14 States where no minister of religion is permitted, the question naturally arises whether a similar inquiry might not be made . . . through the American Embassy and American consular officials. The undersigned members of Congress, together with the full membership of the committee, believe that some simple and constructive measure ought to be taken in order to ascertain the facts of this situation, evidencing an affirmative interest in the religious rights of American citizens of all faiths and creeds.[53]

The petition included an appended note in which the signatories enumerated justifications for the measure. First and foremost, the ad hoc subcommittee strove to make it crystal clear that they were "unalterably opposed to any semblance of interference or intervention in Mexico."[54] After all, the congressmen noted, when Roosevelt inspired a Senate protest against the persecution of Jews in Germany on June 19, 1933, no one claimed that the act constituted "intervention" or "interference." Most important, the petitioners requested "some overt statement" on the matter, because the time for "official silence" on the matter had long since passed. It was time for action.[55]

Notice how the language used in this petition accomplished the same purposes as the Borah resolution, but omitted the condemnatory comments that, in the Borah legislation, belied a foregone conclusion. Higgins, Fenerty, and the others, in passing around the petition, collected signatures from 250 members of the House of Representatives—two-thirds of whom were not Catholic—indicating overwhelming support for this sort of "simple and constructive measure" to discover the truth of the conditions in Mexico.[56]

On July 16, 1935, a committee of twenty-one representatives accompanied Fenerty and Higgins and presented the petition to Roosevelt. Roosevelt and Hull accepted the petition, and the president authorized Fenerty to publicize a statement with which he acknowledged the import of the petition: "The President stated that he is in entire sympathy with all people who make it clear that the American people and the Government believe in freedom of religious worship not only in the United States but also in all other nations."[57]

There is a certain degree of controversy regarding the reception Hull afforded the petition. Jesuit activist Michael Kenny claimed that the committee had the rug pulled out from underneath it when it met with the secretary of state, when Hull claimed that "the Bishops and Church representatives had assured him of their satisfaction with the action of the President and himself in regard to Mexico and also that [the] Congressional Committee did not represent the views of the Church in the matter." These congressmen, according to Kenny in a letter to Apostolic Delegate Cicognani, were "beginning to lose confidence in the Bishops regarding the proper action to take."[58] Kenny wrote to convince Cicognani to prevent the NCWC's interference in the Mexican issue. However, one must wonder how put off the representatives actually were, since one of the primary petitioners, Higgins, was not a Catholic, and neither were the majority of those who signed the document. Moreover, the issue of whether the petitioners felt concerned about the leadership of the bishops is certainly a matter of debate. By this time, the NCWC Administrative Committee had decided to refrain from supporting the Borah resolution in the Senate; Kenny's reaction to the alleged statement from the secretary of state evidently arose out of frustration with this decision.

Others soon joined Kenny in his frustration. One of the resolution's primary backers in the Senate, David I. Walsh of Massachusetts, was similarly alarmed. Early in 1935, Walsh had begun a correspondence with Archbishop Curley, in which he tried to ascertain whether or not he could count on the support of the Administrative Committee in debate over the resolution in the Senate Foreign Affairs Committee. Walsh indicated that this support would be "most helpful," although he had heard that the committee was disinclined to provide such official backing.[59] Later, Walsh wrote to Curley that he had been informed that the Administrative Committee had indeed decided not only to refrain from offering its support of the resolution, but had chosen to actively oppose its passage. Walsh claimed that the only hope for eventual success of the measure, in the face of this considerable opposition, was "a careful, scientific organization of our forces, as well as . . . something like a long-range plan." The result of this "careful" effort at organization was "a nation-wide committee of one hundred lay men and women to constitute a National Committee for the Defense of American Rights in Mexico [NCDARM]."[60]

Walsh based his confidence in the eventual success of the resolution on the volume of support for the measure flowing from the four corners of the nation. Various state legislatures expressed their hope that the Borah resolution would be passed, including those in Arizona, New York, Illinois, and Massachusetts. In fact, the Illinois resolution noted that any failure to protest would "reflect on the integrity of any governing body that failed to raise its voice in just protest."[61] Even local governing boards joined in the hue and cry for the resolution. Both the Los Angeles and the Baltimore Board of Supervisors called for an official investigation into the persecution of Catholics in Mexico.[62]

While several representatives and senators received letters from their constituencies expressing support for the Borah resolution, an even louder cry arose in outrage in response to Daniels's ill-informed comments of 1934. Dozens, if not hundreds, of senators and representatives forwarded these protests to the State Department for response.[63] Most of these letters were from individuals who, in the words of protester Martha Holbrock, considered Daniels's actions "a flagrant misrepresentation of the spirit of our Constitution and the sympathies of our people."[64] In fact, such an uproar erupted from the floor of the House of Representatives that the editor of the *New York Times* was prompted to ask, with a tinge of irony: "What can have happened to turn a kindly and benevolent man, as we all know Josephus Daniels to be, into an enemy of democracy and humanity?"[65]

In the end, there was, indeed, an uproar from the congressional floor. In the first six months of 1935, the House debated fourteen resolutions on the floor demanding that the Roosevelt administration respond to the crisis in Mexico. Most dictated that the United States investigate the facts behind the persecution; two called on Daniels to be returned to the United States, and one boldly demanded that Hull assert the American claim that freedom of religion must reign in Mexico.[66] One of the main instigating factors for this plethora of legislative activity was correspondence to Washington from groups at home—groups which were actively interested in remedying the situation in Mexico.

Organized Laic Effort

Many of the organizations that acted as catalysts for change in Mexico were established strictly for that purpose. Most of these organizations had a common goal—the establishment of a public opinion that would place pressure on both the United States government to act on behalf of the ideal of religious freedom, and on the Mexican government to end the persecution. While these groups, which constitute a dizzying sea of acronyms, had similar goals, they employed different tactics to achieve them. Two of these groups, the National Committee for the Protection of Religious Rights in Mexico

(NCPRRM) and the Association for the Protection of Religious Rights in Mexico (APRRM), were both founded in mid-1926; while the former was officially the offspring of the National Catholic Welfare Conference, the latter became most clearly associated with its charismatic president, Judge Alfred Talley.

As discussed earlier, Fr. John J. Burke was instrumental in establishing the NCPRRM under the auspices of the NCWC's National Councils of Catholic Men and Women. After Archbishop José Mora y del Río of Mexico City called for active American protests in 1926, Burke recognized that it was "obligatory upon us to arouse and inform our fellow-citizens and to help create a moral sentiment that will make impossible the continuation of the Calles regime in Mexico."[67] Burke directed the National Council of Catholic Men (NCCM) and the National Council of Catholic Women (NCCW) to form a committee to "assist in securing and distributing of information on the situation in Mexico [in order to] create a right public opinion on the persecution of the Church therein and to meet the needs resulting from that persecution."[68] Catholic Judge Morgan J. O'Brien, chair of the NCPRRM, assisted Burke in soliciting participation in the committee's work by sending form letters to prominent Catholics throughout the United States seeking members. To convince a large number of prominent Catholics to participate, O'Brien identified the committee's goals: the publishing and distribution of pamphlets explaining the situation in Mexico, the planning and promotion of public meetings throughout the nation where the persecution would be discussed by well-informed panels, and an effort to secure financial resources necessary to meet the needs of refugee priests and other clergy.[69] O'Brien placed great urgency on the conditions making the committee necessary. He believed that the Mexican government was nothing less than a "standing menace and challenge to our Christian civilization. If we love our country, our liberty and our civilization, we have a paramount duty imposed upon us of arousing our countrymen to the menace and danger of such a scourge on our very borders."[70] He also laid out the challenge which faced the committee: "Our committee will seek to awaken on this continent a public opinion that will show how thoroughly America condemns Mexico's un-Christian laws and the enforcement of its program of religious persecution."[71]

Although Burke's files contain long lists of more than two hundred members who welcomed the opportunity to meet Burke's invitation and O'Brien's challenge to become members of the committee—most of whom were corporate presidents, judges, and attorneys—his files also contain angry refusals protesting the committee's goals and even its very existence. This antagonism hindered the organization's efforts in its first year. In his summing up of the committee's 1926 activities, O'Brien noted that in its efforts at accomplishing its ambitious agenda, "the Committee has not been wholly successful. . . ." The committee published and distributed two pamphlets and had provided information for other organizations' meetings, but had not yet mobilized to provide support for the Mexican refugees then streaming across the border. O'Brien was frustrated about a rising tide of "sentiment against the scattered activities of many groups" trying to secure a "right public sentiment in the United States. . . ." The committee, and indeed all of these organizations, would be more effective and efficient if the committee were vested with the authority to direct all such efforts, including those of the Knights of Columbus and others.[72]

One organization not under the control of the NCPRRM, the Association for the Protection of Religious Rights in Mexico (APRRM), had a slightly more finely focused goal. This group, the brainchild of Judge Alfred Talley, was active only in New York City, although he anticipated branch groups for other cities. Talley sought to exercise influence through the sheer weight of crowds. With a membership of two hundred thousand in New York City, Talley wrote with some authority to New York's senators, James Wadsworth and Royal Copeland, seeking their help in his effort to convince the United States government to break diplomatic relations with Mexico. Copeland responded that "within the limits of international law it is the manifest duty of this Government to intervene for the prevention of civil and religious conflict in Mexico."[73] Of course, the sticky wicket of international law prevented interference short of treaty violations, but this did not stop Talley from using Copeland's bold proclamation to foment public support for the APRRM.

Talley was the mouthpiece for the APRRM, and made sure that his opinions were constantly before the public's eyes. His two main arguments were that the Mexican government was a front for the Russian Communists in the Western Hemisphere, and that Mexican consular agents in the United States, by spreading propaganda at the public's expense, had softened the American resistance to that incursion. In testimony before the House Committee on Foreign Affairs, Talley warned that unless the United States severed its recognition of the "Sovietized" Mexican government, the Russian menace presented a threat to all of the ideals that Americans held so dear. "Mexico," warned Talley, "in her Sovietized program, is giving warning to us." And he asked: "Will we heed that warning?"[74]

One indication, in Talley's mind, that the American government refused to acknowledge that warning was its inactivity. Coolidge refused to move beyond espousing platitudes to taking real action. Talley maintained that "one word of warning" from Coolidge would be sufficient to end the persecution, but since Coolidge neglected to utter that word, the Mexican government felt free to "go ahead with impunity" in its anticlerical program, "a system of religious persecution without parallel in recent times" through which Calles "outdoes Russia."[75] Coolidge's refusal to do whatever was necessary to stem the tide of propaganda flowing out of the Mexican consulates in the United States stood as further proof of his negligence. In spite of a long list of precedents wherein American secretaries of state, from 1797 to 1915, criticized and arranged the recall of foreign officials who addressed themselves directly to the American people, Kellogg refused to act.[76]

These two organizations, the NCPRRM and the APRRM, painted their goals and ideals with relatively broad brushes. Senator David I. Walsh of Massachusetts formed another organization with a very closely delineated purpose. Walsh established the National Committee for the Defense of American Rights in Mexico (NCDARM) solely to get the Borah resolution passed in 1935. In fact, the official statement of purpose for the NCDARM indicates its single objective. Sympathetic community leaders had formed it for the express purpose of "collecting information and facts available to aid in supporting the Borah Resolution to assist the persecuted Christians of Mexico."[77]

In maintaining this single-minded goal, the NCDARM naturally came into direct conflict with Roosevelt, who wholeheartedly opposed the investigation authorized by the resolution. When Roosevelt made it clear to the members of the Senate Foreign Relations Committee that the resolution was not one he could support, discussion of the measure quietly ceased. An NCDARM statement called Roosevelt on the carpet for what it considered the administration's official refusal to face the reality of the violation of human rights in Mexico. Moreover, the NCDARM claimed that Roosevelt had earlier pulled a similar stunt that resulted in the end of discussion of the violation of religious rights in Russia. By doing so, the Roosevelt administration had embraced "the sorry role of a protector of tyrants and an obstacle to the truth."[78] To counter the administration's argument that such an investigation would amount to intervention into the affairs of another nation, the NCDARM asserted that Americans opposed intervention. However, the United States, as the guarantor of liberty under the Monroe Doctrine and the Roosevelt Corollary, owed it to the hemisphere to investigate allegations of the abuse of rights. From the perspective of the NCDARM, neglecting this responsibility afforded Calles support, which in and of itself constituted illegitimate intervention.[79]

This was the argument that served as the central justification for the Friends of Catholic Mexico, later known as the Friends of Mexican Freedom. The long legacy of interference in Mexico's affairs by aid to rulers who stood opposed to the interests of the Mexican people convinced the Friends that the United States government was ultimately responsible for the conditions prevailing in Mexico. This responsibility drove the Friends of Catholic Mexico to work for the "relief, protection and advancement of the Mexican people."[80] Such an effort as that begun by the Friends, according to Robert R. Hull, corresponding secretary of the Friends, complied fully with the work and the will of Archbishop Ruiz, the apostolic delegate to Mexico. In asserting this unity of purpose, Hull intended to assure others that any cleavage between the ideals espoused by Ruiz and the activities of American Catholics existed in the bowels of the Church of the United States, that is, the hierarchy and the clergy.[81]

Hull's organization dedicated itself to healing that cleavage to provide a united front. This effort to unite American Catholic action held the promise of success where other such efforts had fallen to failure. Since none of the previous activities, including the ill-fated *modus vivendi* of 1929, achieved long-lasting results, the Friends decided in 1935 that it was time for more direct action. Complicity on the part of the United States government made this course of action clear: the Friends needed to assert such pressure on the government that it would finally withdraw its support for the despotic regime which had Mexico in its grip. The Friends sought to build this pressure with the help of Catholic journal editors, the clergy, and the hierarchy in the United States. In order to garner their assistance, the organization assured the clergy that "the FRIENDS OF CATHOLIC MEXICO agree to assume the responsibilities of action, [thereby] leaving the Church, the Hierarchy and the priesthood free from public censure."[82]

The Friends of Catholic Mexico adopted as two of its three primary goals the standards of the American Catholic effort: the passage of the Borah resolution and the recall of Daniels. In spite of an all-out effort to get the Borah measure through the Senate, to which Hull pledged his organization's support, little was accomplished. In fact, other than a general appeal for support for the measure and a resolution passed in the Friends's annual meeting, there is little evidence that the organization's best efforts amounted to much in the fight for the resolution.[83] As far as the recall of Daniels was concerned, Hull considered the ambassador simply a pawn in the hands of an interventionist administration. Like the organization's work on behalf of the Borah resolution, the extent of work by the Friends on the Daniels issue was limited to a call for general support for the recall of the ambassador, and a resolution passed at the 1935 annual meeting demanding that Daniels be replaced with "a man who will represent the United States and not Mexico."[84]

The third project behind which the Friends threw their support was an effort to economically isolate Mexico. The main thrust of this project was a memo the Friends sent to all representatives of Latin American nations, save Mexico, which included a checklist of thirty-eight basic commodities that the United States imported from Mexico. The letter asked the representatives to check off which of these commodities, ranging from livestock and produce to oil and minerals, that their countries might provide, and in what annual quantities they might be available. This letter, a clear effort to secure sources for these goods from outside Mexico, thereby isolating it economically, concerned Najera, the Mexican ambassador to the United States. Under Secretary of State William Phillips effectively short-circuited the move by the Friends by assuring Najera that proximity would insure that the United States would remain Mexico's best customer.[85]

The Friends of Catholic Mexico, in concert with other organizations designed to aid the Mexican Catholics, such as the National Committee for the Protection of Religious Rights in Mexico, the Association for the Protection of Religious Rights in Mexico, and the National Committee for the Defense of American Rights in Mexico, fought to improve the conditions facing Mexico's Catholics. These were, however, necessarily temporary efforts, as the entire identities of these groups centered on the crisis in Mexico.[86] As such, they fought with an intensity born of their temporary nature, but they did not have the depth necessary to carry through with long-range plans. Each of these organizations had a membership limited to a relatively few individuals who chose to become active in the effort to aid the Mexican Catholics. Other groups were more broadly and deeply planted, as they were extant before the American Catholics became involved in the Mexican crisis. As such, their effort to aid the Mexican Catholics involved more substance and presented a more broad-based response to the crisis in Mexico. The long-lived groups constituting this effort included the Holy Name Society, the National Council of Catholic Women, and the National Council of Catholic Men.

The Holy Name Society was by far the oldest Catholic lay organization that interested itself in the crisis in Mexico. While it had a 650-year background by the outbreak of the Mexican Revolution, it was a localized organization without a national headquarters to direct its activities.[87] It claimed a remarkable number of men in each of its local societies—its motto was, and is, "Every Catholic Man a Holy Name Man"—and its influence arose out of the sheer bulk of its membership. Resolutions from diocesan, archdiocesan, and local chapters of the Holy Name Society in protest against Daniels and the persecution fill State Department records. Protests carried with them the support of sixty thousand men in Los Angeles and San Diego, fifty thousand men in Baltimore, and 2.5 million men across the country.[88] The Holy Name men also cooperated with the Knights of Columbus (undoubtedly there was overwhelming overlap in their memberships). One editorial in the Knights' journal maintained that if Knights of Columbus councils and Holy Name Societies continued to flood Washington with protest resolutions, a miscarriage of justice could be averted, for the "State Department is ready to sign the death certificate [for the Church in Mexico] and the slightest slackening of the wave of protest will be eagerly accepted as evidence that the patient has stopped breathing."[89]

Although the Holy Name Society claimed a huge membership, they suffered from a lack of a central voice, and their cry was inevitably lost among the din arising from other local clubs and organizations. Conversely, the lay arms of the NCWC's Department of Lay Organizations, namely the National Councils of Catholic Women and Men, could put forth protests focused through a national organization that coordinated and stimulated the activities of their own impressive memberships.

The National Catholic Welfare Conference established the National Council of Catholic Women (NCCW), along with its male counterpart, in 1920 with the mission of working "to unite all organizations of Catholic Women in the United States in purpose and action in religious, educational, social, and economic fields."[90] As a national organization, with constituent groups in nearly every parish in the country, the NCCW mounted extensive and broad-based protests against the United States' response, or lack thereof, to the Mexican crisis. Letters sent to President Calvin Coolidge and to various congressmen protesting the persecution, and resolutions passed in local and national meetings of the NCCW comprise the most notable of these protests. Agnes Regan, executive secretary of the NCCW, effectively disseminated the resolutions passed in the organization's annual meetings; the October 1926 resolution is a case in point. The resolution called on the government to heed ancient American ideals, to take responsibility for the special position of the United States in the Mexican situation, and to express, "in terms that are clear and unmistakable, the abhorrence in which the people of this country hold the attempt that is being made in Mexico by a Government ... to root out in that great nation, the principles of liberty and justice and the institutions of democracy which we hold sacred."[91] Regan mailed the resolution to virtually every governmental office, including all of the cabinet offices and the offices of the members of Congress. Hundreds of responses to Regan's letters fill the files of the NCCW, acknowledging the receipt of the resolution. In 1932, Regan began sending the NCCW's annual protest resolutions not only to every major office in the United States government, but also to the offices of the Latin American legations in the United States, to the Pan-American Union, to the German and Italian embassies in Washington, and to the offices of sixty Catholic women's organizations throughout Europe and South America.[92]

The NCCW letters to the president received similar international publicity. Mary G. Hawks, president of the NCCW, sent a letter to Coolidge dated December 27, 1927, in which she expressed her organization's frustration with the lack of backbone with which the United States received news of the persecution. Hawks, and the NCCW as a whole, viewed Lindbergh's 1928 goodwill flight to Mexico City, and news of a growing relationship between Calles and Ambassador Dwight Morrow, as "the most unusual evidence of good will ... by our Government towards the Calles regime." The world, Hawks cautioned, interpreted this evidence "as condoning, if not approving, the method by which the Calles government seeks to destroy liberty of religion, liberty of the press and liberty of education."[93] Praise for Hawks's letter to Coolidge flowed into the NCCW's offices from across the United States, as well as from Catholic women's organizations in Budapest, Poland, Austria, Spain, Argentina, and Denmark. Typical of the adulation heaped on the letter was a comment from the Argentine vice president of the League of Catholic Women: "You have added a beautiful page to the annals of Catholicism by intervening in such a direct and efficacious manner in favour of our unfortunate brethren in Mexico."[94]

The letters and resolutions from the NCCW, protesting the conditions in Mexico and the lack of strong response thereto from the United States government, were in response to the NCWC Administrative Committee's call on the NCCW to help foster the creation of a strong public opinion. This strong public opinion, according to Fr. John J. Burke, would establish the basis for a protest by the government by demonstrating "how thoroughly the United States condemns the persecution of the Church in Mexico."[95] Moreover, the NCCW membership maintained that the United States was in a special position to help mold public opinion around the world; if the United States exercised this power, persecution could not long stand in Mexico. The NCCW found inspiration in its effort to engender a sympathetic public opinion in the words of none other than Daniel Webster:

> We think that nothing is powerful enough to stand before autocratic, monarchical or despotic power. There is something strong enough, and, if properly exerted, will prove itself so—and that is the power of intelligent public opinion in all the nations of the earth. There is not a monarch on earth whose throne is not liable to be shaken by the progress of opinion and the sentiment of the just and intelligent part of the people. It becomes us, in the station which we hold, to let that public opinion, as far as we form it, have a free course. Let it go out, let it be pronounced in thunder tones, let it open the ears of the deaf, let it open the eyes of the blind and let it everywhere be proclaimed what we of this great Republic think of the general principle of human liberty and of that oppression which all abhor.[96]

Clearly, the NCCW held great faith in the power of that opinion, and fought to see that the truth about Mexico spread throughout the United States. The National Council of Catholic Men (NCCM), in its work in publishing and disseminating information, provided great assistance in the effort to proclaim the truth as loudly and forcefully as possible.

The NCWC established the NCCM to act as the hierarchy's liaison to the lay community by unifying Catholic attitudes and action in the United States. In fact, John T. McNicholas, archbishop of Cincinnati, claimed that there was a great need "for solidarity among [Catholic men] on all moral questions affecting the public welfare" and that the NCCM could be "the greatest medium of this solidarity."[97] One of the ways the NCCM could accomplish this was to take advantage of its members' coincidental membership in numerous other Catholic groups in the country.[98]

The NCCM's most important activity in working for the unification of American Catholic action was serving as a clearinghouse to keep all of these groups informed about the progress of the persecution in Mexico. The NCCM supplied affiliated organizations with the data they needed both to hold effective educational meetings, which were necessary to mold public opinion, and to launch appeals to the White House calling for action to protect religious freedom. This information enabled the American Catholics to fulfill the duty of the NCCM to "keep constantly before our Government the menace of Mexico's denial of . . . the principles of human rights which the founders of our republic gave their lives and their fortunes to preserve."[99]

The NCCM formed an effective network throughout the American Catholic community with which to disseminate this information. The organization's national office oversaw the establishment, on the local and diocesan levels, of committees comprised of representatives from various lay Catholic societies in the diocese. These local and diocesan committees cooperated with the central office in the preparation and distribution of informational literature, thereby maximizing the effectiveness of Catholic protests.

The NCCM strove, above all, to educate the public, particularly through publishing monthly updates on the condition in Mexico in the *N.C.W.C. Bulletin,* and still more significantly through their information bulletin series on the persecution of religion in Mexico. A survey of the special bulletins' titles provides a thumbnail sketch of the issues with which the NCCM hoped to stimulate intelligent protests: "Sections of the [Mexican] Constitution on which Calles Based [Anticlerical] Regulations,"[100] "The Church in Mexico is Fighting for Fundamental Principles Upon which Our Own Country is Founded," by John J. Burke,[101] "British View Mexico Dispute as Evidence of Bolshevism," by Sir Philip Gibbs,[102] and "International Aspects of the Mexican Religious Controversy," by Judge Morgan O'Brien (chair of the NCPRRM).[103] The NCCM printed nearly two hundred thousand of each of these pamphlets, and distributed them to local committees and groups throughout the country. In addition to the NCCM's special informational bulletins, the group printed and distributed tens of thousands of copies of Pope Pius XI's encyclical *Iniquis Afflictisque* and the hierarchy's 1926 pastoral letter on the Mexican crisis. While it is difficult to draw a direct conclusion as to the efficacy of the NCCM's publishing activities, it is nonetheless clear that the work of this group to foster informed public opinion and intelligent protest demonstrated its desire to alter the relationship between the United States and Mexico.

As we have seen in the earlier analyses of this work, a gap exists between what lay Catholics, whether they be individuals or organizations, sought to accomplish and what they in fact succeeded in doing. In fact, it is fair to say that these lay Catholics failed to meet the variety of their most concrete goals, from Montavon's work towards a settlement between the Mexican Church and the Mexican government in 1929, to the work of the NCDARM to secure a successful passage of the Borah resolution through Congress, and the effort by the Friends of Catholic Mexico to get Ambassador Daniels recalled. Nonetheless, they succeeded in creating a political, emotional, and spiritual climate within the United States characterized by the official interest in a settlement of the Mexican crisis as outlined in previous chapters. Other symptoms of that climate included official and informal statements of dedication to religious freedom such as that with which Franklin Roosevelt greeted the congressional petition in 1935. Chief among the factors that contributed to the American government's interest in the plight of Mexican Catholics were those which sought to educate and arouse the American public, such as Montavon's eloquent arguments against the legality of the *callista* reforms, the visceral alarms of Representative Gallivan and the efforts of Representatives Boylan and Fenerty to paint the Mexican reforms in Red tones, and finally the efforts of the NCPRRM and other organizations to foster educated public opinion and protests. Through these various works, lay Catholics undertook the challenge to counter the apparent indifference with which the American people received the news of the persecution of their co-religionists in Mexico. It was this indifference that presented one of the most fundamental challenges to the Catholic effort to guide public policy. As an interest group, these Catholic laymen and women worked to bring to the fore their ultimate goal—the essence of that which Americans held most dear—the right of religious freedom.

chapter 8

THE BROADER SIGNIFICANCE OF CATHOLIC ACTIVISM

W<small>HEN THE MEXICAN REVOLUTIONARIES LAUNCHED THEIR BATTLE</small> against the old order, they chose as their initial target the traditional foe of the Mexican liberals—the archetype of that order—the Roman Catholic Church. In their onslaught against the Church, they pursued what they believed to be their ultimate charge: the conquest of Mexico for the Mexicans. Catholics, both American and Mexican, however, viewed this attack as a direct threat to their faith. This was not a challenge most Catholics were willing to let go unanswered. To the Catholics in the United States, this assault on the Church in Mexico was also a challenge to what they believed to be one of the founding ideals upon which this country was established: the fundamental and universal human right to worship freely. Catholics in the United States believed this was a right that knew no boundaries. American Catholics responded to the persecution suffered by their Mexican co-religionists in a variety of ways that they believed both recognized and reflected the political and religious realities of their lives as Americans. The struggle with which American Catholics waged a war against intolerance was, like most things in life, mixed. It is a story of neither unmitigated successes nor unqualified failures.

An assessment of American Catholics' relative successes and failures in their struggle to win for the Mexican Catholics the right to worship as they saw fit requires first an examination of the goals they pursued and the methods they employed in that effort. The stated aims of the American Catholics essentially amounted to efforts to place sufficient pressure upon the government of Mexico that it would back down from its execution of the anticlerical provisions of the Mexican Constitution of 1917. Two of their goals, they believed, if met, would have brought about the fall of the revolutionary government. First, the lifting of the arms embargo, which confined the legal export of American-made arms and munitions to government forces, would have freed the Catholic majority in Mexico to try to oust the revolutionary government. Many Catholics believed that if the Catholic rebels were sufficiently armed, their struggle would end the persecution. Mexican Catholic rebels solicited aid for their cause, unsuccessfully, from the Catholics in the United States. This move, however, was doomed from the start, since papal proscriptions strictly forbade any action that would have resulted in further bloodshed in Mexico. The second effort Catholics in the United States made to bring about the downfall of the Calles-inspired government was their attempt to convince the United States government to sever diplomatic recognition of the Mexican government. This reflected the popular, though mistaken, assumption in the early twentieth century that Latin American governments required the recognition of the United States to remain in power.

American Catholics' remaining objectives revolved around what historian Robert Ferrell maintained was one of the "basic assumptions" of United States foreign policy in the late 1920s and early 1930s. Ferrell noted that policy makers recognized that the old paradigm of the use of military force to bring about peace had given way to the influence of moral force wielded by public opinion.[1] In their pursuit of this public opinion, Catholics not only organized themselves as a private interest group to issue protests ranging in scope from the individual to nationwide organizations, but they also sought to procure strong protests from both Presidents Calvin Coolidge and Franklin Roosevelt in the form of official statements from the White House, the recall of Ambassador Josephus Daniels, and the passage and implementation of the Borah resolution.

If we maintain that many people embraced this assumption as to the power of public opinion, we begin to understand, to a degree, the resistance on the part of the Coolidge and Roosevelt administrations to issue these strong protests. Open and forceful statements of protest against the Mexican persecution, within the context of this understanding of the power of public opinion, would have amounted to the United States government buckling under the weight of pressure from a private interest group. That may not have been so remarkable—government policy in the United States frequently reflects the will of private interests. In this case, however, the divided nature of this particular interest group, and the group's inability to make its goals clear, made a simple interest group policy decision impossible for the Coolidge and Roosevelt administrations.

Chief among the examples of the activist American Catholics' inability to make its ultimate goals clear were the two issues of whether or not the Catholics desired intervention or interference in Mexican affairs, and whether or not Roosevelt needed to abandon his Good Neighbor policy. State Department officials remained keenly aware of the breakdown of logic in the Catholic argument. Secretary of State Frank Kellogg demonstrated this awareness in a memorandum he prepared for Coolidge on August 26, 1926, in the wake of a meeting with the leading Knights of Columbus. He noted that Supreme Knight "Flaherty made a statement the other day in the press that they [the Knights] did not seek intervention by the United States ... *but* I believe he did add something about their desire to have the United States make a protest."[2] Kellogg's emphasis on the last phrase seems to convey his belief that in spite of the Knights' pledge, they did, indeed, seek intervention. Catholics' confusion on so central a point made policy decisions much easier for the government. Under the Roosevelt administration, it was further unclear whether American Catholics wanted the president to abandon the Good Neighbor policy altogether. Catholic pressure vis-à-vis Mexico was the first challenge to the policy. Activist Catholics hoped that Mexico, as an apparently atheistic, Communistic, subversive influence (if the critics were to be believed), would cause Roosevelt to re-examine the Good Neighbor policy. Did American Catholics intend a return to interventionism throughout Latin America, or just in Mexico? In the end, Roosevelt chose to weather the Catholic domestic political challenge in favor of sustaining his new policy of non-intervention and "good neighborliness" in Latin America.

As an aid in the process of assessing the relative successes and failures of American Catholics, it is helpful to examine the variety of methods they used to achieve their ends. As we have seen, American Catholics employed a number of means to bring about an end to the persecution in Mexico, ranging

from simple prayer and statements of protest against the Mexican government and the persecution itself, to political threats and attacks on the president of the United States for ignoring the violation of American ideals. Within
this spectrum lie the local and mass protest rallies sponsored by the Knights
of Columbus and other groups that attracted the support of a number of
prelates.

With these ends and means in mind, it takes little analysis to note that
the American Catholics failed to reach their stated goals. The Borah resolution was never reported out of committee. The United States did not sever
diplomatic relations with Mexico. Josephus Daniels continued to serve as the
United States ambassador until 1941. Neither Calvin Coolidge nor Franklin
Roosevelt issued the stinging protests to the Mexican government that many
Catholics demanded. That these major goals were never met is really not surprising, as any one of them could easily be perceived as an openly hostile act
of the United States. Moreover, Catholics even failed to achieve their most
important intermediate goal when the political threat to the re-election of
Roosevelt in 1936 never materialized. Of all of these goals, it seems that this
last was the only one that had even a remote chance for success.

In late 1936, the editor of the Jesuit journal *America* claimed that American Catholics could, as citizens, demand that the Roosevelt administration
cease its continued intervention into Mexican affairs. If the administration
failed to respond to this demand, Catholic voters could "express their disap-
probation at the polls" in November.[3] Political scientist Ralph Levering noted
that the voting booth was, indeed, the locus of power available to the mass
public, and that "retribution at the polls is . . . likely to come from voters with
strong convictions about an issue."[4] Also, in their examination of interest
group "clout," Clive Thomas and Ronald Hrebnar explain that the primary
factor in determining political influence is how much the group is "needed
by politicians and the government."[5] We can use Levering's, Thomas's, and
Hrebnar's conclusions to test the resolve of American Catholics facing the
harsh persecution of their fellow Catholics south of the Rio Grande and the
influence they may have wielded because of their importance to the Roosevelt administration. The results of that test are clear. In its confrontation
with the Catholic political threats, the Roosevelt electoral machine emerged
victorious.

There were several reasons why this Catholic bloc vote failed to materi-
alize. First, as much as American Catholics hated the persecution of Mexican
Catholics and as terrible as that situation was, Americans were preoccupied

with their own socioeconomic crisis in the depths of the Depression. Second, by the time of the election, the church-state tensions in Mexico had subsided as President Lázaro Cárdenas ousted the violently anti-Catholic officials from his government and turned his government's attention to solving Mexico's own fiscal troubles. Josephus Daniels, the focal point of most American Catholics' invective and the whipping boy of those working to mobilize a bloc vote, actually proved that he was a powerful ally of Mexican Catholics. He worked closely with the Mexican president to loosen restrictions on the Church. The ambassador demonstrated his dedication to Mexican Catholics in his work to gain the right of Catholics to hold a funeral procession (strictly forbidden as a public religious ceremony) following the death of his friend Archbishop Pascual Díaz of Mexico City in May 1936. Third, a voting bloc has power only to the degree to which it can present a real threat to a politician's continued tenure. Activist Catholics were simply unable to mobilize that threat. Chief among the conditions that mitigated this threat was the fact that the Catholic lobby was "automatically cancelled out" by those who believed the Catholic Church was the biblical "whore of Babylon." If the administration undertook any overt cooperation with the Catholics, it would have inflamed the passions of anti-Catholic Protestants and others who could interpret a policy move that Catholics requested or demanded as an effort by the Roosevelt White House to pander to Rome.[6] Simply put, there was too great a domestic downside to buckling under to Catholic bloc vote threats. Fourth, the Catholics in the United States failed to achieve a bloc vote protest simply because Catholics were badly divided on the proper policy for the United States and Mexico. The clearest example of this division is the rivalry between two princes of the Church, Archbishop Michael Cardinal Curley of Baltimore, who was first to pose the political threat to Roosevelt, and Archbishop George Cardinal Mundelein of Chicago, who eagerly awarded Roosevelt an honorary doctorate at the University of Notre Dame and who counted himself as one of the president's most loyal backers. Clearly, the Catholic leadership in this country was far too factionalized to pose any realistic political threat in the 1920s and 1930s.

Perhaps the most fundamental hurdles for those who would have used Catholics as a voting bloc were the inherent problems of wielding the weapon of bloc voting. Noted political scientist V. O. Key Jr. asserted that endorsements as often repel voters as attract them: "Those who rated the CIO [Congress of Industrial Organizations] and the Catholic Church as organizations whose advice they were most likely to take were far outnumbered by those who placed these groups among those whose advice they were least likely to take."[7] Moreover, the perception of the power of the people at the voting box to shape foreign policy by either electing or voting out certain candidates is largely overblown. Blocs, even well-organized ones, can exert only very limited influence through the ballot particularly because the major foreign policy officials are beyond the reach of the electorate. Also, because of the relatively small number of voters who would change their votes based on displeasure with a president's foreign policy—so small is the "attentive" public—presidents tend to find it relatively easy to ignore bloc opinions when they cannot be otherwise neutralized.[8]

This is not to say that all the efforts of American Catholics fell to dismal defeat. This private interest group's primary efforts centered on the formation of an informed public opinion. There is long-standing support for the influence a strong public opinion is capable of exerting. Former Secretary of State Elihu Root once noted that public opinion was "the real power behind international as well as national progress towards better conditions" and "the power behind all human law and all custom."[9] Mexicans themselves were aware of the power of American public opinion. Rene Capistran Garza, a representative of the Liga Nacional de Defensora de la Libertad Religiosa in the United States, reported to the NCWC Administrative Committee that "in order to form such an irresistible public opinion that would assure a real friendship between Mexico and the United States, [based] . . . principally on spiritual relations, we need to count, above all, on the Bishops of the United States. Having their support, we can count on the clergy and, counting on the clergy, we could count on Catholics at large, and these will be the leaven that will ferment the great mass of the American people."[10]

Wilfrid Parsons likewise noted the power of United States public opinion to influence policy: "every Mexican politician pays more attention to it than to public opinion at home." Parsons also cautioned that this power implied responsibility as well as the ability to mold policy. Catholics in the United States needed to educate the public because American public opinion in the late 1920s was "compounded in about equal parts of ignorance, misinformation and prejudice. For this state of affairs, our own newspapers are to blame, of course."[11]

John J. Burke and others were well aware of the potential of this power and the responsibility for educating the public. Their efforts to rally the American Catholics behind the cause of freedom of religion in Mexico reached into the experience of practically every parish in this country. An example was

Burke's work to establish the National Committee for the Protection of Religious Rights in Mexico under the National Councils of Catholic Men and Women to "assist in securing and distributing of information on the situation in Mexico [to] create a right public opinion on the persecution of the Church therein."[12] Organizations such as these initiated letter-writing campaigns that flooded the White House and the State Department. These letters of protest that reflected the growing influence of the Catholic interest group over public opinion were not without effect. Secretary of State Frank Kellogg met with Mexican Ambassador Manuel Tellez to apprise him of the volume of correspondence flowing in from Catholics across the United States, and to inform him that "the Mexican laws and regulations put out by President Calles [restricting the practice of religion were] creating a very unfortunate sentiment in this country not only among Catholics but among other classes of people." This demonstrated that not only was the State Department sensitive to the Catholic protests, but that State Department officials believed that those protests represented the "sentiment in this country."[13] An example of the effect this growing public opinion had on the Roosevelt administration was when Secretary of State Cordell Hull met with Mexican Ambassador Francisco Castille Najera on March 5, 1935, seeking moderation by the Mexican government in the face of rising protests in the United States.[14]

The general successes won by the Catholics in the United States effectively provided a backdrop to their more specific failed efforts. Smaller successes formed an atmosphere in the United States which helped to change the American approach to Mexican anticlericalism—successes such as: the approaches described above by Kellogg and Hull to the Mexican ambassadors in the interest of creating a sensitivity in Mexico to the rising tide of public opinion in the United States; the Knights of Columbus's use of their $1 million fund to educate the American Catholics as to the conditions prevailing in Mexico; the attention focused on the Mexican situation through the loud cries in favor of the Borah resolution by the Knights and others; the statement of the American dedication to the right of religious freedom with which Roosevelt received the Fenerty-Higgins congressional petition; and Roosevelt's speech in San Diego on October 2, 1935, in which he again articulated the American desire for all people to enjoy the blessings of religious liberty. All of these succeeded in creating a political, emotional, and spiritual climate in the United States through which official concern (at best) or interest (at least) was focused on the Mexican persecution of Catholics. Within the context of this climate, it is clear that the American Catholics actually accomplished a great deal by convincing the chief articulator of the Good Neighbor policy to reverse himself by taking an active interest in the plight of persecuted Catholics in Mexico.

This involvement of the American Catholics in the relations between the United States and Mexico was not the only time a religious interest group sought to force the American government to intervene in the affairs of another nation during this period. Two other issues in which American Catholics involved themselves were the 1933 debate over the recognition of the Russian government and the American policies toward the Spanish Civil War beginning in 1937. In the first of these affairs, American Catholics sought to have the Roosevelt administration insist that the Soviet government insure the freedom of all Catholics, American and Russian, to exercise their religion in Russia.[15] As in the Mexican affair, John J. Burke and Edmund A. Walsh were in the center of the controversy. Burke met extensively with Undersecretary of State William Phillips in order to convey to the Roosevelt administration the desire of the NCWC that the United States government refrain from granting recognition without some concessions by the Soviet government. Walsh not only carried on a hectic lecture schedule in which he opposed the unqualified recognition of the Soviet Union, he also met with Roosevelt at the White House in late October 1933. At the meeting, Walsh strove to impress upon the president his conviction that if religious liberty were not guaranteed in any negotiations over Russian recognition, "the liberties now being assailed in Russia will never be restored," and this failure would violate American ideals and would prove "abhorrent to Christian instincts."[16] In the end, Roosevelt responded to the Catholic opinion, but had to compromise with the Russian negotiator, Maxim Litvinov. On November 16, 1933, hours before granting diplomatic recognition to the Soviet Union, Roosevelt and Litvinov exchanged statements in which the Soviet Union pledged to recognize American citizens' religious freedom in that nation; there was no mention of Russians' own religious liberties.

American Catholics became interested in the Spanish Civil War following the Russian decision to send a modest amount of aid to the Loyalist forces battling the Nationalist army under General Francisco Franco, who was backed in a much more substantial way by both Hitler and Mussolini. American Catholics feared that this Soviet aid was an initial effort to spread the plague of Communism across the Iberian Peninsula, and moved to convince Roosevelt to see that the United States remained neutral, thereby aiding, in effect, Franco's forces. Essentially, the American Catholics worked to see that the Neutrality Law of 1937, the renewed version of the 1935 Neutrality Law, which prohibited arms shipments and loans to belligerents, was not over-turned. The closest that the neutrality law came to being reversed was as it neared its May 1939 expiration date. Catholics mobilized to see that the neu-trality law was renewed yet again. An organization known as the "Keep the Spanish Embargo Committee," numbering some 4 million Catholics in twenty different organizations, worked to flood Washington, D.C., with letters, reso-lutions, and telegrams. The NCWC also joined in the effort, and by January 14, 1939, more than four hundred thousand cards and letters littered the House and Senate. Father Charles Coughlin, "the Radio Priest," used his forum to get Catholics to express their support for the embargo, and by February 5, more than 1.7 million Catholics had made their opinion known at the Capitol.[17]

American Catholics were not alone among religious groups who sought to influence United States foreign policy. Franklin Roosevelt was surrounded by Jews. From his advisor, law professor and future Supreme Court Justice Felix Frankfurter, and Associate Justice Louis Brandeis, to Samuel Rosenman, a Roosevelt speechwriter and editor of the Roosevelt public papers, a number of Jews were close to the center of the administration. And, they used this po-sition to their own benefit. As Arab attacks on Jewish migrants to Palestine in-creased in 1936, these influential Jews conveyed the American Jewish concern to Roosevelt. The president decided to act, and on July 27, 1936, Hull and Roo-sevelt authorized American Ambassador Robert Bingham in London to infor-mally and unofficially approach Anthony Eden, the British foreign minister, about the United States government's concern over the treatment of Jews in Palestine. Hull and Roosevelt made it clear that they wanted Bingham to men-tion the "deep concern" manifested by "influential Jewish circles in the United States."[18] The British government thanked Bingham for bringing the American concerns to its attention, but took no immediate action. Two months later, after the British government announced its intention to suspend Jewish immi-gration into Palestine, Roosevelt told Hull to again send Bingham to the for-eign office to intercede on behalf of the Jews. Hull informed Bingham of the intensity of the emotion arising out of the Jewish community in the United States, and noted that "as you know, there are three or four million of them," many of whom enjoyed "personal influence" with both Hull and Roosevelt.[19] After Bingham conveyed to the foreign secretary the American concern, plans for the suspension of immigration were called off.

From the perspective gained from these two important issues, it is clear that American religious groups enjoyed a significant amount of influence over

United States relations with other nations. Just as the methods employed are the same, that is, a combination of personal influence by prominent churchmen and the exercising of the muscle provided by public opinion created by interest groups, the responses to these overtures was similar. Personal, unofficial diplomacy, under the auspices of the president and the secretary of state, addressed the fundamental issues that lay at the core of the concerns of these interest groups.

The general successes achieved by religious interest groups in influencing foreign policy contribute well to this study's attempt to demonstrate the connection between public policy and public opinion formed by active interest groups. In this study, we have examined the reaction among Catholic opinion makers to stimuli from without. The expression of that reaction and of potential policies, that is, the specific Catholic goals which would mitigate the crisis in Mexico, to the interested public and the methods that public employed to express to the policy makers its preference of those potential policies is fairly clear. The resulting changes in public policy, or, in the case of this study, the changes in official attitudes which resulted from that expression of opinion, are a clear indication of both the relationship between public policy and interest group formation of opinions in general and of the influence of an informed public on foreign policy in particular.

As this study draws to a close, it is important to recognize that religious groups such as Catholics and Jews did not enjoy exclusivity in their efforts to mold United States–Mexican policy. Commercial groups, such as American oilmen, also worked to influence this country's relations with Mexico. Indeed, oil interests were American Catholics' closest analogue in their effort to shape international policy.[20]

United States oil interests viewed the Mexican Constitution of 1917 in general, and Article 27 in particular, as a threat to their economic resources in Mexico.[21] The offending article would have seized for Mexico the subsoil mineral rights that Porfirio Díaz had alienated in his late-nineteenth-century effort to modernize and industrialize Mexico. The article asserted for Mexico ownership of subsoil rights, and established mechanisms for reconcessioning applications and requiring that concession holders improve their claim. The ultimate fear, for American oil interests, was the doctrine of retroactivity, whereby the Mexican government could challenge the legality of their concessions and thereby deprive these companies of the oil wealth they had come to expect. Clearly, the oil interests had to respond to the fearsome article.

Oil executives recognized early on that a concerted and united front would win more for them than even the most active individual efforts. In 1918, oil company executives formed the Association of Petroleum Producers in Mexico (APPM) to coordinate corporate strategies and pool their resources. In addition to this cooperative effort, oil interests took advantage of sympathetic individuals in the United States government. It was, of course, helpful that such former government officials as Franklin K. Lane, former secretary of the interior, and Mark Requa, former director of the United States Fuel Administration, served on oil corporate boards of directors. Such personalities counted among their friends and associates Ambassadors Henry Fletcher and James R. Sheffield.[22]

In the early 1920s, the APPM found a focused target for this significant mobilization of resources. Among the efforts of the government of Alvaro Obregón to earn for Mexico the best return on Mexican oil was a proposed export tax increase that would, in part, offset a proposed United States tariff on Mexican petroleum. In response to what they saw as a punitive tax increase, the APPM employed tactics that Catholics would attempt to use later: an economic boycott and efforts to press the United States ambassador in Mexico for help. The oil boycott of 1921 involved member companies cutting off oil shipments and withdrawing tankers from service in Mexico. The embargo caused localized economic hardships in and around the main oil port, Tampico. To forestall potential hostilities directed against oil properties, Secretary of State Charles Evans Hughes asked that two United States warships be stationed off the port. When no hostilities arose, Hughes asked that the ships be recalled, so that they could not be used as a pretext for deeper United States involvement on behalf of the oil companies. Hughes made it clear to the APPM that the United States would not be sucked into direct involvement, and pressed the companies to negotiate their way out of their problems.[23]

As part of his 1926 shake-up of the revolution, Plutarco Calles issued a decree requiring that new oil concessions applications be filed by December 31, 1926. Any oil company that refused to comply faced harsh penalties, including having Mexican federal troops cap unauthorized wells. Several United States oil companies broke the seals and resumed operations illegally. When Calles threatened legal recourse, the APPM fled for support to Ambassador James Sheffield, in whom they found a receptive ear. Sheffield endorsed the companies' defiant stand, and in fact opined that the State Department needed to take a more active role in protecting the oil corporate interests. Sheffield even went so far as to urge the lifting of the arms embargo so Calles's enemies could gain access to sufficient arms to overthrow him.[24] An angry Secretary of State Frank B. Kellogg, who had earlier ordered Sheffield not to advise the APPM, called the ambassador on the carpet and personally instructed him to avoid pushing the APPM policy objectives.

In an August 1927 meeting, Kellogg told the APPM personally that they could not look to Washington for the help they desired. He tersely refused their requests for both a severance of diplomatic relations with Mexico and armed intervention.[25] Personally, however, Kellogg himself was coming to the realization that a settlement was long overdue. To facilitate that settlement, Kellogg decided to replace Sheffield with a personality better suited to the delicate negotiations—one who was not tainted with earlier advocacy of the APPM—Dwight Whitney Morrow.

Morrow, as we know, employed a warm style of personal diplomacy. It clearly worked. His military attaché, Colonel Alexander MacNab, claimed that within a short time of his arrival in Mexico City, the ambassador had the ear of every ministry and bureau with influence over United States interests and even took the treasury minister "under his wing and taught him finance."[26]

As he had in his efforts to settle the church-state dispute, Morrow met the oil situation head-on by conferring first with the interested parties in the United States before meeting with Calles. In November 1927, Morrow met with oil company executives and pledged to make a case to the Mexican president for a settlement. Morrow and Calles hammered out the framework of a settlement during a mid-November tour of the northern Mexican states. Morrow suggested that the Mexican Supreme Court uphold a lower court ruling affirming the doctrine on non-retroactivity. Calles agreed with Morrow, and on November 17, 1927, the Mexican high court handed down a decision to that effect.[27]

The APPM initially resisted accepting this "half-a-loaf" solution, because the Mexican court's decision neglected to address the APPM's fundamental complaint—the Constitution of 1917 still required oil companies to seek the Mexican government's confirmation of their subsoil rights. Morrow convinced the oil executives to settle their differences with the Mexican government through a negotiated compromise. By 1929, most issues had been handled, but the oil companies found new complaints in tax rates and the Mexican government's favor of organized labor. Morrow, however, had had enough. He angrily informed the APPM that the Unites States government had gone as far as it was willing to go, and that any further pushing by the oil companies would surely fall on deaf ears. Faced with an apparent stonewall, the APPM finally accepted a negotiated settlement.

Parallels between the United States oil interests and the Catholic Church in their dealings with the Mexican government are more apparent than real. Historian Lorenzo Meyer points to a common goal shared by both the Catholics and the oilmen: "to create an image of an atheistic communistic state that was threatening moral and material values in the hemisphere."[28]

In pursuit of this goal, both groups followed two main programmatic tracks: (1) using sympathetic officials close to the United States presidency, and (2) forming organizations to mobilize their resources as effectively and efficiently as possible.

Both the activist Catholics and oil interests took advantage of prominent personalities who could champion their causes from positions close to the presidency. For Catholics, most of their strongest advocates either served in Congress—John Boylan, Clare Gerald Fenerty, David Walsh, and William Borah, for example—or were outside government altogether (but who could still make forceful appeals to the government), such as William Franklin Sands and Patrick Callahan. Ironically, the most highly placed Catholic in this period, Postmaster General James Farley, used his position in Franklin Roosevelt's cabinet to *obstruct* Catholic efforts.[29] For oil interests, their champions enjoyed much more immediate access to the seat of power. Chief examples include Coolidge's secretary of the treasury, oil magnate Andrew Mellon, former Secretary of the Interior Franklin K. Lane, and Ambassadors Henry Fletcher and James R. Sheffield.

The second programmatic track, Catholics' and oil interests' use of organizational structures to maximize their influence, seems more parallel, at least on the surface. Catholics' organizations—the National Committee for the Protection of Religious Rights in Mexico (NCPRRM), the Association for the Protection of Religious Rights in Mexico (APRRM), the National Committee for the Defense of American Rights in Mexico (NCDARM), and the Friends of Catholic Mexico—worked much like the oil companies' APPM to mobilize financial resources to present a united front to both the United States and the Mexican governments. Unlike the various Catholic organizations, however, the APPM was much more focused on a single issue, enjoyed a secure source of funds, and represented a homogenous perspective. This allowed the APPM to make unwavering demands because there was no need to accommodate the conflicting attitudes of a diverse membership.[30] This was, as we have seen, a degree of unanimity simply beyond the ability of activist American Catholics.

Noted political scientist Robert A. Dahl defined "influence" as a relationship in which "one person or a group of persons causes another person or group of persons to do something that they otherwise would not do."[31] If we accept Dahl's definition, the APPM failed to exercise real influence on foreign policy. Rather, the State Department influenced the oil companies to accept negotiation to which they remained opposed. On the other hand, if we use Dahl's standard to the work of American Catholics interested in Mexico, then it seems clear that they reached a profound level of influence: the power to mold consciousness.[32] Catholics influenced Coolidge's and Roosevelt's consciousnesses, resulting in the governmental awareness of or sensitivity to the plight of Mexican Catholics.

The purpose of this study has been twofold. First, it examined the efforts made by American Catholics to resolve a crisis in Mexico that endangered the lives, spiritual and physical, of their Mexican co-religionists. Second, and perhaps more important, this work was intended to provide a case study of the attempts of a special interest group to exert influence on public policy to the end that public policy would become responsive to its specific concerns. It was not the design of this work to express alarm at the degree to which any private interest group can pull the appropriate strings in Washington, D.C., to get what it wants out of the foreign policy of the United States. In all practicality, the only degree of responsiveness by the policy maker that can be expected by any interest group is not that the public policy maker would simply do the bidding of that group, but rather that the policy maker would address the general concerns which lie behind the specific demands. Thus by addressing those overarching interests, the policy maker might adopt a general awareness or sensitivity of the issues that most concern that group. Judged by this yardstick, the American Catholic private interest group succeeded in influencing United States–Mexican relations and as a result, helped to end the religious suffering of their brothers and sisters in Mexico. The degree of success that American Catholic activists achieved, in the end, reflected the degree to which they could link their protests and initiatives to that which this interest group believed was worth fighting for—the right of all Catholics to worship their God freely.

appendix a

TEXT OF SENATE RESOLUTION 70,
THE "BORAH RESOLUTION"

RESOLUTION

Whereas serious antireligious outbreaks have occurred in Mexico under the
regime of the National Revolutionary Party now in control of the Government of Mexico; and

Whereas the persecutions of Christians of all faiths now being practiced in
Mexico have aroused indignation and protest throughout the civilized
world; and

Whereas American citizens of the Christian faiths have been outraged and re-
viled, their homes invaded, their civil rights abridged, and their lives
placed in jeopardy; and

Whereas the vindictive antireligious policy of the present Mexican Government has arbitrarily and unwarrantably restricted the number of ministers, priests, and rabbis, permitted to officiate in some States within the
boundaries of Mexico, and has, in other States, entirely forbidden and
prohibited the ordinary spiritual ministrations of clergymen of all creeds,
thus resulting in the complete denial of the right of the people to practice the religion of their own choosing; and

Whereas it has been the national policy of the Government and the dominant revolutionary party of Mexico to discourage religious profession and obliterate religious worship; and

Whereas the present Mexican Government prohibits the time-honored practice of private religious instruction and education of children and compels parents as an only alternative to ignorance to educate their children in schools teaching hostility to orthodox religion; and

Whereas such antireligious activity in Mexico is contrary to the traditions of freedom of conscience and liberty of religious worship which are the cherished attributes of all civilized government; and

Whereas many distinguished leaders of the Protestant, Jewish, and Catholic faiths as well as outstanding religious and interdenominational organizations and societies have emphatically denounced and registered protest against such policies of the present Government of Mexico; and

Whereas the Government of Mexico has even encouraged an economic boycott against those sincerely professing and practicing the Christian religion; and

Whereas Christians are expelled from public office and driven from professions; and

Whereas Christian residents of Mexico who complain of such intolerance are flagrantly mistreated and abused: Now, therefore, be it

Resolved, That the Senate of the United States deems it fitting and proper to protest the antireligious campaign and practices of the present rulers of Mexico; and that it views with the gravest concern such ruthless persecution of helpless men and women who have become the innocent victims of antireligious persecution; be it further

Resolved, That it strongly condemns the cruelties and brutalities that have accompanied the campaign of the present Mexican Government against the profession and practice of religious beliefs by our nationals of all religious faiths now domiciled in Mexico; be it further

Resolved, That it calls upon the Government of Mexico in the name of humanity to cease denying fundamental and inalienable rights to those of our nationals who may be resident in Mexico regardless of religious convictions; and be it further

Resolved, That the Committee on Foreign Relations of the United States Senate, or a subcommittee thereof, be authorized to conduct hearings and receive such evidence as may be presented relating to religious persecution and antireligious compulsion and agitation in Mexico for the purpose of determining the policy of the United States in reference to this vital problem and in what way we may best serve the cause of tolerance and religious freedom.

For the purposes of this resolution the committee, or any duly authorized subcommittee thereof, if authorized to hold such hearings, to sit and act at such times and places during the sessions and recesses of the Senate in the Seventy-fourth Congress, to employ such clerical and other assistants, to require by subpoena or otherwise the attendance of such witnesses and the production of such books, papers, and documents, to administer such oaths, to take such testimony, and to make such expenditures, as it deems advisable. The cost of the stenographic services to report such hearings shall not be in excess of 25 cents per hundred words. The expenses of the committee, which shall not exceed $10,000, shall be paid from the contingent fund of the Senate upon vouchers approved by the chairman.

Source: United States Department of State, Records of the Department of State Relating to Internal Affairs of Mexico, 1910–1929, 1930–1939, Decimal File 812.404. See record 812.404/1505.

appendix b

THE BURKE-CALLES
EXCHANGE STATEMENTS

Fr. John J. Burke's letter to Mexican President Plutarco Elías Calles,
March 29, 1928.

From persons whom I have reason to consider well informed, I have
learned that you have stated that it has never been your purpose to destroy
the identity of the Church nor to interfere with its spiritual functions, but in
view of the constitution and the laws of Mexico, your purpose in enforcing
the same has been, and will be, to keep ecclesiastics from being implicated in
political struggles while at the same time leaving them free to dedicate themselves to the welfare of souls.

The Mexican bishops have felt that the constitution and the laws, particularly the provision which requires the registration of priests and the provision which grants the separate states the right to fix the number of priests, if
enforced in a spirit of antagonism threatened the identity of the Church by
giving the State the control of its spiritual offices. I am satisfied that the
Mexican bishops are animated by a sincere patriotism, and that they desire

a true and lasting peace. I am satisfied, also that they desire to resume public worship if that can be done consistently with their loyalty to the Republic of Mexico and their consciences. I think it could be done if they were assured of a tolerance within the law permitting the Church freedom to live and to exercise its spiritual offices. This would involve their leaving to the Mexican people, acting within the law through their duly constituted authorities, the adjustment of other questions in dispute.

If you felt that you could in full accord with your constitutional duties make a declaration that it is not the purpose of the constitution and laws, nor your purpose, to destroy the identity of the Church, and that in order to avoid unreasonable applications of the laws the government would be willing to confer from time to time with the authorized head of the Church in Mexico, I am confident that no insurmountable obstacle would remain to prevent the Mexican clergy from forthwith resuming their spiritual offices. It might well be that each in an atmosphere of good will would suggest at a later time changes in the laws which both the Republic of Mexico and the Church might desire.

If you feel that such an adjustment might meet the situation, I would be very glad to come to Mexico for the purpose of discussing confidentially with you the practical steps to be taken to bring such an adjustment into operation. I remain, with sentiments of esteem,

Most respectfully yours,
(signed) John J. Burke, C.S.P.

President Plutarco Elías Calles's letter to Fr. John J. Burke, April 28, 1928.

Dear Señor:
Through your favor of March 29 and the interview which I have had with you to-day, I am advised of the desire of the Mexican bishops to renew public worship, and I take advantage of the opportunity to declare with all clearness, as I have already done on other occasions, that it is not the purpose of the Constitution nor of the laws, nor my own purpose, to destroy the identity of any church, nor to interfere, in any form, in its spiritual functions.

In accordance with the oath of office which I took when I assumed the Executive Power of the nation, to observe and cause to be observed, the General Constitution of the Republic and the laws derived therefrom, my purpose has been to fulfill honorably said oath and to see that the law be applied in a spirit of reasonableness and without any prejudice, being myself as well as my collaborators, always disposed to hear from any person, be he a dignitary of some church or merely a private individual, the complaints they may have regarding injustices that may be committed through excess of the application of the laws.

With no other particular, I am your attentive and obedient servant,
(signed) Plutarco Elías Calles

Source: United States Department of State, Records of the Department of State Relating to Internal Affairs of Mexico, 1910–1929, 1930–1939, Decimal File 812.404. See 812.404/ 931-2/12.

appendix c

STATEMENTS OF PRESIDENT
EMILIO PORTES GIL AND
ARCHBISHOP LEOPOLDO
RUIZ Y FLORES, JUNE 21, 1929

President Emilio Portes Gil:

I have had conversations with Archbishop Ruíz y Flores and Bishop Pascual Díaz. These conversations took place as a result of the public statement made by Archbishop Ruiz y Flores on May 2 and the statement made by me on May 8th.

Archbishop Ruiz y Flores and Bishop Díaz informed me that the Mexican bishops have felt that the constitution and the laws, particularly the provision which requires the registration of ministers and the provision which grants the separate states the right to determine the maximum number of ministers, threaten the identity of the church by giving the state the control of its spiritual offices.

They assure me that the Mexican bishops are animated by a sincere patriotism and that they desire to resume public worship if this can be done consistently with their loyalty to the Mexican Republic and their consciences. They stated that it could be done if the church could enjoy freedom within the law to live and exercise its spiritual offices.

I am glad to take advantage of this opportunity to declare publicly and very clearly that it is not the purpose of the constitution, nor of the laws, nor of the government of the Republic to destroy the identity of the Catholic Church or of any other, or to interfere in any way with its spiritual functions. In accordance with the oath of office which I took when I assumed the provisional government of Mexico to observe and cause to be observed the constitution of the Republic and the laws derived therefrom, my purpose has been at all times to fulfill honestly that oath and to see that the laws are applied without favor to any sect and without any bias whatever, my administration being disposed to hear from any person, be he a dignitary of some church or merely a private individual [any] complaints in regard to injustices arising from undue application of the laws.

With reference to certain provisions of the law which has been misunderstood, I also take advantage of this opportunity to declare:

One. That the provision of the law which requires the registration of ministers does not mean that the Government can register those who have not been named by the hierarchical superior of the religious creed in question or in accordance with its regulations.

Two. With regard to religious instruction, the constitution and the laws in force definitely prohibit it in primary or higher schools, whether public or private or [*sic*] but this does not prevent ministers of any religion from imparting its doctrines, within church confines, to adults or their children who may attend for that purpose.

Three. That the constitution as well as the laws relating to the country guarantee to all residents of the Republic the right of petition and therefore the members of any church may apply to the appropriate authorities for the amendment, repeal or passage of any law.

Archbishop Leopoldo Ruiz y Flores:

Bishop Díaz and myself have had several conferences with the President of the Republic the results of which are set forth in the statement which he issued today.

I am glad to say that all of the conversations have been marked by a spirit of mutual good will and respect. As a consequence of said statement made by the President the Mexican clergy will resume religious services pursuant to the laws in force.

I entertain the hope that the resumption of religious services may lead the Mexican people, animated by a spirit of mutual good will, to cooperate in all moral efforts made for the benefit of all the people of our fatherland.

Source: United States Department of State, Records of the Department of State Relating to Internal Affairs of Mexico, 1910–1929, 1930–1939: Memorandum by George Rublee of the United States Embassy in Mexico City, "The Religious Conflict and Its Adjustment," DSR 812.404/1040, 84–85.

appendix d

INTERNATIONAL CATHOLIC TRUTH
SOCIETY STATEMENT

The list of "truths" to be spread by Catholics "on every occasion":

1. For 300 years, 1524–1824, the Catholic Church Christianized and civilized the people of Mexico.

2. The Catholic Church has nothing to apologize for during these three hundred years.

3. For nearly one hundred years the Catholic Church has been outlawed by godless governments in Mexico.

4. The Catholic Church is therefore not responsible for the conditions in Mexico today.

5. There is no freedom of speech, freedom of elections, no freedom of assemblage, no freedom of the press and no freedom of conscience in Mexico today.

6. The present godless constitution of Mexico was never passed upon or accepted by the Mexican people.

7. The present President of Mexico was never legitimately elected.

8. The present Federal Congress of Mexico does not represent the Mexican people. It is the tool and slave of the National Revolutionary Party.

9. Of the last 72 governments in Mexico, since the beginning of the nineteenth century, only 12 have had legal origin.

10. Bullets and not ballots explain the presence of tyranny in Mexico today.

11. The program of the Mexican government is the same as the program of Moscow. Children are being made slaves of the State through sex and socialistic education.

12. There is religious persecution in Mexico today.

13. In 14 States no priest is permitted to minister to the hundreds of thousands of Catholics residing therein.

14. Less than 500 priests are permitted to minister to 14,000,000 Catholic Mexicans.

15. All property devoted to any purpose of religion or to any purpose of religious charity, such as schools, hospitals and asylums, has been confiscated by the Mexican government without compensation.

16. In the State controlled elementary schools children are taught to despise religion and to deny the existence of God.

17. Over 90 per cent of the Mexican people are Catholic. They are good Catholics and devoted Catholics and loyal Catholics. Today they are suffering and dying for their faith.

18. Over 90 per cent of the colleges and universities and libraries and hospitals and asylums and art and scientific accomplishments of Mexico are the results of the Church's labors long ago.

19. The Catholic Church is not seeking special favors in Mexico. The Church is demanding that the fundamental rights of Mexicans as human beings be recognized and respected.

20. The Mexican people want peace.

They want to worship God in the Faith of their fathers.

They want suffering priests to minister to them.

They want the right to educate their children.

They want the freedom of speech, freedom of assemblage and freedom of press.

They want a government that represents their traditions and aspirations.

They want an American Ambassador who understands their history and their condition.

They want the same rights south of the Rio Grande as we possess north of the Rio Grande.

*   *   *   *

Pray for Mexico!   Speak for Mexico!

Act for Mexico!

Help the I. C. T. S. help Mexico!

NOTES

Preface

1. Most notable works include E. David Cronon, *Josephus Daniels in Mexico* (Madison: University of Wisconsin Press, 1960); John W. F. Dulles, *Yesterday in Mexico: A Chronicle of the Revolution, 1919–1936* (Austin: University of Texas Press, 1961); P. Edward Haley, *Revolution and Intervention: The Diplomacy of Taft and Wilson with Mexico, 1910–1917* (Cambridge: MIT Press, 1970); and Alan Knight, *U.S.-Mexican Relations, 1910–1940: An Interpretation* (San Diego: Center for U.S.-Mexican Studies and the Tinker Foundation, 1987).

2. See especially Sr. M. Elizabeth Ann Rice, OP, "The Diplomatic Relations between the United States and Mexico, as Affected by the Struggle for Religious Liberty in Mexico, 1925–1929" (published Ph.D. dissertation, Catholic University of America, 1959); Robert E. Quigley, *American Catholic Opinions of Mexican Anticlericalism, 1910–1936* (Cuernavaca, Mexico: Centro Intercultural de Documentación, 1969); E. David Cronon, "American Catholics and Mexican Anticlericalism, 1933–1936," *Mississippi Valley Historical Review* 65 (September 1958): 201–230; and Douglas J. Slawson, CM, "The National Catholic Welfare Conference and the Church-State Conflict in Mexico, 1925–1929," *The Americas* 47 (July 1990): 55–93. A notable recent addition to the study of the place of the Catholic Church in Mexico is Randall S. Hanson,

"The Day of Ideals: Catholic Social Action in the Age of the Mexican Revolution, 1867–1929" (Ph.D. dissertation, Indiana University, 1994).

3. James Yoho, "The Evolution of a Better Definition of 'Interest Group' and its Synonyms," *The Social Science Journal* 35:2 (April 1988): 231. See also Arthur F. Bentley, *The Process of Government: A Study of Social Pressures* (Cambridge: Belknap Press, 1967), 211.

4. Mark Rozell and Clyde Wilcox, *Interest Groups in American Campaigns: The New Face of Electioneering* (Washington, DC: Congressional Quarterly Press, 1999), 7. Such political goals include lobbying and working to influence elections.

5. V. O. Key, Jr., in his landmark book, distinguishes between "special publics" and the "general public" in issues such as those this study addresses. See Key, *Public Opinion and American Democracy* (New York: Alfred A. Knopf, 1964), 9–10. Key further advances these distinctions by noting the existence of "attentive publics" which coalesce around particular issues. See Key, 544–545.

6. See, for example, Walter Lippmann, *Public Opinion* (New York: Harcourt, Brace and Co., 1922); Thomas Bailey, *The Man in the Street* (New York: Macmillan Co., 1948); and H. R. Mahood, *Interest Group Politics in America: A New Intensity* (Englewood Cliffs, NJ: Prentice Hall, 1990).

7. Key, *Public Opinion*, 14–15.

8. James N. Rosenau, *Public Opinion and Foreign Policy: An Operational Formulation* (New York: Random House, 1961), 11–12.

9. Jean-Guy Vaillancourt, *Papal Power: A Study of Vatican Control over Lay Catholic Elites* (Berkeley: University of California Press, 1980), 3.

10. Carol Bodensteiner, "Special Interest Group Conditions: Ethical Standards for Broad-Based Support Efforts," *Public Relations Review* 23:1 (Spring 1977): 31. Bodensteiner notes, also, that more often than not, private interest group agenda are "seldom in the interests of the public as a whole."

11. Douglas Little, "Antibolshevism and American Foreign Policy, 1919–1939: The Diplomacy of Self-Delusion," *American Quarterly* 35 (Fall 1983): 390.

chapter 1
Mexican Church-State Conflict and the Origins of Catholic Activism

1. Throughout this work, I will refer to elements, groups, events, and individuals from the United States as "American" and those from Mexico as "Mexican." I understand that inhabitants of the Western Hemisphere can rightly claim the title "American," but for lack of a more appropriate and compact term, the choice of the term "American" is, with all due respect to Latin Americans and Canadians, the best at the present.

2. Frank Tannenbaum, *Peace by Revolution: Mexico after 1910* (New York: Columbia University Press, 1933, 1966), 252.

3. Ralph B. Levering, *The Public and American Foreign Policy, 1918–1978* (New York: William Morrow and Co., 1978), 39.

4. William M. Halsey, *The Survival of American Innocence: Catholicism in an Era of Disillusionment, 1920–1940* (Notre Dame: University of Notre Dame Press, 1980), 51, and James Hennesey, SJ, *American Catholics: A History of the Roman Catholic Community in the United States* (New York: Oxford University Press, 1981), 221.

5. Burke was a member of the Congregation of Missionary Priests of Saint Paul the Apostle; members of his order were more commonly known as "Paulists."

6. Hennesey, *American Catholics,* 225–226. Hennesey noted that some conscientious objectors were Catholic—four out of the 3,989 registered objectors.

7. Many Catholics, such as Father Charles Coughlin and *Catholic World* editor Father James Gillis, staunchly opposed the Court, while Father John A. Ryan (director of the National Catholic Welfare Conference Social Welfare Department) and his assistant, Father Raymond McGowen, favored it; McGowen castigated opponents' "blatant nationalism." See David J. O'Brien, *American Catholics and Social Reform* (New York: Oxford University Press, 1968), 81.

8. For more on the "Americanist" controversy, see Charles Morris, *American Catholic: The Saints and Sinners Who Built America's Most Powerful Church* (New York: Times Books, 1997), 81–112.

9. Jay P. Dolan, *In Search of an American Catholicism: A History of Religion and Culture in Tension* (New York: Oxford University Press, 2002), 133.

10. At the beginning of the nineteenth century, clerics owned or controlled half of Mexico's productive land, as well as owning or mortgaging more than half of the houses in Mexico City. See José Mariano Sánchez, *Anticlericalism: A Brief History* (Notre Dame: University of Notre Dame Press, 1972), 184.

11. Thomas G. Paterson, J. Garry Clifford, and Kenneth J. Hagan, *American Foreign Relations: A History since 1895* (Lexington, KY: D.C. Heath & Co., 1995), 196. Land ownership statistics make the foreign domination of Mexico clearest: in the richest agricultural states of Mexico, between 96.2 and 99.8 percent of the Mexican people were landless; Mexican landlords closely linked to foreign interests and foreign investors themselves owned practically everything. See Hubert Herring, *A History of Latin America from the Beginnings to the Present* (New York: Alfred A. Knopf, 1968), 330–334.

12. Walter LaFeber, *The American Age: U.S. Foreign Policy at Home and Abroad since 1896* (New York: W.W. Norton & Co., 1994), 278.

13. Herring, *History of Latin America,* 330.

14. For a more complete description of the Liberal-Conservative conflict, see J. Lloyd Mecham, *Church and State in Latin America: A History of Politicoecclesiastical Relations* (Chapel Hill: University of North Carolina Press, 1966), 340–415.

15. Randall Scott Hanson, "The Day of Ideals: Catholic Social Action in the Age of the Mexican Revolution, 1867–1929" (Ph.D. dissertation, Indiana University, 1994), 6.

16. Patience A. Schell, *Church and State Education in Revolutionary Mexico* (Tucson: University of Arizona Press, 2003), 12. Randall Scott Hanson claims that it was just this revolutionary social agenda that posed the greatest challenge to the Mexican government. By competing with the revolutionary regimes for the support of the masses, this socially active Church forced the imposition of a harsh anticlerical agenda later in the 1920s: "The Church was building a coalition almost exactly like that of the Revolution, that is, one that united the middle class with labor and peasants." See Hanson, "Day of Ideals," 480.

17. Unfortunately for the PCN, many of its leaders, urbanites who had profited handsomely from the Porfiriato, supported Huerta in his counter-revolution. This, and a loan that Huerta managed to force out of Archbishop José Mora y del Río of Mexico City to support his counter-revolutionary coup, contributed to the radical revolutionaries' suspicion that the Church stood in stark opposition to the revolution itself. Schell, ibid.

18. Britain, Germany, Spain, Norway, Japan, Italy, Portugal, Belgium, China, Argentina, Brazil, and Chile did, however, offer Huerta recognition. Wilson successfully used Huerta's self-nomination for re-election, in violation of the Mexican Constitution, as evidence to argue that the regime did not merit recognition. Wilson furthermore convinced Britain to withdraw its recognition. Powerful Americans favored recognition to secure their investment of well over $250 million in Mexican mining claims and $15 million in oil, which boomed to nearly $60 million by 1917. See Mark T. Gilderhus, "The United States and Carranza, 1917: The Question of De Jure Recognition," *The Americas* 29 (October 1972): 216.

19. This seizure, which Wilson envisioned as a liberating move for Mexico, had an expensive price tag: ninety American and as many as five hundred Mexican casualties. The move was ostensibly an effort to force reparations for an incident in Tampico in which some American naval personnel were arrested and briefly detained. See Robert E. Quirk, *An Affair of Honor: Woodrow Wilson and the Occupation of Veracruz* (Lexington, KY: Mississippi Valley Historical Association by the University of Kentucky Press, 1962); Alan Knight, *U.S.-Mexican Relations, 1910–1940: An Interpretation* (San Diego: Center for U.S.-Mexican Studies, and the Tinker Foundation, 1987); and Kendrick Clements, "Woodrow Wilson's Mexican Policy, 1913–1915," *Diplomatic History* 4 (1980): 113–136, for more on the Veracruz occupation and its background.

20. Department of State Press Release, October 27, 1915, Farley Correspondence File I-18, Papers of Archbishop John Murphy Cardinal Farley, Archives of the Archdiocese of New York, Dunwoodie, New York. The last sentence of this pledge, as we shall see, was the subject of intense debate.

21. See Luis Araquistain, *La Revolución Mejicana: Sus Origines, Sus Hombres, Su Obra* (Madrid: Renacimiento: 1929), 272.

22. Douglas Richmond, *Venustiano Carranza's Nationalist Struggle, 1893–1920* (Lincoln: University of Nebraska Press, 1983), 108.

23. Mexican law requires a separate order for the implementation of laws and accompanying provisions for penalties—Carranza did not see to it that these legal

maneuvers were executed. For more on the constitution and Carranza's efforts to react to the radical provisions, see Douglas Richmond, "The First Chief and Revolutionary Mexico: The Presidency of Venustiano Carranza, 1915–1920" (Ph.D. dissertation, University of Washington, 1976), 221–283.

24. Historian David C. Bailey called Obregón "Mexico's Accommodating President," because of his struggles to stabilize the revolutionary government following a decade of warfare. See Bailey's "Obregón: Mexico's Accommodating President," in George Wolfskill and Douglas Richmond, eds., *Essays on the Mexican Revolution: Revisionist Views of the Leaders* (Austin: University of Texas Press, 1979), 81–99.

25. Apostolic delegates are the Vatican's representatives to a nation's Catholic population. Papal (apostolic) nuncios have full diplomatic representation to another nation's government. Ernesto Filippi was Mexico's last until the 1930s; the United States had three in the period under examination: Giovanni Bonzano (1911–1922), Pietro Fumasoni-Biondi (1922–1933), and Amleto Cicognani (1933–1958).

26. Robert E. Quirk, *The Mexican Revolution and the Catholic Church* (Bloomington: Indiana University Press, 1973), 132.

27. Bailey, "Obregón," 90.

28. Hanson, "Day of Ideals," 495–496.

29. Ibid., 507.

30. Sr. M. Elizabeth Ann Rice, OP, "The Diplomatic Relations between the United States and Mexico, as Affected by the Struggle for Religious Liberty in Mexico, 1925–1929" (published Ph.D. dissertation, Catholic University of America, 1959), 58.

31. Pérez, the leader of the schismatic movement, was a former priest, previously a soldier of fortune, a member of a Masonic lodge, and a married man (all conditions that placed him outside the priesthood). The use of the title Caballeros de Guadalupe was not only a bid to attract the support of Mexican nationalists devoted to Mexico's patroness, the Virgin of Guadalupe. It was also an effort to bleed supporters away from the Mexican branch of the Knights of Columbus, the Caballeros de Colón. Calles, under pressure from the neighborhood residents, relocated the schismatic church to another part of the capital, but instead of allowing Roman Catholic services to return to La Soledad, he converted the confiscated church into a public library. See Schell, *Church and State,* 176, and Hanson, "Day of Ideals," 513–514.

32. The Mexican hierarchy disclaimed any connection to the Liga, and the organization accepted its own responsibility for its actions. See Harriet Denise Joseph, "Church and State in Mexico from Calles to Cardenas, 1924–1938" (Ph.D. dissertation, North Texas State University, 1976), 42.

33. Ibid., 52–53.

34. Schell, *Church and State,* 179.

35. The archbishops and bishops of the United States, when referred to collectively in this work, will be referred to variously as "prelates," the "hierarchy," or simply as "bishops."

36. In 1926, there were no more than several hundred Cristeros under arms, and but three thousand in January 1927, spread out over the states of Jalisco, Michoacán,

Durango, Colima, Zacatecas, Coahuila, Nayarit, Guanajuato, Aguascalientes, Guerrero, San Luis Potosí, and Mexico. By December 1927, their number swelled to twenty-five thousand in eighteen states, and by 1929, there were an estimated fifty thousand Cristeros in the field. See Joseph, "Church and State," 104–105, 132, 315. Other authorities on the rebellion include David C. Bailey, *¡Viva Cristo Rey!: The Cristero Rebellion and the Church-State Conflict in Mexico* (Austin: University of Texas Press, 1974); and Jean A. Meyer, *The Cristero Rebellion: The Mexican People between Church and State, 1926–1929* (Cambridge: Cambridge University Press, 1976).

37. Peter Lester Reich, *Mexico's Hidden Revolution: The Catholic Church in Law and Politics since 1929* (Notre Dame: University of Notre Dame Press, 1995), 13–14.

38. Pope Pius XI may have been convinced of the need for the encyclical in part because of letters he had received from Mexican prelates outlining the failures of the settlement. For example, Bishop Leopoldo Lara y Torres of Tacámbaro wrote to the pope that between 1929 and 1931, the Church in Mexico had steadily lost power, prestige, and influence over the people, as the government violated the agreement with apparent impunity. This caused, among other things, an eroding of the people's confidence in the Church's ability to protect their rights, and an expansion of the power and presence of the Protestant churches. See copy of a letter from Leopoldo Lara y Torres to Pope Pius XI, October 12, 1931, Leopoldo Lara y Torres, *Documentos para la Historia de la Persecución Religiosa en México* (México: Editorial Jus, 1954), 817–818.

39. Rodríguez was Calles's handpicked choice to replace Pascual Ortiz Rubio in 1932. Ortiz Rubio was, in turn, the man Calles chose to succeed Emilio Portes Gil in 1930. Calles's influence in Mexican politics would make itself known again in 1934 when he chose Lázaro Cárdenas to replace Rodríguez. Although Calles was president only from 1924 to 1928, by manipulating the top office and by seeing that his hand-picked candidates became president (Portes Gil, Ortiz Rubio, Rodríguez, and Cárdenas), he controlled Mexican politics from 1924 until Cárdenas threw him out in 1935.

40. Timothy Clarke Hanley, "Civilian Leadership of the Cristero Movement: The Liga Nacional Defensora de la Libertad Religiosa and the Church-State Conflict in Mexico, 1925–1938" (Ph.D. dissertation, Columbia University, 1977), 579. The Mexican Supreme Court responded to this initiative almost immediately by striking down the law that allowed states to limit the number of priests; ibid., 580.

41. Claude Pomerleau, "El problema de las Relaciones Iglesia-Estado en Mexico," *Estudios Internacionales* 20 (1987): 231.

42. Statement of Franklin Roosevelt following his receipt of the congressional petition, July 16, 1935, Editorials, Columbia 15 (July 1935): 13.

chapter 2
The Efforts of the American Catholic Hierarchy as a Whole

1. "Letter of Sympathy From the Hierarchy of the United States to the Archbishops, Bishops, Priests, and Laity of Mexico," Raphael M. Huber, STD, OFM Conv.,

Our Bishops Speak: National Pastorals and Annual Statements of the Hierarchy of the United States, 1919–1951 (Milwaukee: Bruce Publishing Co., 1952), 188–189. See also *Baltimore Catholic Review*, September 17, 1926 (hereafter cited as "*BCR*").

2. Boston *Pilot*, September 25, 1926.

3. "The Hierarchy of the United States Pastoral Letter on Mexico," Huber, *Our Bishops Speak*, 66–97; see also file: "The *Pastoral Letter* on Mexico by the American Hierarchy and *Church and State in Mexico*, Opinion of William D. Guthrie," National Catholic Welfare Conference Archives, Catholic University of America, Washington, DC (hereafter cited as "NCWCA"), 31, *N.C.W.C. Bulletin* 8 (January 1927): 30–39, and the *BCR*, December 24 and 31, 1926.

4. Huber, *Our Bishops Speak*, 68.

5. Ibid, 70.

6. Ibid, 94.

7. Ibid. Few claimed that the Church sought armed intervention; the letter does not, in fact, deny a desire for other types of intervention.

8. *New York World*, December 16, 1926.

9. "Statement of the Hierarchy of the United States on 'Anti-Christian Tyranny in Mexico,'" Huber, *Our Bishops Speak*, 205–209; see also *Catholic Action* 16 (December 1934): 3–4, and *The Catholic Mind* 32 (1934): 454–458. The *N.C.W.C. Bulletin* was briefly succeeded by the *N.C.W.C. Review* as the official organ of the NCWC, but only for 1930–1931. *Catholic Action* followed the *Review*.

10. Huber, *Our Bishops Speak*, 208–209; *Catholic Action* 16: 4.

11. Josephus Daniels, *Shirt-Sleeve Diplomat* (Chapel Hill: University of North Carolina Press, 1947), 519.

12. "Speeches, Writings, Related Materials, Speech File, 1934," Josephus Daniels Papers, Library of Congress Manuscripts Division, Washington, DC (hereafter cited as "Daniels Papers"), 4. See also Christopher Kauffman, *Faith and Fraternalism: The History of the Knights of Columbus, 1882–1982* (New York: Harper & Row, 1982), 207.

13. Daniels, *Shirt-Sleeve Diplomat*, 182. See also Daniels to Hull, January 22, 1935, "Subject File: Mexico Church-State Relations, 1934," Daniels Papers, 1.

14. Personal letter, Daniels to Roosevelt, November 6, 1934, "Diplomatic Correspondence Mexico 1933–1935," President's Secretary File, Franklin D. Roosevelt Library, Hyde Park, New York.

15. Patience Schell has demonstrated that in reality, this threat was more potential than reality. Indeed, even after Calles began his crackdown on the Church in 1926, the Church and state cooperated in educating Mexico's youth to an impressive degree. Schell identifies several examples in which the state, through the Secretaría de Educación Pública (SEP—the Ministry of Public Education), and the Church, through the Unión de Damas Católicos Mexicanas (UCDM—the Union of Catholic Mexican Ladies), cooperated to keep some essential schools open. Schell notes that "the SEP was clearly willing to look the other way as long as its regulations were observed on paper." See Patience A. Schell, *Church and State Education in Revolutionary Mexico* (Tucson: University of Arizona Press, 2003), 187. SEP inspectors feared that an inflexible

enforcement of Article 3 of the Constitution of 1917 would throw millions of children out into the streets where they would receive no education at all.

16. Ibid. See also *BCR*, November 23, 1934; *The Catholic Mind* 32 (1934): 58; and *New York Times*, November 17, 1934.

17. *BCR*, December 7, 1934.

18. Catholic News Service file: "Mexico—US Hierarchy—Mexico," NCWC News Service Press Release, January 25, 1936, Catholic News Service Library, United States Catholic Conference/National Conference of Catholic Bishops, Washington, DC (hereafter cited as "CNS").

19. Leo V. Kanawada, *Franklin D. Roosevelt's Diplomacy and American Catholics, Italians and Jews* (Ann Arbor: UMI Research Press, 1982), 44.

20. Thomas W. Spalding, *The Premier See: A History of the Archdiocese of Baltimore, 1789–1989* (Baltimore: Johns Hopkins University Press, 1989), 352. See also John B. Sheerin, CSP, *Never Look Back: The Career and Concerns of John J. Burke* (New York: Paulist Press, 1975), 169.

21. For more detail on Burke and his role in the NCWC, see chapter 4.

22. John J. Piper, "Father John J. Burke, C.S.P., and the Turning Point in American Catholic History," *Records of the Catholic Historical Society of Philadelphia* 92 (1981): 102–103.

23. The archbishop of Baltimore traditionally stood at the head of the hierarchy, since Baltimore was the Premier See, the first diocese in the United States, established when John Carroll was named the first bishop in the United States in May 1789.

24. Jay P. Dolan, *The American Catholic Experience: A History from Colonial Times to the Present* (Garden City, NY: Image Books, 1985), 353.

25. Elizabeth McKeown, "The National Bishops' Conference: An Analysis of its Origins," *The Catholic Historical Review* 66 (1980): 574–575. Note how Muldoon incorrectly assumed that a permanent organization could direct the institutions of public opinion: press, teachers, and even legislatures.

26. Huber, *Our Bishops Speak*, xvi–xvii.

27. Minutes of the Annual Meetings of the American Hierarchy, September 24, 1919, 9, NCWCA.

28. *BCR*, October 4, 1919.

29. The Administrative Committee was authorized to speak on behalf of the membership as a whole between meetings of the entire NCWC. Under Burke, the office of the general secretary, in turn, frequently spoke on behalf of the Administrative Committee. This gave rise to misconceptions on the part of some prelates that Burke was speaking and acting on behalf of the American hierarchy as a whole. These criticisms will be discussed in more detail in chapter 4. For the balance of the present chapter, Burke will be referred to only when he acted in his official capacity as general secretary; chapter 4 deals with his personal attitudes and activities.

30. Sheerin, *Never Look Back*, 66.

31. Minutes of the Annual Meetings of the American Hierarchy, September 28, 1922, NCWCA, 6; see also John Tracy Ellis, *American Catholicism* (Chicago: University of Chicago Press, 1956), 140–141. "Council" carries particular meaning, since the Church's original meetings at Nicaea, Trent, and Rome were official councils that determined the nature of the Church itself. The term "conference" also indicated that the NCWC's powers were advisory, not jurisdictional; "it could recommend, but not enjoin." Huber, *Our Bishops Speak*, xxi.

32. CNS Press Release, December 24, 1927.

33. As early as April 15, 1926, the minutes of the bishops' annual meeting noted that "the Archbishop of Mexico desires that protests be made by American Catholics." See April 15 minutes, NCWCA, 105.

34. Douglas J. Slawson, CM, "The National Catholic Welfare Conference and the Church-State Conflict in Mexico, 1925–1929," *The Americas* 47 (July 1990): 61.

35. "Formal Statement of the NCWC Administrative Board on 'Mexican Injustice to the Church,'" Huber, *Our Bishops Speak,* 268–270.

36. Ibid., 270.

37. *Southern Messenger* (San Antonio), May 27, 1926.

38. Statement of Appeal from NCWC to NCCW and NCCM councils, August 1926, file: "Newspaper Statements, 1926–1927," NCWCA.

39. Burke to Judge Morgan J. O'Brien, September 14, 1926, file: "Statements, Letters: 1925–26," Burke Mexico Files, National Catholic Welfare Conference/United States Catholic Conference Archives, Catholic University of America (hereafter cited as "Burke Mexico Files").

40. For more information on the NCPRRM, see chapters 4 and 7.

41. NCWC to Coolidge, April 15, 1926, United States Department of State, Records of the Department of State Relating to Internal Affairs of Mexico, 1910–1929, 1930–1939, 812.404/413, 2 (hereafter cited as "DSR 812.404/***").

42. Gunther memorandum of Burke meeting with Kellogg, April 21, 1926, DSR 812.404/502, 2.

43. Sister M. Elizabeth Ann Rice, OP, "The Diplomatic Relations between the United States and Mexico, as Affected by the Struggle for Religious Liberty in Mexico, 1925–1929" (published dissertation, Catholic University of America, 1959), 82.

44. Draft of letter from NCWC to Coolidge, April 23, 1926, DSR 812.404/439, 2.

45. This issue did not disappear, however, as in a statement of protest from the NCWC Administrative Committee dated May 1, 1935, the committee maintained that the whole basis of United States recognition on October 19, 1915, was the promise by Arredondo that the Mexican government would insure religious freedom. See CNS Press Release, May 6, 1935.

46. Memorandum of Burke interview with Franklin Mott Gunther, May 14, 1926, Interview Book I, Burke Mexico Files, 1.

47. Ibid. Burke protested Gunther's opposition, since Kellogg had already intimated to Burke that the revised letter was, indeed, acceptable. See Burke letter to Kellogg, May 14, 1926, DSR 812.404/460.

48. Gunther's memorandum of meeting with Burke, May 14, 1926, DSR 812.404/464, 2.

49. See NCWC to Coolidge, April 15, 1926, DSR 812.404/413; NCWC to Coolidge, April 24, 1926, 812.404/439; and Gunther memorandum of meeting with Burke and Montavon, May 14, 1926, 812.404/464.

50. Report, Weddell to State Department, February 1, 1926, DSR 812.404/371, 10.

51. Peter Guilday, ed., *The National Pastorals of the American Hierarchy (1792–1919)* (Washington, DC: National Catholic Welfare Council, 1923), 288.

52. *BCR,* July 27, 1928.

53. Rice, "Diplomatic Relations," 168–169.

54. *Catholic Action* 15 (February 1933): 5.

55. *Catholic Action* 17 (January 1935): 3–4.

56. For the text of the Borah resolution of 1935, see appendix A.

57. Claudius O. Johnson, *Borah of Idaho* (New York: Longmans, Green & Co., 1936), 194. Borah's comments of 1915 made it clear that the Mexican issue was high on his agenda. Upon hearing of the sinking of *Lusitania* in May, Borah declared that "to my mind the sinking of the steamship of a foe upon which happened to be found American citizens is by no means to be compared with the act of hunting out, robbing, assaulting and murdering American citizens in a neighboring country [Mexico]." See Marian C. McKenna, *Borah* (Ann Arbor: University of Michigan Press, 1961), 140. See also *New York Times,* May 9, 1915.

58. Leroy Ashby, *The Spearless Leader: Senator Borah and the Progressive Movement in the 1920s* (Urbana: University of Illinois Press, 1972), 212. The irony of the comment became clear in a longer quote. Borah continued: "The first step toward justice is to stop making false and unfair statements about Mexico." See *New York Times,* March 21, 1927.

59. Johnson, *Borah,* 342. See also George Q. Flynn, *American Catholics and the Roosevelt Presidency, 1932–1936* (Lexington: University of Kentucky Press, 1968), 157.

60. *New York Times,* February 2, 1935. That the Senate's leading isolationist would agree to sponsor such legislation has been a curiosity from then to the present. Christopher Kauffman, in *Faith and Fraternalism,* claims that the Supreme Council was "convinced that the Senator was animated only by a sincere concern for human rights in Mexico," 302. Others have speculated that the fact that some influential Catholics supported Borah in his battle against the World Court has something to do with his willingness to sponsor an investigation into the Mexican situation. See E. David Cronon, "American Catholics and Mexican Anticlericalism, 1933–1936," *Mississippi Valley Historical Review* 65 (1958): 216.

61. Hull to Senator Key Pittman, chair of the Senate Foreign Relations Committee, February 12, 1935, SC-11-2-21, Knights of Columbus Archives, New Haven, Connecticut (hereafter cited as "KCA"), 1.

62. Ibid., 2.

63. Ibid., 3.

64. Ibid., 5.

65. Ibid., 6.

66. See *New York Times,* February 14, 22, and March 2, 1935, respectively.

67. Cronon, "American Catholics," 216–217.

68. Ibid.

69. Statement, Mexican Embassy to Burke, January 31, 1935, file: "Administrative Committee Meeting, Chicago, 1935, July," Burke Mexico Files.

70. Statement, Burke, Secretary General, NCWC, February 1, 1935, ibid., 1. See also "Mexican Persecution, Reverend John J. Burke, CSP, NCWC, 1935," SC-11-2-8, KCA.

71. United States Department of State, *Papers Relating to the Foreign Relations of the United States,* 1935 (Washington, DC: United States Government Printing Office, 1953), 4:794–796, for Hull and Najera statements.

72. Statement of the NCWC Administrative Committee on "Government's Silence on Mexico," May 1, 1935, in Huber, *Our Bishops Speak,* 309. See also *Catholic Action* 17 (June 1935): 3–4.

73. *BCR,* May 10, 1935.

74. See undated telegram, Rome to NCWC, Interview Book IV, Burke Mexico Files. The *New York Times,* on June 1, 1929, considered the Ruiz appointment a great stride toward peace.

75. An indication of the mixed signals coming out of the Vatican was when the Vatican denied any knowledge of the naming of Ruiz as apostolic delegate. According to Vatican officials, "it is thought possible that Archbishop Ruiz . . . had been charged with confidential negotiations with the Mexican Government . . . but that would in no wise imply his appointment as Apostolic Delegate." *New York Times,* June 2, 1929. Two days later, Fumasoni-Biondi, the Vatican's official representative to the United States, declared that there were absolutely "no negotiations in progress between the Church and the [Mexican] government." *New York Times,* June 4, 1929.

76. Kanawada, *Roosevelt's Diplomacy,* 29.

77. Ibid., 30.

78. Burke memorandum of meeting with Sumner Welles, May 15, 1935, Interview Book VI, Burke Mexico Files, 3.

79. Burke memorandum of meeting with McIntyre, June 6, 1935, Interview Book VI, Burke Mexico Files, 2.

80. Kanawada, *Roosevelt's Diplomacy,* 32.

81. Ibid., 34.

82. Burke memorandum of meeting with Welles, December 14, 1935, Interview Book VI, Burke Mexico Files, 2. This claim's patronizing tone demonstrated that it was clearly intended to impress the United States.

83. *Catholic Action* 17 (November 1935): 4–5.

84. *N.C.W.C. Bulletin* 8 (November 1926): 6, 28.
85. Piper, "Father John J. Burke," 112–113.
86. *N.C.W.C. Bulletin* 10 (March 1929): 15, 23.

chapter 3
Leading Voices among the Hierarchy

1. John Tracy Ellis, *The Life of James Cardinal Gibbons, Archbishop of Baltimore: 1834–1921*, 2 vols. (Milwaukee: Bruce Publishing Co., 1952), 2:212.
2. Ibid.
3. Gibbons interview with Baltimore *American,* July 23, 1914, 114 A5, Gibbons Correspondence File, Archives of the Archdiocese of Baltimore (hereafter cited as "Gibbons/AABalt"), 1, 2.
4. Gibbons to Bishop John W. Shaw of San Antonio, August 4, 1914, 114 B6, Gibbons/AABalt.
5. Maas to Gibbons, July 31, 1914, 114 A13, 1–2, Gibbons/AABalt.
6. Gibbons to Wilson, August 18, 1914, 114 I4, Gibbons/AABalt.
7. Wilson to Gibbons, August 21, 1914, 114 C6, Gibbons/AABalt.; see also *Baltimore Catholic Review,* August 27, 1926 (hereafter cited as "*BCR*").
8. Bryan to Gibbons, August 20, 1914, United States Department of State, Records of the Department of State Relating to Internal Affairs of Mexico, 1910–1929, 1930–1939, 812.404/8 (hereafter cited as "DSR 812.404/***").
9. Gibbons to Kelley, October 29, 1914, 114 K8, Gibbons/AABalt.
10. Kelley to Gibbons, November 13, 1914, Gibbons/AABalt.
11. See Gibbons to "The Archbishop of Mexico & all the Archbishops of that Republic," November 9, 1914, 114 K25, Gibbons/AABalt; and Gibbons to Archbishop John Cardinal Farley of New York, October 16, 1914, Farley Correspondence File, Archives of the Archdiocese of New York, Dunwoodie, New York.
12. *New York Times,* October 2, 1915. Gibbons was referring to the huge outpouring of support for a molested missionary in Armenia earlier in the year.
13. Gibbons to Smith, May 15, 1917, 119 E8, Gibbons/AABalt.
14. John Tracy Ellis, *American Catholicism* (Chicago: University of Chicago Press, 1956), 136–137.
15. Elizabeth McKeown, "The National Bishops' Conference: An Analysis of Its Origins," *Catholic Historical Review* 66 (1980): 570.
16. Roosevelt to Gibbons, January 5, 1917, 118 G8, Gibbons/AABalt.
17. Kelley to Curley, June 22, 1922, K-214, Curley Correspondence File, Archives of the Archdiocese of Baltimore (hereafter cited as "Curley/AABalt"), 2.
18. See Curley to Kenny, February 25, 1935, K-626, Curley/AABalt, 2.
19. *BCR,* March 5, 1926.
20. Michael Cardinal Curley, *Mexican Tyranny and the Catholic Church: An Analysis of the Assault upon Freedom of Conscience, Freedom of Worship, Freedom of the*

Press, and Freedom of Education in Mexico during the Past Ten Years (Brooklyn: International Catholic Truth Society, 1926).

21. *BCR*, February 19, 1926; see also Catholic News Service file: "Mexico—US Hierarchy—Mexico," NCWC News Service Press Release, February 22, 1926, Catholic News Service Library, United States Catholic Conference/National Conference of Catholic Bishops, Washington, DC (hereafter cited as "CNS").

22. *BCR*, February 26, 1926.

23. Ibid.

24. Curley to Bishop Edward Ledvina of Corpus Christi, March 6, 1926, L-492, Curley/AABalt.

25. *BCR*, April 2, 1926; March 12, 1926.

26. Curley to Fumasoni-Biondi, March 19, 1926, Curley file: "Roman Letters, 1921–1930," Curley/AABalt.

27. *BCR*, March 19, 1926; April 9, 1926. Curley's longtime correspondent, Constantine McGuire, was little more confident in the Calles administration. He gave them six months; see Curley to McGuire, April 9, 1926, Mc-734, Curley/AABalt.

28. Curley to McGuire, April 9, 1926, Mc-734, and Curley to Ledvina, April 9, 1926, L-492, Curley/AABalt.

29. *BCR*, May 21, 1926. See also *BCR*, May 7, 1926: "Diplomacy Done in Oil."

30. *BCR*, July 9, 1926; see also John B. Sheerin, CSP, *Never Look Back: The Career and Concerns of John J. Burke* (New York: Paulist Press, 1975), 111.

31. *BCR*, October 12, 1934. This exposé was a long series of articles by Fr. Michael Kenny, SJ, later collected and published under the title *No God Next Door*, which one scholar considered "more inflammatory" than Francis C. Kelley's *Blood-Drenched Altars*. See Thomas W. Spalding, *The Premier See: A History of the Archdiocese of Baltimore, 1789–1989* (Baltimore: Johns Hopkins University Press, 1989), 537.

32. *BCR*, November 2, 1934.

33. *Washington Post*, February 14, 1935.

34. Hanna to Curley, March 8, 1935, H-227, Curley/AABalt. According to Administrative Committee member Bishop John T. Noll of Fort Wayne, this refusal and the refusal to endorse the activities of the Knights of Columbus Supreme Council were intended to free Roosevelt's hands, so that he could appear to have taken the initiative in issuing a statement of protest without being forced by the hierarchy; see Leo V. Kanawada, *Franklin D. Roosevelt's Diplomacy and American Catholics, Italians and Jews* (Ann Arbor: UMI Research Press, 1982), 31.

35. Curley to Hanna, March 9, 1935, H-228, Curley/AABalt.

36. Curley to Kenny, February 25, 1935, K-626, Curley/AABalt, 1.

37. *BCR*, April 19, 1935.

38. Curley before the Washington Sodality Union, April 19, 1935, CNS Press Release, April 22, 1935.

39. Mahan to Curley, March 26, 1935, "Mexican file," AABalt (hereafter cited as "Mex/AABalt"), 1–2.

40. *New York Times*, March 26, 1935, and *BCR*, March 29, 1935.

41. Curley CNS Press Release, April 22, 1935.

42. E. David Cronon, "American Catholics and Mexican Anticlericalism, 1933–1936," *Mississippi Valley Historical Review* 65 (1958): 220.

43. McManus to Curley, March 31, 1935, Mex/AABalt, 3.

44. Curley to Fr. Michael Kenny, April 5, 1935, K-629, Curley/AABalt.

45. Curley to J.N. Pride [real name: Jorge Nunez], leader of the Liga in Washington, DC, April 4, 1935, P-898, Curley/AABalt.

46. Holland to Curley, n.d., Mex/AABalt, 2.

47. Burke to Curley, February 27, 1936, B-2097, Curley/AABalt, 2.

48. Curley to Burke, February 28, 1936, B-2098, Curley/AABalt.

49. Francis Clement Kelley, *The Bishop Jots It Down: An Autobiographical Strain on Memories* (New York: Harper & Bros., 1939), 184.

50. *New York Times*, December 6, 1914; see also Theodore Roosevelt, *Fear God and Take Your Own Part* (New York: George H. Doran Co., 1916), 231–232, and Kelley, *Jots*, 190–191.

51. Kelley editorial letter, *America* 12 (1914): 5–6.

52. Francis C. Kelley, *The Book of Red and Yellow: Being a Story of Blood and a Yellow Streak* (Chicago: The Catholic Church Extension Society of the United States of America, 1915), 88, 91.

53. Ibid., 69.

54. Deborah J. Baldwin, *Protestants and the Mexican Revolution: Missionaries, Ministers, and Social Change* (Urbana/Chicago: University of Illinois Press, 1990), 134, 138. Catholics in the United States noted that most Protestant-run religious schools remained open throughout the revolution, in clear violation of constitutional Articles 3 and 130, which Catholics interpreted as more proof that the revolution was anti-Catholic rather than anti-Christian.

55. Bryan to Kelley, March 20, 1915, Woodrow Wilson Papers, Library of Congress Manuscripts Division, Washington, DC (hereafter cited as "LC/Wilson"), 2–3. See also Bryan to Kelley, 114 X10, Gibbons/AABalt; and DSR 812.404/85.

56. Kelley to Bryan, April 17, 1915, LC/Wilson, 1–2.

57. See Kelley to Walsh, January 30, 1917, LC/Wilson, and memorandum, Wilson to Tumulty, n.d., ibid.

58. James P. Gaffey, *Francis Clement Kelley and the American Catholic Dream*, 2 vols. (Bensenville, IL: The Heritage Foundation, 1980), 2:31, 38.

59. Ibid., 5.

60. Ibid., 47–48.

61. Kelley sent a March 23, 1919, report to Archbishop George Cardinal Mundelein of Chicago, claiming that little could be accomplished in Paris, primarily because the American delegation did "not want any advise from anyone, much less an American." Kelley could get in to meet with representatives of any of the other delegations, but "the doors of the American Commissioners [were] barred—very busy." See Gaffey, *Kelley*, 51–52.

62. Memorandum, Kelley to Borah, April 3, 1929, Interview Book III, Burke Mexico Files, National Catholic Welfare Conference/United States Catholic Conference Archives, Catholic University of America, 2–3.

63. "The Hierarchy of the United States Pastoral Letter on Mexico," in Raphael M. Huber, STD, OFM Conv., *Our Bishops Speak: National Pastorals and Annual Statements of the Hierarchy of the United States, 1919–1951* (Milwaukee: Bruce Publishing Co., 1952), 69–77.

64. Boston *Pilot,* October 9, 1926.

65. Huber, *Our Bishops Speak,* 95, from Kelley, *The Book of Red and Yellow,* 74.

66. Francis C. Kelley, *Blood-Drenched Altars* (Milwaukee: Bruce Publishing Co., 1935).

67. Gaffey, *Kelley,* 90.

68. Martin Carmody, "Supreme Knight's Annual Report, Proceedings of the Supreme Council, 1935," Knights of Columbus Archives, New Haven, Connecticut, 81.

69. Ibid., 89–90.

70. Curley to Kelley, March 29, 1935, K-246, 1, Curley/AABalt.

71. Gaffey, *Kelley,* 90.

72. Kelley, *Altars,* 347.

73. *BCR,* November 22, 1935.

74. Gaffey, *Kelley,* 97.

75. In 2005 dollars, these figures represent $337,096.77 and $237,844.25, respectively. See inflation conversion charts maintained by Dr. Robert Shari of Oregon State University, oregonstate.edu/Dept/pol_sci/fac/sahr/sahr.htm, November 21, 2003.

76. Ibid., 80–81.

77. O'Connell to Bonzano, May 9, 1922, Chancery Central Subject File, M-299: "NCWC, 1911–1940," Archives of the Archdiocese of Boston, Massachusetts (hereafter cited as "AAB"), 2, 3.

78. O'Connell to Bonzano, June 14, 1922, M-299, AAB, 1.

79. Ibid., 1–2. Fr. Ryan, a prominent professor at The Catholic University of America, was Burke's assistant in the NCWC.

80. O'Connell to Archbishop Edward Hanna, NCWC Administrative Committee Chair, December 16, 1922, M-299, AAB, 3.

81. Fumasoni-Biondi to O'Connell, October 20, 1932, M-299, AAB.

82. William Cardinal O'Connell, "The Injustice of the Mexican Government," in *Sermons and Addresses of His Eminence William Cardinal O'Connell, Archbishop of Boston* (Boston: Pilot Publishing Co., 1930), 9:141–144. See also Boston *Pilot,* August 7, 1926.

83. See letter from O'Connell to all archdiocesan churches, May 22, 1935, to be read at all masses on May 26, 1935, M-1647, AAB.

84. Notes for reply to Fumasoni-Biondi letter of May 15, 1925, May 17, 1925, M360/35, AAB.

85. *BCR,* April 23, 1926.

86. *BCR,* December 16, 1927.

87. *BCR,* December 14, 1934.

88. Vatican orders made San Antonio a province August 27, 1926, thus elevating Drossaerts from bishop to archbishop.

89. Michael Kenny, *No God Next Door: Red Rule in Mexico and Our Responsibility* (New York: William J. Hirten Co., 1935), iv–v.

90. *BCR,* March 19, 1926.

91. Sermon: "Blessing Churches at Los Angeles and New-Westphalia, 17 October 1926," Drossaerts Collection: Sermons, 1904–1926, Occasional Sermons, 1912–1926, Catholic Archives of San Antonio, Texas (hereafter cited as "CASA"), 3.

92. Drossaerts's public response to Consul-General Enrique Santibarrey's invitation to speak across the border in Mexico, May 19, 1928, Archives of the Archdiocese of San Antonio, 1–2; see also *BCR,* June 1, 1928.

93. Drossaerts's eulogy for Valdespino, May 15, 1928, CASA; see also CNS Press Release, May 21, 1928.

94. Speech, American Board of Catholic Missions, 1929, "Drossaerts, Arthur J., Most Reverend, Speeches, Vol. 2 (1928–1940)," CASA.

95. Ibid.

96. Edward R. Kantowicz, "Cardinal Mundelein of Chicago and the Shaping of Twentieth-Century American Catholicism," *Journal of American History* 68 (1981): 65–66.

97. Mundelein was not alone in his criticism. The British Catholic journal *The Month* used the ceremony to observe that "the Knights of Columbus' estimate of the President's conduct is not the view of all Catholics. . . ." See memo, William D. Hassett to Stephen Early, March 28, 1936, OF146a, "Mexico Miscellaneous, 1936–1938," Franklin D. Roosevelt Library, Hyde Park, New York.

98. George Q. Flynn, *American Catholics and the Roosevelt Presidency, 1932–1936* (Lexington: University of Kentucky Press, 1968), 185. Curley's outrage at this ceremony is curious, since Mundelein was not the first to so honor Roosevelt. The president was awarded an honorary Doctor of Laws degree from Catholic University of America on June 15, 1933, *from Curley himself.* See *BCR,* June 16, 1933.

99. Daniels to Roosevelt, December 4, 1936, President's Safe File, "Mexico," Franklin D. Roosevelt Library, Hyde Park, New York.

100. These divisions parallel similar rifts in the Mexican hierarchy. The two main factions were the militants, such as José de Jesús Manríquez y Zárate (Huejutla), José Maria Gonzalez y Valencia (Durango), Pascual Díaz (Tabasco), and Leopoldo Lara y Torres (Tacámbaro), and the accommodationists, such as Miguel de la Mora (San Luis Potosí), Rafael Guízar Valencia (Veracruz), and Leopoldo Ruiz y Flores (Morelia). See Patience A. Schell, *Church and State Education in Revolutionary Mexico City* (Tucson: University of Arizona Press, 2003), 180.

101. Kelley to Curley, April 2, 1935, Mex/AABalt.

chapter 4
John J. Burke, CSP

1. Quoted from Castle's personal diary in L. Ethan Ellis, "Dwight Morrow and the Church-State Controversy in Mexico," *Hispanic American Historical Review* 38 (November 1958): 484 n. 5.

2. Burke also served as the chair of the secretary of war's "Committee of Six"—comprised of one Catholic (Burke), four Protestants, and a Jew—who convened to advise the secretary on religious and moral issues of the war. For this service, the War Department awarded Burke the Distinguished Service Medal in 1919; Raphael M. Huber, STD, OFM Conv., *Our Bishops Speak: National Pastorals and Annual Statements of the Hierarchy of the United States, 1919–1951* (Milwaukee: Bruce Publishing Co., 1952), xvi.

3. John J. Piper, "Father John J. Burke, CSP, and the Turning Point in American Catholic History," *Records of the American Catholic Historical Society of Philadelphia* 92 (1981): 110.

4. John B. Sheerin, CSP, *Never Look Back: The Career and Concerns of John J. Burke* (New York: Paulist Press, 1975), 60–61.

5. Quoted in Servando Ortoll, "Catholic Organizations in Mexico's National Politics and International Diplomacy (1926–1942)" (unpublished Ph.D. dissertation, Columbia University, 1987), 84.

6. Sheerin, *Never Look Back,* 111. Burke was referring to the ceremony in which prelates assume the office of cardinal. His Vatican conspiracy model found support, in his mind, in the events of mid-1926. Curley and Representative John J. Boylan (New York) wrote a resolution that Boylan introduced in the House, calling for a severance of United States diplomatic relations with Mexico. Burke feared this would be a prelude to war. Also, when the Liga (the National League for the Defense of Religious Liberty) moved beyond its failed economic boycott into armed resistance (the Cristero Rebellion) in December 1926, Burke was ever more convinced of the effort to force Calles from the presidency.

7. Memorandum of Burke interview with Franklin Mott Gunther, May 14, 1926, 1, Interview Book I, Burke Mexico Files, National Catholic Welfare Conference/United States Catholic Conference Archives, Catholic University of America (hereafter cited as "Burke Mexico Files").

8. United States Department of State, Records of the Department of State Relating to Internal Affairs of Mexico, 1910–1929, 1930–1939, Decimal File 812.404 (hereafter cited as "DSR 812.404/***"). See NCWC to Coolidge, April 15, 1926, DSR 812.404/413; NCWC to Coolidge, April 24, 1926, 812.404/439; and Gunther memorandum of meeting with Burke and Montavon, May 14, 1926, 812.404/464. See also Douglas J. Slawson, CM, "The National Catholic Welfare Conference and the Church-State Conflict in Mexico, 1925–1929," *The Americas* 47 (July 1990): 64, and Sister M. Elizabeth Ann Rice, OP, "The Diplomatic Relations between the United States and

Mexico, as Affected by the Struggle for Religious Liberty in Mexico, 1925–1929" (published dissertation, Catholic University of America, 1959), 84–85.

9. Burke to Kellogg, July 19, 1926, file: "U.S. Department of State, 1926, July–Dec.," Burke Mexico Files, 1, 3.

10. Independent handwriting experts examined photostat copies of the entry log that Caruana allegedly signed when entering Mexico (he claimed to have signed no logs). These experts verified that the Spanish word for "Catholic" (*catolico*) had been rather clumsily altered to appear as the Spanish word for "Protestant" (*protestante*). Also, both experts claimed that the signatures on the sheets were nothing like Caruana's own signature. See *Baltimore Catholic Review* (hereafter cited as "*BCR*"), August 9, 1926. The *BCR* closely followed the saga of Caruana's exile; see *BCR*, May 7, 1926, through August 6, 1926. See also memo to Morrow from Department de Gobernación, May 14, 1926, Series X, Box 9, Dwight Whitney Morrow Papers, Amherst College Library and Special Collections, Amherst College Library (hereafter cited as "Morrow Papers"), and *Revista Católica*, July 25, 1926.

11. Gunther memorandum, May 27, 1926, DSR 812.404/486.

12. Telegram, Kelley to Coolidge, May 19, 1926, file: "Protests to Government Against Expulsion of Archbishop Caruana from Mexico, 1926," Burke Mexico Files. Kelley based his statements on a misinterpretation of the "Arredondo Pledge" of 1915.

13. See file: "Protests to Government Against Expulsion of Archbishop Caruana from Mexico, 1926," Burke Mexico Files. See also United States Department of State, *Papers Relating to the Foreign Relations of the United States*, 1926 (Washington, DC: United States Government Printing Office, 1941), 705 (hereafter cited as "FRUS").

14. Memorandum of Burke meeting with Kellogg, July 3, 1926, file: "U.S. Department of State, 1925–26," Burke Mexico Files, 3.

15. "Not a Catholic Question," *Wall Street Journal*, July 9, 1926. See also an editorial by William Montavon, *Wall Street Journal*, July 10, 1926.

16. Statement, William Green, August 11, 1926, file: "Statements, Letters: 1925–26," Burke Mexico Files, 1, 2. See also Catholic News Service press release, March 22, 1926.

17. Burke to Green, August 13, 1926, Burke Mexico Files, 1.

18. Green to Burke, August 14, 1926, ibid., 1; see statement August 8, 1926, 2.

19. Burke to Judge Morgan J. O'Brien, September 14, 1926, ibid., 3.

20. Minutes of the Meeting of the Administrative Committee, National Catholic Welfare Conference, April 15, 1926, 105, National Catholic Welfare Conference Archives, Catholic University of America, Washington, DC (hereafter cited as "NCWCA"); Burke to Charles F. Dolle, Executive Secretary of the NCCM, August 1926, file: "National Committee for the Protection of Religious Rights in Mexico, 1926," Burke Mexico Files.

21. Mullen to Burke, August 16, 1926, "National Committee for the Protection of Religious Rights in Mexico, 1926," Burke Mexico Files, 2.

22. Callahan to Burke, August 21, 1926, ibid. For more on Patrick Callahan, see chapter 7 below.

23. Mumm to Burke, August 20, 1926, ibid., 1–2.

24. Burke to Mumm, September 20, 1926, ibid. Clearly, Mumm was referring to political and diplomatic intervention, which Burke evidently did not consider "interference."

25. Manton to Burke, August 18, 1926, ibid., 1.

26. Burke to Manton, September 20, 1926, ibid.

27. John W. F. Dulles detailed the loose connections between the Pro brothers and the would-be assassins. Humberto Pro owned the car used in the assault, but he had sold it to the conspirators just days before the attempt on Obregón's life. Dulles claimed that Calles himself wanted the Pro brothers and the two others in custody shot "to set an example." John W. F. Dulles, *Yesterday in Mexico: A Chronicle of the Revolution, 1919–1936* (Austin: University of Texas Press, 1961), 313–315. Carleton Beals considered the executions "drastic measures," which were based on "presumptive, but not at all conclusive" evidence. The evidence against Miguel Pro, moreover, was "scarcely presumptive." Carleton Beals, *Rio Grande to Cape Horn* (Boston: Houghton Mifflin Co., 1943), 77.

28. Memorandum on Burke meeting with Coolidge, November 26, 1927, Interview Book I, Burke Mexico Files, 2.

29. Memorandum on Burke meeting with Kellogg, November 28, 1927, file: "U.S. Department of State, 1927, July–December," Burke Mexico Files, 2.

30. Page 43 of report, ibid.

31. Slawson, "National Catholic Welfare Conference," 71. In retirement, Sheffield held that Kellogg, who the ambassador felt had been most unsupportive, "had an unholy fear that I was going to get the United States embroiled in war—the last thing on earth I wanted." Ibid., n. 51.

32. In this, Morrow concurred with Walter Lippmann, who noted in the December 29, 1927, edition of the *New York World* that "Americans, regardless of their own religious affiliation, cannot be indifferent to the [Mexican-American] question. For until there is peace between church and state in Mexico there will not be complete peace in Mexico, and there will not be an untroubled understanding between Mexico and the United States." Lippmann considered Morrow's appointment "the most extraordinary appointment made in recent years." Ronald Steel, *Walter Lippmann and the American Century* (Boston: Little, Brown and Co., 1980), 239.

33. Morrow justified his decision to join Calles on the trip in a personal and confidential letter to Olds: "I went on the trip . . . with reluctance because I realized that some Catholics might consider my trip an endorsement of the act of the Government, however unreasonable such a conclusion would be. . . . It was impossible . . . to avoid taking the trip at this time without peremptorily declining an invitation from the head of the government to which I am accredited." See Morrow to Olds, December 9, 1927, Series X, Box 10, Morrow Papers, 2.

34. See letter, Morrow to Olds, December 9, 1927, Series X, Box 10, Morrow Papers, 5.

35. See memoranda of Burke-Olds meetings, December 20 and 29, 1927, Interview Book I, Burke Mexico Files.

36. Slawson, "National Catholic Welfare Conference," 76.

37. Burke meeting with Olds, January 4, 1928, Interview Book I, Burke Mexico Files, 1.

38. Burke meeting with Fumasoni-Biondi, January 5, 1928, ibid., 2–3.

39. These observations were not unique to Morrow. Sheffield had made note of Calles's irrational, visceral response to the religious issue. Calles, according to Sheffield, "lost control of himself" whenever the church-state crisis was discussed. See Randall Scott Hanson, "The Day of Ideals: Catholic Social Action in the Age of the Mexican Revolution, 1867–1929" (Ph.D. dissertation, Indiana University, 1994), 524.

40. Burke meeting with Morrow, January 17, 1928, Interview Book I, Burke Mexico Files, 3, 9.

41. Burke meeting with Morrow, January 18, 1928, ibid., 3.

42. Burke meeting with Mora, January 19, 1928, ibid., 1–3.

43. Steel, *Walter Lippman,* 241–242. Lippmann and Morrow modeled their proposed *modus vivendi* on other successful efforts. Lippmann sent Morrow a copy of the *modus vivendi* between the Catholic Church and the government of Czechoslovakia titled "Exposé concerning the Modus Vivendi between the Czechoslovak Republic and the Vatican, delivered by Dr. Edward Benes [Czech Foreign Minister], February 1, 1928" in a personal letter, Lippmann to Morrow, April 16, 1928, Series X, Box 5, Morrow Papers.

44. Jack Starr-Hunt, "Mexico Studies Report of Parley As Path to Early Church Truce," *New York Herald-Tribune,* February 10, 1928.

45. Burke to Hanna, February 13, 1928, file: "Hanna, Edward J., Archbishop, 1927–1932," Burke's Private Files on Mexico, National Catholic Welfare Conference/United States Catholic Conference Archives, Catholic University of America, 2.

46. Burke meeting with Olds, March 12, 1928, ibid., 1–2. See also telegram, Morrow to Kellogg, March 13, 1928, DSR 812.404/872 for drafts of the letters.

47. Burke meeting with Olds, ibid.

48. Lippmann briefed Burke on how to approach Calles: "My own impression of the President is that he is a clearheaded man, resolute, and reliable in the sense that he would abide by any understanding which might be reached. He looks like the kind of man who would not leave you in doubt as to where he stood." See letter, Lippmann to Burke, March 7, 1928, Series X, Box 10, Morrow Papers.

49. Burke meeting with Lippmann, March 24, 1928, Interview Book I, Burke Mexico Files, 1–3. See also confidential memo from Morrow to Olds, March 9, 1928, Series X, Box 10, Morrow Papers.

50. See appendix B for the full texts of the Burke-Calles correspondence.

51. Morrow to Olds, April 10, 1928, Series X, Box 6, Morrow Papers.

52. Memorandum of first meeting, Burke and Calles, April 4, 1928, Interview Book II, Burke Mexico Files, 4. See also excerpt from Burke's diary included in a personal letter, Olds to Morrow, April 18, 1929, Series X, Box 6, Morrow Papers, 3.

53. Personal letter, Daniels to Roosevelt, October 13, 1934, "Diplomatic Correspondence Mexico, 1933–1935," President's Secretary File, Franklin D. Roosevelt Library, Hyde Park, New York (hereafter cited as "FDR Library").

54. Memorandum, Weddell to Kellogg, February 1, 1926, DSR 812.404/371, 6–9. See also Olds to Morrow, April 19, 1928, Series X, Box 1, Morrow Papers, and Morrow to Clark, October 19, 1928, DSR 812.404/931-6/12.

55. Rice, "Diplomatic Relations," 129.

56. Burke meeting with Olds, May 10, 1928, Interview Book II, Burke Mexico Files.

57. Burke memorandum, May 12, 1928, ibid.

58. Memorandum of Burke meeting with Montavon, Ruiz, Calles, and James and Albert Smithers, May 17, 1928, ibid., 3–4.

59. Burke informed Calles that he would travel to Rome "to expedite the conclusion of the matter and advise on personnel"; Morrow to Clark, October 5, 1928, DSR 812.404/931-2/12. See also memo, Ryan to Morrow, Morrow Papers.

60. Burke private memorandum, May 19, 1928, Interview Book II, Burke Mexico Files, 5. When Fumasoni-Biondi heard that Olds would be standing by, waiting for a cable from Rome, he confided to Burke's assistant, Father James Ryan, that "these Americans are crazy. They want to rush things. It can't be done. Rome does not act in that way. She is eternal. . . ." Memorandum of Ryan meeting with Fumasoni-Biondi, May 16, 1928, ibid.

61. Sheerin, *Never Look Back*, 137. Morrow was interesting in clarifying the record. In a letter to J. Reuben Clark, Morrow clearly notes that Calles did not make the first move; the Church, through Burke, took the initiative. See personal letter, Morrow to Clark, October 25, 1928, Morrow Papers, Series X, Box 1, 4. In spite of the row over Ruiz's comments, Morrow was confident that Calles maintained "entire confidence in Father Burke." See confidential letter, Morrow to Olds, October 30, 1928, ibid.

62. *New York Times*, July 19, 1928, and Morrow to Kellogg, July 23, 1928, DSR 812.404/895-2/9.

63. Telegram, Burke to Morrow, July 19, 1928, Interview Book II, Burke Mexico Files.

64. This opinion of the official nature of *Osservatore Romano* was reinforced during a conversation between Apostolic Delegate Pietro Fumasoni-Biondi and Morrow. See Morrow memo of meeting, September 11, 1928, Series X, Box 8, Morrow Papers.

65. Slawson, "National Catholic Welfare Conference," 86. The editor of the *BCR*, however, considered the *Osservatore Romano* "the official organ of the Vatican," and as such, would be "the last paper in the world that would publish untrue or unfair accusations. . . . When the *Osservatore Romano* makes . . . a statement it can be accepted as a hundred per cent true, for [it] is considered in a way the mouth-piece of the Holy Father." See *BCR*, August 13, 1926.

66. Kellogg (by Clark) to Morrow, November 16, 1928, DSR 812.404/936a.

67. *New York Times*, May 2, 1929.

68. Memorandum by Arthur Bliss Lane of Morrow and Ruiz meeting at Burke's house, May 28, 1929, DSR 812.404/974-14/17.

69. Memorandum by George Rublee of the United States Embassy in Mexico City, "The Religious Conflict and Its Adjustment," DSR 812.404/1040 (hereafter cited as "Rublee Memorandum"), 46.

70. Personal and confidential letter, Morrow to Clark, November 20, 1928, Series X, Box 1, Morrow Papers, 1. See also Rublee Memorandum, 39.

71. Morrow to Clark, October 5, 1928, DSR 812.404/931-2/12, 3.

72. Rice, "Diplomatic Relations," 180–182.

73. United States Department of State, *Papers Relating to the Foreign Relations of the United States,* 1929 (Washington, DC: United States Government Printing Office, 1953), 3:479–480, and *Southern Messenger* (New Orleans), June 20, 1929. See appendix C for the Portes Gil–Ruiz statements.

74. Rice, "Diplomatic Relations," 182. Peace returned to Mexico very slowly. The Cristeros hesitated to trust the Mexican government to stand by their promises. This distrust, it turned out, was justified, as hundreds of those who had surrendered died at the hands of federal troops.

75. Letter, Ramon Villa and José Tello to Clark, April 5, 1929, enclosed in letter, Clark to Morrow, April 25, 1929, Series X, Box 1, Morrow Papers, 3.

76. Hanson, "Day of Ideals," 612.

77. *BCR,* June 29, 1929.

78. Supreme Knight's Annual Report, 1929, Knights of Columbus Archives, New Haven, Connecticut, 23, and *Columbia* 9 (October 1929): 36.

79. *Columbia* 9 (October 1929): 38. See also Robert E. Quigley, *American Catholic Opinions of Mexican Anticlericalism, 1910–1936* (Cuernavaca, Mexico: Centro Intercultural de Documentacion, 1969), 215, and Series X, Box 2, Morrow Papers for files of congratulatory letters and telegrams.

80. Rublee Memorandum, 94.

81. Sheerin, *Never Look Back,* 154.

82. *The Commonweal* 10 (July 3, 1929): 244. See also Quigley, *Catholic Opinions,* 212.

83. *The Commonweal* 11 (January 1, 1930): 242–243. Many in Mexico remained highly critical of the terms of the settlement. See critical comments of Bishop Leopoldo Lara y Torres of Tacámbaro in chapter 1, note 38 above, and Villa/Tello letter, note 75 above.

84. Letter, Leopoldo Lara y Torres to Archbishop Leopoldo Ruiz y Flores, April 5, 1928, in Leopoldo Lara y Torres, *Documentos para la Historia de la Persecución Religiosa en México* (México: Editorial Jus, 1954), 260.

85. Letter, Leopoldo Lara y Torres to Archbishop Leopoldo Ruiz y Flores, April 11, 1930, ibid., 740.

86. *BCR,* August 9, 1929.

87. Quigley, *Catholic Opinions,* 157.

88. Burke to Ambassador J. Reuben Clark, Jr., February 3, 1931, DSR 812.404/1043, 2.

89. Memorandum, Clark to Stimson, June 20, 1931, DSR 812.404/1052. Clark succeeded Morrow as ambassador in 1933.

90. Bustos was ostensibly an agent of the Liga in the United States, seeking funding and other support for the rebellion. In reality, he was a secret agent of Díaz, work-

ing to *block* Liga fund-raising efforts in the United States. See Ortoll, "Catholic Organizations," 113–114.

91. Ibid., 118.

92. Quigley, *Catholic Opinions,* 158.

93. Burke memorandum of meeting with Daniels, April 3, 1933, 2–4, Interview Book V, Burke Mexico Files.

94. Burke memorandum of meeting with Apostolic Delegate Fumasoni-Biondi, May 14, 1934, Interview Book V, Burke Mexico Files, 2.

95. Burke memorandum of meeting with Roosevelt, May 2, 1935, Interview Book VI, Burke Mexico Files, 3.

96. Josephus Daniels, *Shirt-Sleeve Diplomat* (Chapel Hill: University of North Carolina Press, 1947), 519.

97. Daniels to Hull, January 22, 1935, "Subject File: Mexico Church-State Relations, 1934," Josephus Daniels Papers, Library of Congress Manuscripts Division, Washington, DC, 1.

98. Burke memorandum of meeting with Roosevelt, October 22, 1934, Interview Book V, Burke Mexico Files, 3–4.

99. Admiral Benson was keenly aware of the impact of anti-Catholicism on Catholics in the United States: "[Catholics] meet bigots in their work, in their neighborhood life, in the organizations to which they belong. If they are teachers, they are in danger in many instances of being discharged. If they are in public life, their religion loses them votes and prevents them, perhaps, from giving their full service to their city, state or country. In some way or other we [Catholics] are all handicapped." See Jay P. Dolan, *In Search of an American Catholicism: A History of Religion and Culture in Tension* (New York: Oxford University Press, 2002), 135.

100. E. David Cronon, *Josephus Daniels in Mexico* (Madison: University of Wisconsin Press, 1960), 210.

101. Burke memorandum of meeting with Roosevelt, October 22, 1934, Interview Book V, Burke Mexico Files, 3–4.

102. Memorandum by Edward L. Reed of the State Department's Division of Mexican Affairs to William Phillips, Undersecretary of State, October 24, 1934, DSR 812.404/1301 1/2, 3.

103. Ibid., 25. See also Burke memorandum of meeting with Roosevelt, October 22, 1934, Interview Book V, Burke Mexico Files, 3–4, and Sheerin, *Never Look Back,* 162–163.

104. Burke memorandum of meeting with Phillips, October 27, 1934, Interview Book V, Burke Mexico Files, 1.

105. Pinkman to Burke, November 1, 1934, file: "Protest Letters, 1928–1937," Burke Mexico Files.

106. Burke to Pinkman, November 5, 1934, ibid., 1–2.

107. Memorandum of Burke-Callahan meeting, January 22, 1935, file: "Administrative Committee Meeting, Chicago, 1935, July," Burke Mexico Files, 3.

108. Statement, Mexican Embassy to Burke, January 31, 1935, file: "Administrative Committee Meeting, Chicago, 1935, July," Burke Mexico Files.

109. Burke's Statement, February 1, 1935, ibid., 1. See also "Mexican Persecution, Reverend John J. Burke, CSP, NCWC, 1935," SC-11-2-8, Knights of Columbus Archives, New Haven, Connecticut.

110. Burke memorandum of meeting with Walsh, July 11, 1935, Interview Book VI, Burke Mexico Files.

111. Burke memorandum of meeting with Callahan, February 1, 1935, ibid., 3. See also Minutes of the Meeting of the Administrative Committee, National Catholic Welfare Conference, March 12, 1935, NCWCA, 291.

112. Burke memorandum of meeting with Murphy, March 8, 1935, ibid., 3.

113. Burke memorandum of meeting with Murphy, March 20, 1935, ibid., 1.

114. Welles to Burke, November 5, 1935, Sumner Welles Papers, Box 27, folder 01, FDR Library.

115. McIntyre memorandum to Burke, May 18, 1935, sparked by Noll's May 16, 1935, letter to Roosevelt; see "Selected Materials From the Papers of Franklin D. Roosevelt *Re:* Roman Catholic Church Matters," Catholic University of America Archives, Washington, DC (hereafter cited as "RC Church Matters").

116. Secretary of state memorandum, May 6, 1935, ibid.

117. Burke's memorandum of meeting with McIntyre, June 6, 1935, Interview Book VI, Burke Mexico Files, 2.

118. Leo V. Kanawada, Jr., *Franklin D. Roosevelt's Diplomacy and American Catholics, Italians, and Jews* (Ann Arbor: UMI Research Press, 1982), 35.

119. Memorandum of meeting between Sumner Welles and Najera, December 12, 1935, DSR 812.404/1829a, 1.

120. Personal letter, Daniels to Roosevelt, April 7, 1936, "Mexico" file, President's Secretary File, FDR Library.

121. Kanawada, *Roosevelt's Diplomacy,* 1.

122. Welles to Roosevelt, June 17, 1936, "Mexico" file, President's Secretary File, FDR Library.

123. FDR Press Statement, October 30, 1936, RC Church Matters.

chapter 5
Individual Activist Clerics

1. Jay P. Dolan, *The American Catholic Experience: A History from Colonial Times to the Present* (Garden City, NY: Image Books, 1985), 352.

2. *America* 34 (1926): 583.

3. *America* 35 (1926): 557.

4. *America* 41 (1929): 108.

5. *America* 35 (1926): 270.

6. *America* 37 (1927): 197.

7. Ibid., 248–249.

8. Ibid., 149. The Mexican Supreme Court, in fact, ruled favorably for the Texas Oil Company in 1927.

9. *America* 38 (1927): 230.

10. Ibid., 287.

11. *America* 54 (1935): 170. See also *The Catholic Mind* 33 (1935): 471–472.

12. *America* 55 (1936): 511.

13. *America* 51 (1934): 459.

14. Ibid., 554–555.

15. *America* 52 (1935): 324. This is a curious charge, since Calles was the power behind the presidential chair, but was not the officially elected president.

16. Ibid.

17. *America* 52 (1935): 437.

18. *America* 55 (1935): 362.

19. Wilfrid Parsons, SJ, *Mexican Martyrdom* (New York: Macmillan Co., 1936), 272. The Knights of Columbus did not find the statement "sufficient."

20. *America* 55 (1936): 542.

21. Undoubtedly these articles brought a tidy sum to the paper, as implied by the New Year teaser, in which Kenny's articles were promoted. According to the advertisement, beginning with the January 25, 1935, issue, "his articles will exceed in vigor anything he has written. Nothing like them has ever been published in this country.... In his articles he will show the perfidy [*sic*] of our own government ... in its approval and indorsement [*sic*] of the lowest strata of humanity, the men who are waging war on religion in Mexico. He will spare no official, no matter how high he may be, for his conduct in the Mexican affairs. He will make suggestions that will rock this country and Mexico. He will expose conditions that should make every real American blush for shame...." See *Baltimore Catholic Review* (hereafter cited as "*BCR*"), January 18, 1935.

22. *BCR*, November 16, 1934. This article provides an example of Kenny's Mason paranoia. This paranoia is also well-developed in his book, *No God Next Door,* in which he claimed that it was the influence of Masonic lodges which got Ambassador James Sheffield ("the friend of liberty and justice") recalled and replaced by Morrow, who was "as acceptable to the Calles clique as to ministers and Masons and interested bankers." See Michael Kenny, SJ, *No God Next Door: Red Rule in Mexico and Our Responsibility* (New York: William J. Hirten Co., 1935), 128.

23. *BCR*, December 7, 1934.

24. *BCR*, December 14, 1934.

25. Kenny, *No God*, 65.

26. *BCR*, November 9, 1934.

27. Kenny to Fitzpatrick, January 14, 1935, "Mexican file," Archives of the Archdiocese of Baltimore.

28. *BCR*, April 12, 1935.

29. *BCR*, April 19, 1935.

30. Kenny, *No God,* 178.

31. Kenny to Noll, April 6, 1935, file: "Kenny, Michael, SJ," Burke's Private Files on Mexico, National Catholic Welfare Conference/United States Catholic Conference Archives, Catholic University of America, 1.

32. Ibid., 2.

33. Noll to Kenny, April 9, 1935, ibid.

34. Burke to Noll, April 13, 1935, ibid.

35. His first involvement was in 1926 when he represented President Coolidge in an appeal to Archbishop Curley to refrain from attacking the administration.

36. Memorandum by George Rublee of the United States Embassy in Mexico City, "The Religious Conflict and Its Adjustment," United States Department of State, Records of the Department of State Relating to Internal Affairs of Mexico, 1910–1929, 1930–1939, Decimal File 812.404/1040 (hereafter cited as "Rublee Memorandum"), 39. Walsh's connections to the Vatican stem from cordial relations between the priest and the pope that arose out of Walsh's leadership of the Papal Relief Mission during the Russian famine in 1922. See *Washington Post,* June 10, 1929, Box 12, folder 775: 1929 Clipping File, Reverend Edmund A. Walsh Papers, Georgetown University (hereafter cited as "Walsh Papers"). Cruchága proved invaluable for Walsh's efforts. He convinced the Chilean government to provide Walsh with diplomatic papers (including diplomatic immunity) and the help of the first secretary of the Chilean embassy in Mexico, Sergio Montt y Rivas; see "Rapport du Révérend Père Edmund Walsh, S.J. sur le reglement du conflit religieux au Mexique," Box 6, folder 400, Walsh Papers, 1.

37. "Rapport du Révérend Père Edmund Walsh," ibid.

38. Rublee Memorandum, 62. The news of Walsh's work in Mexico broke on June 10, 1929, in the *Washington Post.* The paper reported that Walsh was involved in the negotiations and that he had been in Mexico City for nearly six weeks. When questioned, Father W. Coleman Nevils, president of Georgetown University, refused to discuss Walsh's visit to Mexico, but did say that "Dr. Walsh has been out of the United States for the past six weeks on a secret mission of importance." See 1929 Clipping File, Walsh Papers.

39. *Washington Post,* July 22, 1929.

40. Telegram, Pietro Cardinal Gasparri to Agustín Legoretta, May 13, 1929, Series X, Box 9, Dwight Whitney Morrow Papers, Series X, Box 1, Amherst College Library and Special Collections, Amherst College Library (hereafter cited as "Morrow Papers"). See also Rublee Memorandum, 74.

41. Rublee Memorandum, 76.

42. Sr. M. Elizabeth Ann Rice, OP, "The Diplomatic Relations between the United States and Mexico, as Affected by the Struggle for Religious Liberty in Mexico, 1925–1929" (published Ph.D. dissertation, Catholic University of America, 1959), 183.

43. Burke memorandum, June 19, 1929, Interview Book IV, Burke Mexico Files, National Catholic Welfare Conference/United States Catholic Conference Archives, Catholic University of America. See also Rublee Memorandum, 90.

44. The rationale behind Walsh (already authorized to help in the negotiations) and Ruiz (who, as apostolic delegate had authority to carry on the talks) deciding to cable the settlement proposal to Rome is unclear.

45. Rublee Memorandum, 90. See also Walsh summary of telegram from Holy See, Series X, Box 9, Morrow Papers.

46. Morrow held no hope of the return of property. See personal letter from Morrow to J. Reuben Clark, Undersecretary of State, October 5, 1928, Morrow Papers, 3.

47. Rublee Memorandum, 1.

48. Burke memorandum of meeting with Morrow, October 1, 1929, Interview Book IV, Burke Mexico Files, 1–2.

49. This ambiguity carries over even into Walsh's official biography. The author, Louis J. Gallagher, SJ, could no more than assert "That the three-man special commission [Walsh, Cruchága, and Morrow] was in conference with the archbishop before he issued his final statement is certain, and it may be taken for granted that each of the negotiators played an essential part in the results which were accomplished." See Louis J. Gallagher, SJ, *Edmund A. Walsh, S.J., A Biography* (New York: Benziger Brothers, 1962), 120.

50. Copy of telegram, Edmund Walsh from Chilean Embassy in Mexico to "Culbertson," American Embassy in Chile, n.d., Box 6, folder 398, Walsh Papers. In later years, Walsh's interpretation of the magnitude of his contribution appears to have been inflated by the passage of time. Following an evening with Walsh in 1952, Monsignor Paul Tanner, of Washington, DC, wrote a confidential memorandum to Monsignor H. J. Carroll, also of Washington, conveying Walsh's account of his work in international affairs. In Tanner's recollections of Walsh's stories, the march of events leading to the *modus vivendi* differed radically from other accounts. For instance, Walsh was active in Mexico for "several months" during which a series of dinners enabled him to gain the confidences of the key players of the negotiations. Tanner noted that "after 'eating' his way into the right circles he was able to begin negotiations for a settlement of the impasse." Tanner asserted that "many months were spent in conferences hammering out the simultaneous declarations of the government and the Mexican Hierarchy," and that it was only after "the settlement approached a climax" that Walsh "sent for the Archbishop [Ruiz] and Bishop Díaz, then in the United States," initiated the contact between the two parties, and "then bowed out of the scene." But not before "telling Díaz that he was to be the new Archbishop of Mexico," although most accounts credit Ruiz with telling Díaz of his appointment, while the two were at the shrine to the Virgin of Guadalupe. See Tanner letter to Carroll, March 11, 1952, Burke's Private Files on Mexico, 2–3. This account was followed in the file with a note for Tanner from "TL," dated April 8, 1952. "TL" received an anonymous phone call, which he guessed was from Montavon, intending to correct the record. According to the caller, "Walsh was sent to Mexico by the Holy See . . . to accept the statement of the Government of Mexico. He had no part in the negotiations between the clergy in Mexico with the President of Mexico leading up to the solution of the Church-State problem in Mexico."

51. Gil Borges, Assistant Director of the Pan American Union, to Nevils, June 11, 1929; Walsh Papers, Box 2, folder 109.

52. See note 38 above. Another example of these stories was when the editor of the *Baltimore Catholic Review* claimed that Walsh was in Mexico "with the authority of the Vatican. . . ." See *BCR*, June 28, 1929.

53. This interpretation of Walsh's status arose in part from such evidence as the comments of Papal Secretary of State Pietro Cardinal Gasparri seeking Walsh's help in cooperating "with Msgr. Ruiz and thus assist the action eventually taken by the Holy See." See telegram, Gasparri to Morrow, May 13, 1929, Series X, Box 3, Morrow Papers.

54. See telegram, Interview Book IV, Burke Mexico Files.

55. *Revista Católica*, June 23, 1929. See also *BCR*, June 14, 1929.

56. *Indiana Catholic*, June 14, 1929, and *Washington Post*, June 15, 1929, 1929 Clipping File, Walsh Papers.

57. Francis L. Broderick, *Right Reverend New Dealer, John A. Ryan* (New York: Macmillan Co., 1963), 144. In much the same way, some Catholics turned their faces from Benito Mussolini's invasion of Italians' civil liberties because some of his reforms were more desirable.

58. See John A. Ryan, "American Liberals and Mexican Tyranny," *NCWC Bulletin* 8 (1926): 13–14.

59. See Francis L. Broderick, "Liberalism and the Mexican Crisis of 1927: A Debate between Norman Thomas and John A. Ryan," *The Catholic Historical Review* 41 (1959): 309–326.

60. *Washington Post*, March 28, 1926.

61. Ryan to Colonel Patrick Callahan, February 8, 1927, file: "Ryan Correspondence, A–E," Papers of John A. Ryan, Catholic University of America Archives, Washington, DC (hereafter cited as "CUA/Ryan"), 1. Callahan was acting chair of the Organization Committee of the Catholic Committee on International Peace; Ryan was on the CCIP's Constitution Committee. See also Broderick, "Liberalism," 314, 318.

62. Ryan to Colonel Patrick Callahan, February 8, 1927, CUA/Ryan, 2.

63. Kelly to Ryan, February 25, 1927, file: "Ryan Correspondence, Ke–Na," CUA/Ryan.

64. Callahan to Ryan, February 11, 1927, file: "Ryan Correspondence, A–E," CUA/Ryan.

65. Following a stint in the Far East with the Foreign Service and as the personal political advisor to the emperor of Korea, Sands rejoined the Foreign Service and served in the United States legations in Panama (1905–1907), Guatemala (1907–1908), and Mexico (1908–1909), and was appointed United States minister to Guatemala in 1909. He served until the following year, when he again left the Foreign Service to work as representative to a New York banking firm in Ecuador (1911), and for a Boston sugar refining company in Puerto Rico (1912–1914). See William Franklin Sands, *Our Jungle Diplomacy* (Chapel Hill: University of North Carolina Press, 1944), passim.

66. William Franklin Sands, "Peace With Mexico," *The Commonweal* 3 (1926): 711.
67. Ryan editorial letter, *The Commonweal* 4 (1926): 47.
68. Sands editorial letter, *The Commonweal* 4 (1926): 472.

chapter 6
The Knights of Columbus

An earlier version of this chapter appeared as " 'To Arouse and Inform': The Knights of Columbus and U.S.-Mexican Relations, 1924–1937," *Catholic Historical Review* 88 (July 2002): 489–518.

1. At its peak in this era, the eight-hundred thousand Knights mobilized far more American Catholics than other nationally organized lay groups. The Holy Name Society, which claimed 2.5 million members, was localized and had no central organizational scheme (see chapter 7 for more on the Holy Name Society). Catholics as a whole comprised approximately 16 percent of the population. See United States Bureau of the Census, *Statistical Abstract of the United States* (Washington, DC: United States Government Printing Office, 1922 and 1941).

2. "Mexican Policy of Persecution Stirs Big Meeting," Extra, March 8, 1926, Catholic News Service Library files, United States Catholic Conference, Washington, DC (hereafter cited as "CNS"). See also *Baltimore Catholic Review* (hereafter cited as "*BCR*"), March 5, 1926.

3. For examples of protest resolutions, see United States Department of State, Records of the Department of State Relating to Internal Affairs of Mexico, 1910–1929, 1930–1939, Decimal File 812.404 (hereafter cited as "DSR 812.404/***"): James A. Sullivan, State Deputy, Knights of Columbus of the District of Columbia, to Kellogg, Secretary of State, March 8, 1926, DSR 812.404/341; and Resolution, Knights of Columbus of New York to Kellogg, April 14, 1926, DSR 812.404/414. For a summary of the meeting and resolutions, see *BCR,* March 12, 1926.

4. Christopher Kauffman, *Faith and Fraternalism: The History of the Knights of Columbus, 1882–1982* (New York: Harper & Row, 1982), 292.

5. Servando Ortoll, "Catholic Organizations in Mexico's National Politics and International Diplomacy (1926–1942)" (Ph.D. dissertation, Columbia University, 1987), 57. The Knights were not alone in their belief in the injustice of the embargo. The chancellor of the Archdiocese of Philadelphia, Monsignor Hugh L. Lamb, claimed in the *New York Times* that "if the embargo on arms were lifted and rifles put in the hands of the majority, Calles and his band of minions would be blown to smithereens." See Editorials, *Columbia* 15 (November 1935): 13.

6. *Columbia* 6 (September 1926): 24 ff. See also DSR 812.404/565.

7. *New York Times,* August 7, 1926.

8. *New York Times,* September 2, 1926.

9. C. Dominguez to Flaherty, September 9, 1926, SC-11-2-68, Knights of Columbus Archives, New Haven, Connecticut (hereafter cited as "KCA"), 2.

10. "$1,000,000 for Civilization," in "Red Mexico" (New Haven: Knights of Columbus, 1926), 32. The "Bolshevist" threat was a common theme for the Knights. Joseph Scott, a Knights of Columbus–sponsored speaker, claimed that the United States faced "a steady, persistent effort to Russianize Mexico—to give the brand of communist form of government to an unfortunate and helpless people. . . ." Scott counseled against intervention, which "no sane, patriotic American [would] countenance. . . ." Instead, he contributed to the appeal of efforts such as "Red Mexico" in helping form "an aroused and conscientious democracy" in the United States which could bring change in Mexico. See *BCR,* January 28, 1927. Noted Latin Americanist Hubert Herring criticized the Knights for their Bolshevist accusations. In a December 1927 article in *The World Tomorrow,* he claimed that the Knights "quite obviously know nothing about Mexico, or the United States, or much of anything else. They are having a great time of it, holding mass meetings in which they talk about the Bolshevism of Mexico, and the peril to American Institutions. They are acting for all the world like the Imperial wizard and King Kleagles of the Kluxers. They must be first cousins to these worthies." See copy of article, file: "Ryan References, Le–M," John A. Ryan Papers, Archives of the Catholic University of America, Washington, DC, 512.

11. Cardinal Dougherty to Flaherty, quoted in Flaherty mimeographed reply to questions about assessment, SC-11-2-68, KCA.

12. Robert E. Quigley, *American Catholic Opinions of Mexican Anticlericalism, 1910–1936* (Cuernavaca, Mexico: Centro Intercultural de Documentacion, 1969), 176–177.

13. *The Commonweal* 5 (January 26, 1927): 327.

14. Quigley, *Catholic Opinions,* 178.

15. *Congressional Record,* 69th Congress, 2nd Session, January 14, 1927, 1642. See also *New York Times,* January 15, 1927. Heflin waged a lengthy war in the Senate against the Knights of Columbus. See also *New York Times,* January 15, 1927. Heflin claimed that the Catholics put political pressure on Wilson because he refused to initiate a war with Mexico—pressure that almost cost him re-election in 1916. Similar pressure faced Coolidge. According to Heflin, the part of the 1926 resolution in which the Knights demanded war was when they claimed that "the period of watchful waiting or any such procedure is over."

16. *Congressional Record,* 69th Congress, 2nd Session, January 15, 1927, 1700. See also "Catholic Answer to Senator Heflin's Absurd Charges," January 15, 1927, CNS, 1.

17. *New York Times,* January 15, 1927. For discussion of charges of the Knights using their funds to outfit American troops for an invasion of Mexico, see Sr. M. Elizabeth Ann Rice, OP, "The Diplomatic Relations between the United States and Mexico, as Affected by the Struggle for Religious Liberty in Mexico, 1925–1929" (published Ph.D. dissertation, Catholic University of America, 1959), 100.

18. From 1926 to 1929, sporadic rebellion raged in many of Mexico's northern and western states. At first, there were no more than several hundred Cristeros under arms, and only three thousand in January 1927, spread out over the states of Jalisco, Michoacán, Durango, Colima, Zacatecas, Coahuila, Nayarit, Guanajuato, Aguascalientes, Guerrero, San Luis Potosí, and Mexico. By December 1927, their number swelled to twenty-five thousand in eighteen states, and by 1929, there were an estimated fifty thousand Cristeros in the field. See Harriet Denise Joseph, "Church and State in Mexico from Calles to Cárdenas, 1924–1938" (Ph.D. dissertation, North Texas State University, 1976), 104–105, 132, 315. Other authorities on the rebellion include Ramón Jrade, "Inquiries into the Cristero Insurrection against the Mexican Revolution," *Latin American Research Review* 20 (1985): 53–69; David C. Bailey, *¡Viva Cristo Rey!: The Cristero Rebellion and the Church-State Conflict in Mexico* (Austin: University of Texas Press, 1974); Jean A. Meyer, *The Cristero Rebellion: The Mexican People between Church and State, 1926–1929* (Cambridge: Cambridge University Press, 1976); and Timothy Clarke Hanley, "Civilian Leadership of the Cristero Movement: The Liga Nacional Defensora de la Libertad Religiosa and the Church-State Conflict in Mexico, 1925–1938" (Ph.D. dissertation, Columbia University, 1977).

19. Rice, "Diplomatic Relations," 100, n. 99

20. "Confidential Report," SC-11-2-27, KCA, 2.

21. Santos: *New York Times,* October 16, 1926; Flaherty: *New York Times,* November 6, 1926.

22. Michael Kenny, *No God Next Door: Red Rule in Mexico and Our Responsibility* (New York: William J. Hirten Co., 1935), 117.

23. Supreme Knight's Annual Report, Proceedings of the Supreme Council (hereafter cited as "SCP"), KCA, 1928, 23. See also Kauffman, *Faith,* 297–298.

24. Nemesio García Naranjo, "A Campaign which Defeats its Purpose" (translation from Mexican journal *Excelsior,* February 5, 1927), "Statements, Letters: 1926–27," John J. Burke files, "Mexico, 1921–1943," National Catholic Welfare Conference Archives, Catholic University of America, Washington, DC, 2.

25. Ibid., 3.

26. E. David Cronon, "American Catholics and Mexican Anticlericalism, 1933–1936," *Mississippi Valley Historical Review* 65 (September 1958): 205.

27. Kauffman, *Faith,* 300.

28. "Resolutions," SC-11-2-1, KCA, 2.

29. Editorials, *Columbia* 14 (February 1935): 12, excerpt from letter to *America* (January 12, 1935).

30. Cronon, "American Catholics," 227.

31. George Q. Flynn, *American Catholics and the Roosevelt Presidency, 1932–1936* (Lexington: University of Kentucky Press, 1968), 177.

32. Louisville *Courier-Journal,* January 9, 1935.

33. J. Joseph Leahy to Senator George Chamberlain, December 8, 1914, DSR 812.404/1.

34. SCP, KCA, 1935, 82.

35. *New York Times,* January 22, 1935.

36. Minutes of Supreme Board meeting with Hull, January 21, 1935, file: "Board of Directors, Mexico, 1935," KCA, 2.

37. For a closer look at Borah, see Leroy Ashby, *The Spearless Leader: Senator Borah and the Progressive Movement in the 1920s* (Urbana: University of Illinois Press, 1972), Claudius O. Johnson, *Borah of Idaho* (New York: Longmans, Green & Co., 1936), Marian C. McKenna, *Borah* (Ann Arbor: University of Michigan Press, 1961), and Robert James Maddox, *William E. Borah and American Foreign Policy* (Baton Rouge: Louisiana State University Press, 1969).

38. Hull to Senator Key Pittman, Chair of the Senate Foreign Relations Committee, February 12, 1935, SC-11-2-21, KCA, 2.

39. United States Department of State, *Papers Relating to the Foreign Relations of the United States,* 1891 (Washington, DC: United States Government Printing Office, 1892), 739.

40. Kauffman, *Faith,* 304.

41. Ibid., 303.

42. Hart to Ruiz, March 20, 1935, SC-11-2-115, KCA, 2.

43. Hart to Matt Mahorner, Jr., Associate Counsel of the National Committee for the Defense of American Rights in Mexico (NCDARM), March 23, 1935, SC-11-2-104, KCA. Hart was general counsel for NCDARM.

44. Ibid., 2.

45. Carmody to Curley, March 26, 1935, "Mexico File," Michael Cardinal Curley Papers, Archives of the Archdiocese of Baltimore, Baltimore, Maryland.

46. See CNS Library files for resolutions from Oregon, California, Michigan, and Detroit Knights of Columbus among many others.

47. Truman to Pendergast, February 16, 1935, SC-11-2-119, KCA. The error, while in a letter signed by Truman himself, was presumably one of dictation.

48. Walsh to Roosevelt, April 8, 1935, CNS.

49. See SC-11-2-69, KCA, for copies.

50. "Lovers of Liberty Stay Out of Mexico," The Queen's Work, St. Louis, Missouri, SC-11-2-30, KCA.

51. Hart to Carmody, April 25, 1935, SC-11-2-90, KCA.

52. Knights of Columbus Supreme Board of Directors to Roosevelt, June 23, 1935, SC-11-2-19, KCA, 1.

53. Ibid., 2.

54. Ibid.

55. Ibid., 3.

56. "Memorandum Re: Conference between President Roosevelt and Knights of Columbus Committee on Mexican Affairs, July 8, 1935," SC-11-2-19, KCA, 1.

57. Ibid., 2.

58. Ibid.

59. Ibid., 3.

60. Carmody to Knights of Columbus, undated, "Carmody, Martin, Mexican Persecution, Statements," SC-11-2-70, KCA. See also folder labeled "1935" filled with resolutions to Roosevelt advocating a strong stand, Official File 28, "Knights of Columbus," Franklin D. Roosevelt Library, Hyde Park, New York (hereafter cited as "FDR Library").

61. Carmody news bulletin, February 18, 1935, CNS.

62. *New York Times,* October 3, 1935.

63. Hart to Frank Hall, Director, NCWC News Service, October 12, 1935, SC-11-2-100, KCA, 1.

64. Supreme Board of Directors to Roosevelt, October 25, 1935, SC-11-2-19, KCA, 3. Daniels singled out Carmody, as the supreme knight, as the probable source for the attacks on Roosevelt's San Diego speech. In a letter to Postmaster General James Farley, Daniels implied that Carmody's opposition to Roosevelt's remarks sprung from the fact that Carmody was a Republican; see Daniels to Farley, January 22, 1936, file: "General Correspondence: January-February, 1936," James Farley Papers, Library of Congress Manuscripts Division, Washington, DC. See also confidential memo, Marvin H. McIntyre to Acting Secretary William Phillips, November 1, 1935, on the proper response to Carmody's October 25 letter: "a brief acknowledgement without going into any argument or discussion." See "NCWC," President's Personal File, 2406, FDR Library.

65. Supreme Board of Directors to Roosevelt, October 25, 1935, SC-11-2-19, KCA, 4.

66. Roosevelt to Carmody, undated [November 1935], SC-11-2-19, KCA, 2.

67. Supreme Board of Directors to Roosevelt, December 16, 1935, SC-11-2-19, KCA, 1.

68. The Knights drew a keen distinction between "intervention" or "an interference by one state in the affairs of another state, in order to *enforce* some action or forbearance," and a "remonstrance" or "a strong representation of reasons against a measure, expostulatory counsel or advice." Ibid., 2.

69. Ibid., 6.

70. Ibid., 7; see Theodore Roosevelt, *Fear God and Take Your Own Part* (New York: George H. Doran Co., 1916), chapter 8: "The Sound of Laughter and of Playing Children Has Been Stilled In Mexico," 231–284.

71. See memo, Farley to McIntyre, March 25, 1936, "Mexico Miscellaneous 1936–1938," Official File 146a, FDR Library. Farley, as a Catholic, was curiously uninvolved with the Mexican situation. On each of the five occasions in which he spoke publicly as a Catholic, not once did he ever mention Mexico or the persecution. See public addresses before the Seventh National Eucharistic Conference, the New York Post Office Holy Name Society, the national convention of the National Catholic Alumni Federation, the National Conference of Catholic Charities, and in a radio address with Fr. James H. Ryan. See James Farley Papers, Manuscripts Division of the Library of Congress, Washington, DC.

72. Press release, January 22, 1935, CNS.

73. "K. of C. Units Protest Mexican Persecution," May 27, 1935, CNS; sample resolutions described from Atlanta, Maryland, and Illinois.

74. *BCR*, December 2, 1935.

75. *New York Times*, November 19, 1935.

76. "President Roosevelt and Mexico," *The Commonweal* 23 (November 29, 1935): 114. Williams felt confident that "Germany, Russia, Italy, and all countries controlled by governments which deny or minimize religious liberty will be comforted by this new policy." Ibid., 115.

77. Bakewell to Hart, June 27, 1935, SC-11-2-75, KCA. Pope Leo XIII, in his 1884 encyclical on "Free Masonry," defined the goals of Masonry as those of attacking the Catholic Church and its ideals, and promoting "materialism, Communism and Socialism, . . . [and] Godless public school education. . . ." Bakewell to Hart, October 31, 1935, SC-11-2-75, KCA, 1. The concern over Masonic connections dates not only to Pope Leo XIII's 1884 encyclical, but further back, to the controversy surrounding the first United States envoy to Mexico, Joel Poinsett. Poinsett was in the eye of a storm between conflicting sects of Masons, the York Rite and the Scottish Rite. Catholics viewed both as antithetical to their faith.

78. Hart to Bakewell, June 28, 1935, SC-11-2-75, KCA.

79. Bakewell to Hart, November 9, 1935, SC-11-2-75, KCA, 1.

80. Leo V. Kanawada, Jr., *Franklin D. Roosevelt's Diplomacy and American Catholics, Italians and Jews* (Ann Arbor, MI: UMI Research Press, 1982), 33.

81. See *New York Times*, December 6, 1934.

82. Reisweber to Carmody, October 29, 1935, SC-11-2-69, KCA.

83. See telegram, Kilday to Roosevelt, May 17, 1934, "KC 1935," Official File 28, FDR Library.

84. Callahan to Joyce O'Hara, August 17, 1926, quoted in Quigley, *Catholic Opinions*, 162.

85. Cronon, "American Catholics," 228.

86. Kauffman, *Faith*, 310.

87. *New York Times*, November 4, 1935.

88. Hart to Parsons, November 8, 1935, in Kauffman, *Faith*, 308.

89. Hart recognized that divisions were common in the American hierarchy, thus making a unified statement or attitude difficult. Hart acknowledged that the Knights "would be glad to assist in carrying out any plan that might be agreed upon by the bishops. Up to this time, no such plan has been agreed upon and on account of the divergence of views held in Baltimore, San Antonio, Chicago, and elsewhere, I think it very doubtful whether any plan to assist the Mexican cause can be agreed upon." Hart to Parsons, December 19, 1935, in Kauffman, *Faith*, 309.

90. Kanawada, *Roosevelt's Diplomacy*, 39.

91. "K. of C. Head Replies to Query Concerning Letter to President," November 18, 1935, CNS.

92. Carmody to Sheehy, June 28, 1935, SC-11-2-69, KCA, 1.

93. Dougherty to Donahue, December 8, 1935, SC-11-2-8, KCA. When the *BCR* came under attack from a handful of readers because of the perception that the basis for the attacks on FDR was politically motivated, the editor commented that while Carmody was a Republican, the vast majority of Knights were Democrats, that there were no Republicans on the *BCR* staff, that there were no known Republicans in the building in which the *BCR* was edited, and that none of the editors of the Catholic journals that he knew were Republicans. See *BCR*, February 14, 1936.

94. Carmody to A. Reisweber, June 28, 1935, SC-11-2-69, KCA, 3.

95. *Washington Post*, October 11, 1936.

96. "A Supreme Director Visits Mexico and Reports on the Persecution," *Columbia* 15 (April 1936): 19.

97. Ibid., 10.

98. "The Crusade Goes Forward," The Supreme Knight's Annual Report, *Columbia* 17 (October 1937): 5.

99. Ibid., 10.

100. Memo of Kellogg meeting with Tellez, August 13, 1926, DSR 812.404/586.

101. "American Citizenship Basis for Order's Mexican Protest," *Columbia* 15 (February 1936): 3; see also *BCR*, January 17, 1936.

chapter 7
Catholic Lay Men and Women and Lay Organizations

1. See, for example, William F. Montovan, "Human Rights at Stake in Mexico," *N.C.W.C. Bulletin* 8 (June 1926): 9–10; "Calles and the Church," *N.C.W.C. Bulletin* 8 (August 1926): 7, 20; and "Calles and Constitutionality," *N.C.W.C. Bulletin* 9 (March 1928): 5, 9.

2. Montavon notes for speech in Pittsburgh, 1930, "Montavon News Releases, 1927–1935," William F. Montavon Papers, Catholic University of America, Washington, DC (hereafter cited as "Montavon Papers"), 8–9 (emphasis mine).

3. Montavon, "Human Rights at Stake in Mexico," 10.

4. Catholic News Service Press Release, November 29, 1927, Catholic News Service Library, United States Catholic Conference/National Conference of Catholic Bishops, Washington, DC (hereafter cited as "Catholic News Service").

5. Montavon speech, "Religious Persecution in Mexico—The Facts," *Congressional Record*, 69th Congress, 2nd Session, March 3, 1927, 1.

6. Montavon speech to Baltimore Knights of Columbus Action Guild, November 18, 1932, "Addresses and Lectures, 1926–1937," Montavon Papers.

7. United States Department of State, Records of the Department of State Relating to Internal Affairs of Mexico, 1910–1929, 1930–1939, Decimal File 812.404 (hereafter cited as "DSR 812.404/***"). See telegram, Stimson to American Ambassador in

Rome, April 18, 1929, DSR 812.404/967, and Memorandum by George Rublee of the United States Embassy in Mexico City, "The Religious Conflict and Its Adjustment," DSR 812.404/1040, 49, 52. See also telegram, Undersecretary of State Clark to Morrow, November 19, 1928, DSR 812.404/936b.

8. *N.C.W.C. Bulletin* 11 (July 1929): 3–5, 31.

9. Pietro Cardinal Gasparri, papal secretary of state, to Montavon, August 5, 1929, "Montavon, Letters Received, 1929," Montavon Papers.

10. Daniels to Montavon, September 4, 1934, "Subject File: Mexican Church-State Relations, 1929, 1932, 1933, 1934," Josephus Daniels Papers, Library of Congress Manuscripts Division, Washington, DC, 1 (hereafter cited as "Daniels Papers"). See also United States Department of State, *Papers Relating to the Foreign Relations of the United States, 1935* (Washington, DC: United States Government Printing Office, 1953), 4: 782–783.

11. Daniels to Montavon, November 6, 1934, Daniels Papers, 5. Daniels ended the letter with a postscript: "I will thank you to remember me with regards to Father Burke."

12. Sands had been, at one time or another, assigned to the United States legations in Tokyo, Seoul, Panama City, Guatemala City, and Mexico City, and even rose to the rank of envoy extraordinary and minister plenipotentiary to Guatemala from 1909–1910. See his *Undiplomatic Memories: The Far East, 1896–1904* (New York: McGraw-Hill Co., 1930) and *Our Jungle Diplomacy* (Chapel Hill: University of North Carolina Press, 1944).

13. *The Commonweal* 3 (May 5, 1926): 711.

14. William Franklin Sands, *The Present Conditions of the Church in Mexico* (Washington, DC: James C. Woods, 1935), 22.

15. Ibid., 20.

16. Sands to Patrick H. Callahan, February 7, 1935, DSR 812.404/1613. For similar sentiments, see memo of Sands's meeting with Edward L. Reed, chief of the State Department's Mexican Division, July 24, 1935, DSR 812.404/1770.

17. Sands to Marvin McIntyre, July 25, 1935, Official File 146a, Franklin D. Roosevelt Library, Hyde Park, New York (hereafter cited as "FDR Library"). See also E. David Cronon, *Josephus Daniels in Mexico* (Madison: University of Wisconsin Press, 1960), 106.

18. Editorials, *Columbia* 15 (November 1935): 13.

19. Editorials, *Columbia* 15 (October 1935): 13.

20. Report of delegation from American Committee on Religious Rights and Minorities, September 1935, DSR 812.404/1805, 4.

21. William E. Ellis, *Patrick Henry Callahan (1866–1940): Progressive Catholic Layman in the American South* (Lewiston, NY: Edwin Mellen Press, 1989), 22. Callahan later convinced Daniels to accept the presidency of the William Jennings Bryan Memorial Association, with hopes of making $1 million for a memorial for the fallen leader. Ibid, 55.

22. Cronon, *Daniels*, 97.

23. See Callahan to Beck, January 29, 1935, "Callahan Correspondence," Official File 146a, "Mexico Miscellaneous, 1933–1935," FDR Library.

24. Callahan to Beck, February 27, 1935, ibid.

25. Cronon, *Daniels*, 97.

26. Callahan to Patrick Scanlon, editor of *The Brooklyn Tablet*, February 27, 1935, DSR 812.404/1613, 1–2. He also added that he would follow Daniels's example and befriend Calles, but would say to the Mexican strongman, in his "best Kentucky and Irish vernacular: 'What is the big idea, General, of making life miserable for all of the Catholic people in your own country?'"

27. Callahan to Scanlon, n.d., "Callahan Correspondence," Official File 146a, FDR Library.

28. Callahan to Shannon, n.d., ibid.

29. See "Roman Catholic Church Matters, 1935–1939," Official File 76b, Box 3, FDR Library for copies of numerous such letters.

30. Fitzpatrick to Callahan, December 5, 1934, DSR 812.404/1297-1/2.

31. Callahan to Fitzpatrick, December 11, 1934, ibid.

32. *Baltimore Catholic Review*, January 11, 1935 (hereafter cited as "*BCR*").

33. The volume of the Boylan file in the Curley Papers at the Archives of the Archdiocese of Baltimore is evidence of the active correspondence. In one letter, Curley summarized the effect of this close cooperation: "working together [they had] given the [Mexican] matter national, and almost international publicity." See letter, Curley to Boylan, April 9, 1926, B-1329, Curley Correspondence File, Curley Papers, Archives of the Archdiocese of Baltimore (hereafter cited as "Curley Papers, Baltimore").

34. Catholic News Service Press Release, March 8, 1926.

35. *BCR*, March 19, 1926.

36. *New York Times*, August 14, 1926.

37. Catholic News Service Press Release, June 6, 1926.

38. Catholic News Service Press Release, May 24, 1926.

39. Catholic News Service Press Release, August 12, 1935.

40. "Liberty Dead in Mexico," *Congressional Record*, 69th Congress, 1st Session, June 28, 1926, 12142–12145.

41. Ibid., 12146.

42. James A. Gallivan speech, "America or Mexico, WHICH?" (Washington, DC: United States Government Printing Office, 1927), 3–4.

43. Ibid., 6. Gallivan identified those who would oppose his position: "every minus 100 per cent American, every red communist, every anti-American, every piffling pacifist, every propagandist on Andy Carnegie's Foundation pay roll, and every political eunuch in the community" who would "cheer them and fly to the defense of Calles and his cutthroats." Ibid., 4.

44. Catholic News Service Press Release, March 2, 1935. See also *BCR*, February 8, 1935.

45. Catholic News Service Press Release, April 22, 1935.

46. Excerpts from Fenerty's April 25, 1935, speech before Congress, *The Catholic Mind* 33 (June 8, 1935): 206–207. See also *Congressional Record*, 74th Congress, 1st Session, April 25, 1935, 6420–6433.

47. *Catholic Mind*, 33:218.

48. Ibid., 216.

49. Ibid., 210. See also Josephus Daniels, *Shirt-Sleeve Diplomat* (Chapel Hill: University of North Carolina Press, 1947), 185.

50. *New York Times*, April 26, 1935.

51. *Congressional Record*, 74th Congress, 1st Session, April 25, 1935, 6429.

52. See *BCR*, March 8, 1935, in clipping file, AR-974, "a–d," Folio #2, Sheet #50, Archives of the New Orleans Province of the Society of Jesus. Higgins was a tireless advocate of the Mexican Catholics, introducing House resolutions calling for Daniels's recall and endorsing the Borah resolution, besides co-chairing the congressional committee with Fenerty. Significantly, his Congregationalist faith and Celler's Judaism provided an interdenominational legitimacy to the petition.

53. Rep. John P. Higgins petition to Roosevelt, July 16, 1935, Official File 146a, FDR Library. See also Editorials, *Columbia* 15 (July 1935): 13.

54. Ibid. See also *New York Times*, July 17, 1935, and *BCR*, July 19, 1935.

55. Memo, Congressional Sub-committee on Mexico, July 16, 1935, Official File 146a, FDR Library, 6–7.

56. Ibid. See also *BCR*, July 19, 1935; Catholic News Service Press Release, July 16, 1935; *America* 53 (1935): 362; and Wilfrid Parsons, SJ, *Mexican Martyrdom* (New York: Macmillan Co., 1936), 272. Representative John B. Daly, of Pennsylvania, informed State Department Chief of the Mexican division Edward Reed of the petition as it was circulating the House, and noted that he, Daly, was the only Catholic in the House who refused to sign it. He feared it would place Roosevelt and his administration in a difficult position. Daly expressed his nervousness and anxiety about breaking ranks on such an issue, but Reed assured him that if he did decide to sign, "the Secretary would not fail to understand his motives." See memo of Reed's conversation with Daly, June 20, 1935, DSR 812.404/1724, 3.

57. Ibid.

58. Kenny to Archbishop Amleto Giovanni Cicognani, apostolic delegate to the United States, July 19, 1935, file: "Kenny, Michael," Burke Mexico Files, National Catholic Welfare Conference/United States Catholic Conference Archives, Catholic University of America (hereafter cited as "Burke Mexico Files"), 1.

59. Walsh to Curley, February 23, 1935, W-133, Curley Correspondence File, Curley Papers, Baltimore.

60. Walsh to Curley, March 6, 1935, ibid., 1–2. The NCDARM is discussed in more detail below.

61. Catholic News Service Press Releases, March 5 and March 9, 1935.

62. Catholic News Service Press Releases, February 5 and June 11, 1935.

63. See DSR 812.404/1353 to DSR 812.404/1650 (November 30, 1934, to April 12, 1935), passim.

64. Senator Robert Bulkley (Ohio) to Hull, November 30, 1934, DSR 812.404/1353, forwarding Holbrock's letter to the secretary of state.

65. *New York Times,* February 9, 1935.

66. See *Congressional Record,* 74th Congress, 1st Session, House Joint Resolution 311; Concurrent Resolutions 3, 7, 8, 12, 17, 28; House Resolutions 70, 149, 194, 277, 282, 283, and 286.

67. Letter, Burke to Judge Morgan J. O'Brien, September 14, 1926, file: "Statements, Letters: 1925–26," Burke Mexico Files.

68. Minutes of the Meeting of the Administrative Committee, National Catholic Welfare Conference, April 15, 1926, 105, National Catholic Welfare Conference Archives, Catholic University of America, Washington, DC; Burke to Charles F. Dolle, Executive Secretary of the NCCM, August 1926, file: "National Committee for the Protection of Religious Rights in Mexico, 1926," Burke Mexico Files.

69. *N.C.W.C. Bulletin* 8 (December 1926): 25, 28.

70. "A Call for United Common Action from Hon. Morgan J. O'Brien," August 12, 1926, file: "National Committee for the Protection of Religious Rights in Mexico, 1926," Burke Mexico Files.

71. *N.C.W.C. Bulletin* 8 (September 1926): 18–19.

72. O'Brien to Burke, April 25, 1927, file: "National Committee for the Protection of Religious Rights in Mexico, 1926," Burke Mexico Files, 4. The organization's bylaws stipulate that the NCPRRM would seek the cooperation and alliance of other groups working for similar ends "to insure unity of purpose, harmony of methods, and thus to promote the highest efficiency of the work in which all are engaged." See *N.C.W.C. Bulletin* 8 (December 1926): 28.

73. *BCR,* August 6, 1926, and *New York Times,* August 3, 1926.

74. *BCR,* April 2, 1926. See also *America* 35 (July 3, 1926): 270.

75. *BCR,* July 16, 1926.

76. *BCR,* September 17, 1926.

77. Matt Mahorner, Associate Counsel of NCDARM, to "Dear Reverend Father or Mr. Editor," March 30, 1935, file: "Hart, Luke, Correspondence, Matt Mahorner, Jr.," Archives of the Knights of Columbus, New Haven, Connecticut (hereafter cited as "Knights of Columbus Archives"). The Knights proved instrumental in establishing the NCDARM—Luke Hart, the Knights of Columbus supreme advocate, served as general counsel for the NCDARM.

78. NCDARM statement enclosed in Mahorner letter of March 30, 1935, ibid.

79. *BCR,* May 24, 1935.

80. Constitution of the "Friends of Mexican Freedom," formerly the "Friends of Catholic Mexico," file: "Mexican Persecution, Constitution of the Friends of Mexican Freedom, 1935," Knights of Columbus Archives, 1.

81. Robert R. Hull to Hugh Boyle, Bishop of Pittsburgh, April 22, 1935, Burke Mexico Files, 2.

82. Robert R. Hull and John J. Gorrell of the "Friends of Catholic Mexico," to editors of Catholic journals, November 29, 1935, Burke Mexico Files.

83. Hull to Luke Hart, Supreme Advocate, Knights of Columbus, August 16, 1935, Knights of Columbus Archives.

84. Ibid. See also memo from Frank Hall, Director of the NCWC Press Department, to Burke, December 13, 1935, Burke Mexico Files, 2.

85. Memo of Najera meeting with Phillips, April 12, 1935, DSR 812.404/1666.

86. Other similar groups, with still smaller memberships, included the Society of Mexican Pilgrims and the League for the Spreading of Truth About Mexico. Neither achieved nearly the notoriety or the publicity of the organizations detailed above.

87. Pope Gregory X established the Holy Name Society in 1274; the first local society in the United States opened in 1896. It operated on the diocesan level throughout the United States until the formation of the National Association of the Holy Name Society. The self-espoused purpose of the organization was "the prevention by word and example of the taking of false oaths, the commission of perjury, blasphemy and profanity and the use of obscenity in speech and writing. . . ." See letter, Board of Governors, Holy Name Union of the Diocese of Los Angeles/San Diego, to Roosevelt, January 8, 1935, DSR 812.404/1529.

88. Ibid. See also Leo Lanahan, Secretary of the Holy Name Union of Baltimore to Roosevelt, May 31, 1935, DSR 812.404/1725.

89. Editorials, *Columbia* 14 (May 1935): 12.

90. Kay Esther Haberlack, "An Investigation and Analysis of the International Activities of the National Catholic Welfare Conference," (M.A. thesis, American University, 1962), 41. See also [New Orleans] *Southern Messenger,* May 2, 1926: 4.

91. NCCW 1926 resolution, file: "Foreign Countries—Mexico: Acknowledgments of Convention Resolution," National Council of Catholic Women Archives, Catholic University of America, Washington, DC (hereafter cited as "National Council of Catholic Women Archives"). National Council of Catholic Women Archives files are filled with similar resolutions from local chapters of the organization.

92. NCCW 1932 resolution, file: "Foreign Countries—Mexico: Resolution [1932 and 1934]," National Council of Catholic Women Archives.

93. See *N.C.W.C. Bulletin* 9 (February 1928): 23; *BCR,* December 30, 1927; and *Catholic World* 126 (1927–1928): 698.

94. *N.C.W.C. Bulletin* 9 (April 1928): 12.

95. Memo, Burke to Regan, April 20, 1926, National Council of Catholic Women Archives.

96. NCCW Executive Board Resolution, January 20, 1928, National Council of Catholic Women Archives.

97. *N.C.W.C. Bulletin* 8 (November 1926): 6, 28.

98. A 1927 tally of the 1,086 groups comprising the NCCM included national organizations (321 Knights of Columbus chapters), state organizations (including Catholic groups from Idaho, Oregon, Ohio, Florida, and Georgia), ethnic organizations (Ancient Order of Hibernians, the German Central Verein, and the National Alliance of Bohemian Catholics of America), and professional groups (seventy-five chapters of the Catholic Order of Foresters). See *N.C.W.C. Bulletin* 8 (January 1927): 21.

99. *N.C.W.C. Bulletin* 8 (August 1926): 21.

100. Special Informational Bulletin #1 (Washington, DC: NCWC, August 1926).

101. Special Informational Bulletin #2 (Washington, DC: NCWC, August 1926).

102. Special Informational Bulletin #3 (Washington, DC: NCWC, August 1926).

103. Special Informational Bulletin #4 (Washington, DC: NCWC, November 1926).

chapter 8
The Broader Significance of Catholic Activism

1. Robert H. Ferrell, *American Diplomacy in the Great Depression: Hoover-Stimson Foreign Policy, 1929–1933* (New Haven: Yale University Press, 1957), 20, 26–27.

2. United States Department of State, Records of the Department of State Relating to Internal Affairs of Mexico, 1910–1929, 1930–1939, Decimal File 812.404 (hereafter cited as "DSR 812.404/***"). See Kellogg memo for Coolidge, August 26, 1926, DSR 812.404/638, 2.

3. *Baltimore Catholic Review,* September 4, 1936.

4. Ralph B. Levering, *The Public and American Foreign Policy, 1918–1978* (New York: William Morrow and Co., 1978), 153.

5. Clive Thomas and Ronald Hrebnar, "Who's Got Clout? Interest Group Power in the States," *State Legislatures* 25:4 (April 1999): 30.

6. Alan Knight, *U.S.-Mexican Relations, 1910–1940: An Interpretation* (San Diego: Center for U.S.-Mexican Studies and the Tinker Foundation, 1987), 97–98.

7. V. O. Key, *Public Opinion and American Democracy* (New York: Alfred A. Knopf, 1964), 521–522, 525.

8. Bernard C. Cohen, *The Public's Impact on Foreign Policy* (Boston: Little, Brown and Co., 1973), 185–186.

9. Elihu Root, "Steps Toward Preserving Peace," *Foreign Affairs* 3 (1925): 352–353.

10. Memorandum of Capistran Garza's presentation to NCWC Administrative Committee, September 14, 1926, Minutes of the Meeting of the Administrative Committee, National Catholic Welfare Conference, National Catholic Welfare Conference Archives, Catholic University of America, Washington, DC, 122. Note that Capistran Garza accepted the widespread assumption that "not only was the Roman Catholic Church in the United States guided by a unified hierarcy, but that the opinions of individual Catholics were also molded and manipulated by the prelates." Noting the divisions among the Church above, this assumption is clearly false.

11. Wilfrid Parsons, "New Lessons from Mexico," *America* 41 (1929): 108.

12. Ibid. See also Burke to NCCW and NCCM, April 15, 1926, 105; Burke to Charles F. Dolle, Executive Secretary of the NCCM, August 1926, file: "National Committee for the Protection of Religious Rights in Mexico, 1926," Burke Mexico Files, National Catholic Welfare Conference/United States Catholic Conference Archives, Catholic University of America.

13. Memo of Kellogg meeting with Tellez, August 13, 1926, DSR 812.404/586.

14. United States Department of State, *Papers Relating to the Foreign Relations of the United States, 1935* (Washington, DC: United States Government Printing Office, 1953), IV: 794–796 for Hull and Najera statements.

15. See Leo V. Kanawada, Jr., *Franklin D. Roosevelt's Diplomacy and American Catholics, Italians, and Jews* (Ann Arbor: UMI Research Press, 1982), 3–19.

16. Ibid., 11.

17. Ibid., 69.

18. Ibid., 97.

19. Ibid., 100.

20. Ralph Levering, in *The Public and American Foreign Policy, 1918–1978*, has identified another close analogue for Catholic efforts to mold public opinion in the work of "collective security internationalists" to break down United States isolationism. Efforts such as petition drives, educational programs, and public meetings—similar to those of American Catholics—resulted in similar results: "Although the collective security internationalists and their allies seldom won important legislative fights, such as the effort to have the United States submit disputes to the World Court, they did contribute substantially to the climate of opinion in which the government took steps toward cooperation with international agencies associated with the League." Ibid., 53.

21. In 1926, United States corporations controlled approximately $200 million worth of the Mexican oil industry, by far the largest national investment. See N. Stephen Kane, "Corporate Power and Foreign Policy: Efforts of American Oil Companies to Influence United States Relations with Mexico, 1921–1928," *Diplomatic History* 1 (Spring 1977): 173. Just one of Edward Doheny's Mexican oil companies, Huasteca, accounted for by far the largest production among oil companies doing business in Mexico. In 1922, Huasteca produced nearly 38 million barrels of oil, more than 24 percent of the total production for that year. See Linda B. Hall, *Oil, Banks and Politics: The United States and Postrevolutionary Mexico, 1917–1924* (Austin: University of Texas Press, 1995), 83.

22. Lane was vice president of Edward Doheny's Mexican Petroleum and Pan American Petroleum and Transport Company, and Requa was vice president of the Sinclair Oil Company. Kane, "Corporate Power," 175.

23. Ibid., 178.

24. See Lorenzo Meyer, *Mexico and the United States in the Oil Controversy: 1917–1942*, 2nd ed., trans. Muriel Vasconcelos (Austin: University of Texas Press, 1972), 126.

25. Kane, "Corporate Power," 183.

26. Meyer, *Mexico*, 131.

27. Ibid., 133.

28. Ibid., 121.

29. Recall that Farley considered the Knights of Columbus "terribly discourteous" and recommended that Roosevelt not "bother with them at all." See memo, Far-

ley to McIntyre, March 25, 1936, "Mexico Miscellaneous 1936–1938," Official File 146a, Franklin D. Roosevelt Library, Hyde Park, New York.

30. Kane, "Corporate Power," 195.

31. Robert A. Dahl and Bruce Stinebrickner, *Modern Political Analysis*, 6th ed. (Upper Saddle River, NJ: Prentice Hall, 2003), 13. In their footnotes, Dahl and Stinebrickner offer a more complicated definition for *influence* in a paraphrase of Jack H. Nagel in *The Descriptive Analysis of Power*: "a relation among human actors such that the wants, desires, preferences, or intentions of one or more actors affects the actions, or predispositions to act, of one or more actors in a direction consistent with—and not contrary to—the wants, preferences, or intentions of the influence-wielders." See Dahl and Stinebrickner, 17, n. 9.

32. Dahl identified the four levels of influence: (1) "available options," (2) "agendas," (3) "structures" (institutions, etc.), and (4) "consciousness." See Dahl and Stinebrickner, *Analysis*, 45–47.

BIBLIOGRAPHY

Archival Sources

Amherst College Archives and Special Collections, Amherst College Library, Dwight W. Morrow Papers.
Archives of the Archdiocese of Baltimore: Papers of Archbishops James Cardinal Gibbons and James Cardinal Curley.
Archives of the Archdiocese of Boston: Papers of Archbishop William Henry Cardinal O'Connell.
Archives of the Diocese of Fort Wayne–South Bend: Papers of Bishop John F. Noll.
Archives of the Archdiocese of New Orleans: Papers of Archbishop John William Shaw.
Archives of the Archdiocese of New York: Papers of Archbishops John Murphy Cardinal Farley and Patrick Cardinal Hayes.
Archives of the Archdiocese of San Antonio: Papers of Bishop John William Shaw, Archbishop Arthur Drossaerts, and Bishop E. Ledvina (Corpus Christi, Texas).
Archives of the Catholic University of America: Archives of the National Catholic Welfare Conference, National Councils of Catholic Men and Women, and the Papers of Fr. John J. Burke, CSP, William Montavon, and Fr. John A. Ryan.
Archives of Georgetown University: Papers of Edmund A. Walsh, SJ.
Archives of the Knights of Columbus, New Haven, Connecticut.

Archives of the New Orleans Province of the Society of Jesus.

Archives of Yale University: Papers of Ambassador James R. Sheffield, Sterling Library.

Catholic News Service Library files, United States Catholic Conference/National Conference of Catholic Bishops, Washington, DC.

Franklin D. Roosevelt Archives and Library, Hyde Park, New York.

Library of Congress Manuscripts Division: Papers of Presidents Woodrow Wilson and Calvin Coolidge, Ambassador Josephus Daniels, Postmaster General James Farley, Senator Thomas Walsh, and Assistant Secretary of State Sumner Welles.

National Archives of the United States, United States Department of State, Records of the Department of State Relating to Internal Affairs of Mexico, 1910–1929, 1930–1939, Decimal File 812.404.

Primary/Contemporary Sources

Araquistain, Luis. *La Revolucion Mejicana: Sus Origines, Sus Hombres, Su Obra.* Madrid: Renacimiento, 1929.

Calles, Plutarco Elías. "The Policies of Mexico Today." *Foreign Affairs* 5 (October 1926): 1–5.

Cannon, Bishop James, Jr. "The Church and State Conflict in Mexico—The American Protestant View." *Current History* 24 (1926): 491–496.

Curley, Michael Cardinal. *Mexican Tyranny and the Catholic Church: An Analysis of the Assault upon Freedom of Conscience, Freedom of Worship, Freedom of the Press, and Freedom of Education in Mexico during the Past Ten Years.* Brooklyn: International Catholic Truth Society, 1926.

Daniels, Josephus. *Shirt-Sleeve Diplomat.* Chapel Hill: University of North Carolina Press, 1947.

Ehler, Sidney Z., and John B. Morrall, trans. and eds. *Church and State Throughout the Centuries: A Collection of Historic Documents with Commentaries.* London: Burns & Oates, 1954.

Elias, Arturo M. "Both Sides of the Controversy between the Roman Catholic Church Hierarchy and the Mexican Government." Reprint of *New York World* article, February 5, 1928, printed by author, 1928.

———. *The Mexican People and the Church.* Published by the author, n.d. [1917].

Ellis, John Tracy. *Documents of American Catholic History.* Milwaukee: Bruce Publishing Co., 1962.

Ellis, John Tracy, and Robert Trisco. *A Guide to American Catholic History.* 2nd ed. Santa Barbara: ABC-Clio, 1982.

Guilday, Peter, ed. *The National Pastorals of the American Hierarchy (1792–1919).* Washington, DC: National Catholic Welfare Council, 1923.

Huber, Raphael M., STD, OFM Conv. *Our Bishops Speak: National Pastorals and Annual Statements of the Hierarchy of the United States, 1919–1951.* Milwaukee: Bruce Publishing Co., 1952.

Inman, Samuel Guy. *Building an Inter-American Neighborhood.* World Affairs Books #20. New York: National Peace Conference, 1937.

———. *Christian Cooperation in Latin America: Report of a Visit to Mexico, Cuba and South America, March–October, 1917.* New York: Committee on Cooperation in Latin America, 1917.

———. *Intervention in Mexico.* New York: Association Press, 1919.

———. *Latin America: Its Place in World Life.* New York: Harcourt, Brace and Co., 1942.

———. *Problems in Pan Americanism.* New York: George H. Doran Co., 1925.

———. *Social and International Conflicts in Latin America.* International Peace Series #9. New York: The Church Peace Union, 1933.

Kelley, Francis Clement. *The Bishop Jots It Down: An Autobiographical Strain on Memories.* New York: Harper & Bros., 1939.

———. *Blood-Drenched Altars.* Milwaukee: Bruce Publishing Co., 1935.

———. *The Book of Red and Yellow: Being a Story of Blood and a Yellow Streak.* Chicago: The Catholic Church Extension Society of the United States of America, 1915.

Kenny, Michael, SJ. *No God Next Door: Red Rule in Mexico and Our Responsibility.* New York: William J. Hirten Co., 1935.

Kilpatrick, Carol, ed. *Roosevelt and Daniels: A Friendship in Politics.* Chapel Hill: University of North Carolina Press, 1952.

Knights of Columbus Supreme Council. *Red Mexico: The Facts.* New Haven: Knights of Columbus, 1926.

Lara y Torres, Leopoldo, Bp. *Documentos para la Historia de la Persecución Religiosa en México.* México: Editorial Jus, 1954.

Lippmann, Walter. "Church and State In Mexico: The American Mediation." *Foreign Affairs* 8 (January 1930): 186–207.

McCullagh, Francis. *The Mexican Gang and Mexican Headquarters.* Union City, NJ: The Sign Press, 1928.

———. *Red Mexico, A Reign of Terror in America.* London: Brentano's, 1928.

Macfarland, Charles S. *Chaos in Mexico: The Conflict of Church and State.* New York: Harper & Bros., 1935.

McGuire, Constantine E. "The Church and State Conflict in Mexico—The American Catholic View." *Current History* 24 (1926): 485–490.

Montavon, William F. *The Facts Concerning the Mexican Problem.* Washington, DC: National Catholic Welfare Conference, 1926.

———. *The Religious Crisis in Mexico.* Washington, DC: National Catholic Welfare Conference, 1926.

O'Connell, William Cardinal. *Sermons and Addresses of His Eminence William Cardinal O'Connell, Archbishop of Boston.* Boston: Pilot Publishing Co., vol. 4: 1915, vol. 9: 1930.

Parsons, Wilfrid, SJ. *Mexican Martyrdom.* New York: Macmillan Co., 1936.

———. "New Lessons from Mexico." *America* 41 (1929): 107–109.

Pope Pius XI. "*Acerba Animi*: Encyclical Letter of His Holiness Pius XI on the Present Conditions in Mexico." *The Catholic Mind* 30 (November 1932): 409–419.

Portes Gil, Emilio. *The Conflict between the Civil Power and the Clergy, 1854–1876: Defense of the Civil Power.* Mexico, 1934.

Romero, Matías. *Mexico and the United States.* Vol. 1. New York: G. P. Putnam's Sons, 1898.

Roosevelt, Franklin Delano. "Our Foreign Policy: A Democratic View." *Foreign Affairs* 6 (July 1928): 573–587.

Roosevelt, Theodore. *Fear God and Take Your Own Part.* New York: George H. Doran Co., 1916.

———. "Our Responsibility in Mexico." Broadside flier, 1914.

Root, Elihu. "Steps Toward Preserving Peace." *Foreign Affairs* 3 (1925): 351–357.

Ryan, James H. *The Encyclicals of Pius XI.* St. Louis: B. Herder Co., 1927.

Sands, William Franklin. *Our Jungle Diplomacy.* Chapel Hill: University of North Carolina Press, 1944.

———. *The Present Condition of the Church in Mexico.* Washington, DC: James C. Woods, 1935.

———. *Undiplomatic Memories: The Far East, 1896–1904.* New York: McGraw-Hill Co., 1930.

Seldes, George. *You Can't Print That! The Truth Behind the News, 1918–1928.* Garden City, NY: Garden City Publishing Co., 1929.

Stelzle, Charles, ed. *The Handbook of the Churches, 1931.* New York: J. E. Stohlmann, 1930.

Supreme Knight's Annual Report. *Proceedings of the Supreme Council.* New Haven: Knights of Columbus, 1926–1937.

Tellez, Manuel C. "The Church and State Conflict in Mexico—The Mexican Official View." *Current History* 24 (1926): 496–498.

United States Congress. *Congressional Record, 69th Congress, 1st Session, Proceedings and Debates.* June 28, 1926. Washington, DC: United States Government Printing Office, 1927.

———. *Congressional Record, 69th Congress, 2nd Session, Proceedings and Debates.* January 14–March 3, 1927. Washington, DC: United States Government Printing Office, 1927.

———. *Congressional Record, 74th Congress, 1st Session, Proceedings and Debates.* April 25, 1935. Washington, DC: United States Government Printing Office, 1935.

United States Department of State. *Papers Relating to the Foreign Relations of the United States, 1915–1936.* Washington, DC: United States Government Printing Office, 1924–1954.

Watson, E. O., ed. *Yearbook of the Churches, 1923.* New York: Federal Council of Churches of Christ in America, 1923.

———. *Yearbook of the Churches, 1924–25.* New York: J. E. Stohlmann, 1924.

Watson, Thomas Edward. *The 4th Degree Oath of the Knights of Columbus.* Thomson, GA: Tom Watson Book Co., 1927.

Winchester, Benjamin S., ed. *The Handbook of the Churches (Continuing The Yearbook of the Churches), 1926–27.* New York: J. E. Stohlmann, 1927.

Periodicals

America: 1913–1936
Baltimore Catholic Review: 1919–1937
Boston *Pilot*: 1924–1927
Catholic Action of the South [New Orleans]: 1932–1936
Catholic Mind: 1932–1936
Catholic World: 1926–1936
Columbia: 1920–1937
The Commonweal: 1926–1936
Congressional Record: 1925–1936
Daily States [New Orleans]: 1930–1934
Indiana Catholic: 1929
Light: 1935–1936
The Morning Star [New Orleans]: 1916–1930
The Nation: 1926–1936
NCWC Bulletin/NCWC Review/Catholic Action: 1926–1936
New Orleans *Times-Picayune*: 1926–1936
New York Times: 1914–1935
New York World: 1920–1936
Revista Católica [El Paso, Texas]: 1925–1929
Southern Messenger [New Orleans]: 1926–1929
Washington Post: 1926–1935

Secondary Sources

Abramson, Harold J. *Ethnic Diversity in Catholic America*. New York: John Wiley & Sons, 1973.
Almond, Gabriel. *The American People and Foreign Policy*. New York: Frederick A. Praeger, 1950.
Ashby, Leroy. *The Spearless Leader: Senator Borah and the Progressive Movement in the 1920s*. Urbana: University of Illinois Press, 1972.
Bailey, David C. "Obregón: Mexico's Accommodating President." In George Wolfskill and Douglas Richmond, eds., *Essays on the Mexican Revolution: Revisionist Views of the Leaders*. Austin: University of Texas Press, 1979.
———. *¡Viva Cristo Rey!: The Cristero Rebellion and the Church-State Conflict in Mexico*. Austin: University of Texas Press, 1974.
Bailey, Thomas A. *The Man in the Street: The Impact of American Public Opinion on Foreign Policy*. New York: Macmillan Co., 1948.
Baldwin, Deborah J. *Protestants and the Mexican Revolution: Missionaries, Ministers, and Social Change*. Urbana/Chicago: University of Illinois Press, 1990.

Baudier, Roger. *The Catholic Church in Louisiana.* New Orleans, 1939. Reprint: Louisiana Library Association Public Library Section, 1972.

Beals, Carleton. *Glass Houses: Ten Years of Free-Lancing.* Philadelphia: J. B. Lippincott Co., 1938.

———. *Rio Grande to Cape Horn.* Boston: Houghton Mifflin Co., 1943.

Beelen, George D. "The Harding Administration and Mexico: Diplomacy by Economic Persuasion." *The Americas* 41 (October 1984): 177–189.

Bemis, Samuel Flagg. *A Diplomatic History of the United States.* New York: H. Holt & Co., 1950.

———. *The Latin American Policy of the United States: An Historical Interpretation.* New York: W. W. Norton & Co., 1943.

Bentley, Arthur F. *The Process of Government: A Study of Social Pressures.* Cambridge: Belknap Press, 1967.

Berbusse, Edward J., SJ. "The Unofficial Intervention of the United States in Mexico's Religious Crisis, 1926–1930." *The Americas* 23 (July 1966): 28–62.

Bodensteiner, Carol A. "Special Interest Group Coalitions: Ethical Standards for Broad-Based Support Efforts." *Public Relations Review* 23:1 (Spring 1997): 31–47.

Bokenkotter, Thomas. *Church and Revolution: Catholics in the Struggle for Democracy and Social Justice.* New York: Doubleday, 1998.

Broderick, Francis L. "Liberalism and the Mexican Crisis of 1927: A Debate between Norman Thomas and John A. Ryan." *The Catholic Historical Review* 41 (1959): 309–326.

———. *Right Reverend New Dealer, John A. Ryan.* New York: Macmillan Co., 1963.

Brown, Jonathan C. *Oil and Revolution in Mexico.* Berkeley: University of California Press, 1993.

Bruckberger, R. L., OP. "The American Catholics as a Minority." In Thomas McAvoy, ed., *Roman Catholicism and the American Way of Life.* Notre Dame: University of Notre Dame Press, 1960.

Bryn-Jones, David. *Frank B. Kellogg: A Biography.* New York: G. P. Putnam's Sons, 1937.

Burns, Richard Dean, ed. *Guide to American Foreign Relations since 1700.* Santa Barbara: ABC-Clio, 1983.

Callcott, Wilfrid Hardy. *Liberalism in Mexico, 1857–1929.* Stanford: Stanford University Press, 1931.

Castles, Francis G. *Pressure Groups and Political Culture.* London: Routledge and Kegan Paul, 1967.

Clements, Kendrick A. "Emissary from a Revolution: Luis Cabrera and Woodrow Wilson." *The Americas* 35 (January 1979): 353–371.

———. "Woodrow Wilson's Mexican Policy, 1913–1915." *Diplomatic History* 4 (1980): 113–136.

Cline, Howard F. *The United States and Mexico.* Cambridge: Harvard University Press, 1963.

Cockroft, James D. *Intellectual Precursors of the Mexican Revolution, 1900–1913.* Austin: University of Texas Press, 1976.

Cohen, Bernard C. *The Public's Impact on Foreign Policy.* Boston: Little, Brown and Co., 1973.

———. "The Relationship Between Public Opinion and Foreign Policy Maker." In Melvin Small, ed., *Public Opinion and Historians: Interdisciplinary Perspectives.* Detroit: Wayne State University Press, 1970.

Colson, Charles, and Nancy Pearcey. "Evangelicals Are Not an Interest Group." *Christianity Today* 42:11 (October 5, 1998): 160.

Commager, Henry Steele. *The American Mind: An Interpretation of American Thought and Character since the 1880s.* New Haven: Yale University Press, 1950.

Conger, Robert D. "Porfirio Diaz and the Church Hierarchy, 1876–1911." Ph.D. dissertation, University of New Mexico, 1984.

Cooney, John. *The American Pope: The Life and Times of Francis Cardinal Spellman.* New York: Times Books, 1984.

Cornelius, Wayne A. "Nation Building, Participation, and Distribution: The Politics of Social Reform under Cardenas." In Gabriel Almond, Scott Flanagan, and Robert Mundt, eds., *Crisis, Choice, and Change: Historical Studies of Political Development.* Boston: Little, Brown and Co., 1973.

Costeloe, Michael P. *Church and State in Independent Mexico: A Study of the Patronage Debate, 1821–1857.* London: Royal Historical Society, 1978.

———. *Church Wealth in Mexico: A Study of the "Juzgado de Capellanias" in the Archbishopric of Mexico, 1800–1856.* Cambridge: Cambridge University Press, 1967.

———. "Guide to the Chapter Archives of the Archbishopric of Mexico." *Hispanic American Historical Review* 45 (1965): 53–63.

Cour, Raymond F. "Catholics and Church-State Relations in America." In Thomas T. McAvoy, C.S.C., ed., *Roman Catholicism and the American Way of Life.* Notre Dame: University of Notre Dame Press, 1960.

Cronon, E. David. "American Catholics and Mexican Anticlericalism, 1933–1936." *Mississippi Valley Historical Review* 65 (September 1958): 201–230.

———. *Josephus Daniels in Mexico.* Madison: University of Wisconsin Press, 1960.

Dahl, Robert A., and Bruce Stinebrickner. *Modern Political Analysis.* 6th ed. Upper Saddle River, NJ: Prentice-Hall, 2003.

Dallek, Robert. *The American Style of Foreign Policy: Cultural Politics and Foreign Affairs.* New York: Knopf, 1983.

———. *Franklin D. Roosevelt and American Foreign Policy, 1932–1945.* New York: Oxford University Press, 1979.

Davis, Mollie C. "American Religious and Religiose Reaction to Mexico's Church-State Conflict, 1926–1927: Background to the Morrow Mission." *Journal of Church and State* 13 (1971): 79–96.

De la Fuente, Alberto. "The Oil Industry in Mexico during the 1920s." M. Phil. thesis, Oxford University, 2000.

DeConde, Alexander. *Herbert Hoover's Latin-American Policy.* Stanford: Stanford University Press, 1951.

Dolan, Jay P. *The American Catholic Experience: A History from Colonial Times to the Present*. Garden City, NY: Image Books, 1985.

———. *In Search of an American Catholicism: A History of Religion and Culture in Tension*. New York: Oxford University Press, 2002.

Dulles, John W. F. *Yesterday in Mexico: A Chronicle of the Revolution, 1919–1936*. Austin: University of Texas Press, 1961.

Ellis, John Tracy. *American Catholicism*. Chicago: University of Chicago Press, 1956.

———. *The Life of James Cardinal Gibbons, Archbishop of Baltimore: 1834–1921*. 2 vols. Milwaukee: Bruce Publishing Co., 1952.

Ellis, L. Ethan. "Dwight Morrow and the Church-State Controversy in Mexico." *Hispanic American Historical Review* 38 (November 1958): 482–505.

———. *Frank B. Kellogg and American Foreign Relations, 1925–1929*. New Brunswick, NJ: Rutgers University Press, 1961.

———. *Republican Foreign Policy, 1921–1933*. New Brunswick, NJ: Rutgers University Press, 1968.

Ellis, William E. "Catholicism and the Southern Ethos: The Role of Patrick Henry Callahan." *The Catholic Historical Review* 69 (1983): 41–50.

———. *Patrick Henry Callahan (1866–1940): Progressive Catholic Layman in the American South*. Lewiston, NY: Edwin Mellen Press, 1989.

Erb, Richard D., and Stanley R. Ross, eds. *United States Relations with Mexico: Context and Content*. Washington, DC: American Enterprise Institute for Public Policy Research, 1981.

Ferrell, Robert H. *American Diplomacy: The Twentieth Century*. New York: W.W. Norton & Co., 1988.

———. *American Diplomacy in the Great Depression: Hoover-Stimson Foreign Policy, 1929–1933*. New Haven: Yale University Press, 1957.

Flynn, George Q. *American Catholics and the Roosevelt Presidency, 1932–1936*. Lexington: University of Kentucky Press, 1968.

———. *Roosevelt and Romanism: Catholics and American Diplomacy, 1937–1945*. Westport, CT: Greenwood Press, 1976.

Foster, H. Schuyler. "American Public Opinion and U.S. Foreign Policy." *U.S. State Department Bulletin* 41 (1959): 796–803.

Gaffey, James P. *Francis Clement Kelley and the American Catholic Dream*, 2 vols. Bensenville, IL: The Heritage Foundation, 1980.

Gallagher, John Joseph. "The Theodore Roosevelt Letters to Cardinal Gibbons." *Catholic Historical Review* 44 (January 1959): 440–456.

Gallagher, Reverend Louis J., SJ. *Edmund A. Walsh, S.J., A Biography*. New York: Benziger Brothers, 1962.

Gilderhus, Mark T. *Diplomacy and Revolution: U.S.-Mexican Relations under Wilson and Carranza*. Tucson: University of Arizona Press, 1977.

———. "The United States and Carranza, 1917: The Question of De Jure Recognition." *The Americas* 29 (October 1972): 214–231.

Green, Joseph G. "Patrick Henry Callahan (1866–1940): The Social Role of an American Catholic Lay Leader." Ph.D. dissertation, Catholic University of America, 1963.

Greenleaf, Floyd. "Diplomacy of the Mexican Revolution: Mexican Policy and American Response, 1910–1913." Ph.D. dissertation, University of Tennessee, Knoxville, 1976.

Haberlack, Kay Esther. "An Investigation and Analysis of the International Activities of the National Catholic Welfare Conference." M.A. thesis, American University, 1962.

Haley, P. Edward. *Revolution and Intervention: The Diplomacy of Taft and Wilson with Mexico, 1910–1917.* Cambridge: MIT Press, 1970.

Hall, Linda B. *Oil, Banks and Politics: The United States and Postrevolutionary Mexico, 1917–1924.* Austin: University of Texas Press, 1995.

Halsey, William M. *The Survival of American Innocence: Catholicism in an Era of Disillusionment, 1920–1940.* Notre Dame: University of Notre Dame Press, 1980.

Hanley, Timothy Clarke. "Civilian Leadership of the Cristero Movement: The Liga Nacional Defensora de la Libertad Religiosa and the Church-State Conflict in Mexico, 1925–1938." Ph.D. dissertation, Columbia University, 1977.

Hanson, Randall Scott. "The Day of Ideals: Catholic Social Action in the Age of the Mexican Revolution, 1867–1929." Ph.D. dissertation, Indiana University, 1994.

Harris, Charles H., III, and Louis Sadler. "The 'Underside' of the Mexican Revolution: El Paso, 1912." *The Americas* 39 (July 1982): 69–83.

Henderson, Paul V.N. "Woodrow Wilson, Victoriano Huerta, and the Recognition Issue in Mexico." *The Americas* 41 (October 1984): 151–176.

Hennesey, James, SJ. *American Catholics: A History of the Roman Catholic Community in the United States.* New York: Oxford University Press, 1981.

Herberg, Will. "Religion and Culture in Present-Day America." In Thomas McAvoy, ed., *Roman Catholicism and the American Way of Life.* Notre Dame: University of Notre Dame Press, 1960.

Hero, Alfred O., Jr. *American Religious Groups View Foreign Policy: Trends in Rank-and-File Opinion, 1937–1969.* Durham, NC: Duke University Press, 1973.

Herring, Hubert. *A History of Latin America from the Beginnings to the Present.* New York: Alfred A. Knopf, 1968.

Hill, Larry D. *Emissaries to a Revolution: Woodrow Wilson's Executive Agents in Mexico.* Baton Rouge: Louisiana State University Press, 1973.

Hillam, Ray C., Charles D. Tate, Jr., and Laura Wadley, eds. *J. Reuben Clark, Jr., Diplomat and Statesman.* Provo, UT: Brigham Young University Press, 1973.

Hilton, Stanley E. "The Church-State Dispute over Education from Carranza to Cardenas." *The Americas* 21 (October 1964): 163–183.

Hodges, Donald, and Ross Gandy. *Mexico 1910–1976: Reform or Revolution?* London: Zed Press, 1979.

Holsti, Ole. *Public Opinion and American Foreign Policy.* Ann Arbor: University of Michigan Press, 1996.

Horn, James J. "U.S. Diplomacy and the Specter of Bolshevism in Mexico (1924–1927)." *The Americas* 32 (July 1975): 31–45.

Hughes, Barry. *The Domestic Context of American Foreign Policy.* San Francisco: W. H. Freeman and Co., 1978.

James, Daniel. *Mexico and the Americans.* New York: Frederick A. Praeger, 1963.

Johnson, Claudius O. *Borah of Idaho.* New York: Longmans, Green & Co., 1936.

Jones, Annie Laura. "Diplomatic relations between the United States and Mexico during the Administration of President Wilson, 1913–1921." M. A. thesis, University of Washington, 1937.

Jones, Chester Floyd. "Roots of the Mexican Church Conflict." *Foreign Affairs* 14 (1935–1936): 135–145.

Joseph, Harriet Denise. "Church and State in Mexico from Calles to Cardenas, 1924–1938." Ph.D. dissertation, North Texas State University, 1976.

Jrade, Raymond. "Inquiries into the Cristero Insurrection against the Mexican Revolution." *Latin American Research Review* 20 (1985): 53–69.

Kanawada, Leo V., Jr. *Franklin D. Roosevelt's Diplomacy and American Catholics, Italians, and Jews.* Ann Arbor: UMI Research Press, 1982.

Kane, N. Stephen. "Corporate Power and Foreign Policy: Efforts of American Oil Companies to Influence United States Relations with Mexico, 1921–1928." *Diplomatic History* 1 (Spring 1977): 170–198.

Kantowicz, Edward R. "Cardinal Mundelein of Chicago and the Shaping of Twentieth-Century American Catholicism." *Journal of American History* 68 (1981): 52–68.

Kauffman, Christopher. *Columbianism and the Knights of Columbus: A Quincentenary History.* New York: Simon & Schuster, 1992.

———. *Faith and Fraternalism: The History of the Knights of Columbus, 1882–1982.* New York: Harper & Row, 1982.

———. "The Knights of Columbus: Lay Activism from the Origins through the Great Depression." *U.S. Catholic Historian* 3 (1990): 261–274.

Key, V. O., Jr. *Politics, Parties and Pressure Groups.* New York: Thomas Y. Crowell Co., 1942.

———. *Public Opinion and American Democracy.* New York: Alfred A. Knopf, 1964.

Knight, Alan. *U.S.-Mexican Relations, 1910–1940: An Interpretation.* San Diego: Center for U.S.-Mexican Studies and the Tinker Foundation, 1987.

LaFeber, Walter. *The American Age: U.S. Foreign Policy at Home and Abroad since 1896.* New York: W. W. Norton & Co., 1994.

Lavey, Patrick Bernard. "William J. Kerby, John A. Ryan, and the Awakening of the Twentieth-Century American Catholic Social Conscience, 1899–1919." Ph.D. dissertation, University of Illinois at Urbana-Champaign, 1986.

Lenski, Gerhard. *The Religious Factor: A Sociological Study of Religion's Impact on Politics, Economics, and Family Life.* Westport, CT: Greenwood Press, 1961.

Lerche, Charles. *Foreign Policy of the American People.* 3rd ed. Englewood Cliffs, NJ: Prentice-Hall, 1967.

Levering, Ralph B. *The Public and American Foreign Policy, 1918–1978.* New York: William Morrow and Co., 1978.

Link, Arthur S. *Woodrow Wilson and the Progressive Era, 1910–1917.* New York: Harper & Bros., 1954.

Little, Douglas. "Antibolshevism and American Foreign Policy, 1919–1939: The Diplomacy of Self-Delusion." *American Quarterly* 35 (Fall 1983): 376–390.

Lowry, Philip Holt. "The Mexican Policy of Woodrow Wilson." Ph.D. dissertation, Yale University, 1949.

Mahood, H. R. *Interest Group Politics in America: A New Intensity.* Englewood Cliffs, NJ: Prentice-Hall, 1990.

———. *Interest Groups in American National Politics.* Upper Saddle River, NJ: Prentice-Hall, 2000.

Mancke, Richard B. *El Petroleo Mexicano y los Estados Unidos: Implicaciones Internacionales, Ecónomicas y Políticas.* Mexico, D. F.: Editorial Enero, Anaxagoras 1043–2, 1981.

Manning, William R. *Early Diplomatic Relations between the United States and Mexico.* Baltimore: Johns Hopkins Press, 1916.

McAvoy, Thomas T., CSC. *A History of the Catholic Church in the United States.* Notre Dame: University of Notre Dame Press, 1969.

McKenna, Marian C. *Borah.* Ann Arbor: University of Michigan Press, 1961.

McKeown, Elizabeth. "The National Bishops' Conference: An Analysis of Its Origins." *Catholic Historical Review* 66 (1980): 565–583.

McMullen, Christopher J. "Calles and the Diplomacy of Revolution: Mexican-American Relations, 1924–1928." Ph.D. dissertation, Georgetown University, 1980.

Mecham, J. Lloyd. *Church and State in Latin America: A History of Politicoecclesiastical Relations.* Chapel Hill: University of North Carolina Press, 1966.

———. "A Survey of the Church-State Conflict in Latin American during the First Century of Independence." In Frederick B. Pike, ed., *The Conflict between Church and State in Latin America.* New York: Alfred A. Knopf, 1964.

Melzer, Richard. "Dwight Morrow's Role in the Mexican Revolution: Good Neighbor or Meddling Yankee?" 2 vols. Ph.D. dissertation, University of New Mexico, 1979.

Meyer, Jean A. *The Cristero Rebellion: The Mexican People between Church and State, 1926–1929.* Cambridge: Cambridge University Press, 1976.

Meyer, Lorenzo. *Mexico and the United States in the Oil Controversy: 1917–1942.* 2nd ed. Trans. Muriel Vasconcelos. Austin: University of Texas Press, 1972.

Meyer, Michael. "Arms of the *Ypiranga.*" *Hispanic American Historical Review* 50 (August 1970): 543–556.

Meyer, Michael, and William L. Sherman. *The Course of Mexican History.* 2nd ed. New York: Oxford University Press, 1983.

Miller, Sr. Barbara. "The Role of Women in the Mexican Cristero Rebellion: Las Señoras y Las Religiosas." *The Americas* 40 (January 1984): 303–323.

Morris, Charles R. *American Catholic: The Saints and Sinners Who Built America's Most Powerful Church.* New York: Random House, 1997.

Morrison, Joseph L. *Josephus Daniels: The Small-d Democrat.* Chapel Hill: University of North Carolina Press, 1966.

Murray, Paul V. *The Catholic Church in Mexico.* Vol. 1 (1519–1910). Mexico, D. F., 1965.

Navarrete, Felix. "The Conflict in Mexico between the Civil Power and the Clergy, 1854–1876: Defense of the Clergy." In Frederick B. Pike, ed., *The Conflict between Church and State in Latin America.* New York: Alfred A. Knopf, 1964.

Nicolson, Harold. *Dwight Morrow.* New York: Harcourt, Brace and Co., 1935.

Niemeyer, E. V. "Anticlericalism in the Mexican Constitutional Convention of 1916–17." *The Americas* 11 (July 1954): 31–49.

O'Brien, David J. *American Catholics and Social Reform.* New York: Oxford University Press, 1968.

Olsen, Mancure, Jr. *The Logic of Collective Action.* Cambridge: Harvard University Press, 1967.

Ortoll, Servando. "Catholic Organizations in Mexico's National Politics and International Diplomacy (1926–1942)." Ph.D. dissertation, Columbia University, 1987.

Pastor-Zelaya, Anthony Sean. "The Development of Roman Catholic Social Liberalism in the United States, 1877–1935." Ph.D. dissertation, University of California–Santa Barbara, 1988.

Paterson, Thomas G., J. Garry Clifford, and Kenneth J. Hagan. *American Foreign Relations: A History since 1895.* Lexington, KY: D. C. Heath & Co., 1995.

Piper, John J. "Father John J. Burke, C.S.P., and the Turning Point in American Catholic History." *Records of the American Catholic Historical Society of Philadelphia* 92 (1981): 101–113.

Pomerleau, Claude. "El problema de las Relaciones Iglesia-Estado en Mexico." *Estudios Internacionales* 20 (1987): 223–241.

Quigley, Robert E. *American Catholic Opinions of Mexican Anticlericalism, 1910–1936.* Cuernavaca, Mexico: Centro Intercultural de Documentacion, 1969.

Quirk, Robert E. *An Affair of Honor: Woodrow Wilson and the Occupation of Veracruz.* Lexington, KY: Mississippi Valley Historical Association by the University of Kentucky Press, 1962.

———. *The Mexican Revolution and the Catholic Church.* Bloomington: Indiana University Press, 1973.

Reich, Peter Lester. *Mexico's Hidden Revolution: The Catholic Church in Law and Politics since 1929.* Notre Dame: University of Notre Dame Press, 1995.

Rice, Sr. M. Elizabeth Ann, OP. "The Diplomatic Relations between the United States and Mexico, as Affected by the Struggle for Religious Liberty in Mexico, 1925–1929." Published Ph.D. dissertation, Catholic University of America, 1959.

Rich, Paul, and Guillermo de los Reyes. "The Mexican Revolution and the Caballeros de Colón." *Catholic Southwest* 10 (1999): 60–74.

Richmond, Douglas. "The First Chief and Revolutionary Mexico: The Presidency of Venustiano Carranza, 1915–1920." Ph.D. dissertation, University of Washington, 1976.

———. *Venustiano Carranza's Nationalist Struggle, 1893–1920.* Lincoln: University of Nebraska Press, 1983.

Rosenau, James N. *Public Opinion and Foreign Policy: An Operational Formulation.* New York: Random House, 1961.

Ross, Stanley Robert. "Dwight Morrow and the Mexican Revolution." *Hispanic American Historical Review* 38 (November 1958): 506–528.

Roucek, Joseph S. "American Foreign Politics & American Minorities." *The Indian Journal of Political Science* 17 (July–September 1956): 241–260.

Rozell, Mark J., and Clyde Wilcox. *Interest Groups in American Campaigns: The New Face of Electioneering.* Washington, DC: Congressional Quarterly Press, 1999.

Sanchez, José Mariano. *Anticlericalism: A Brief History.* Notre Dame: University of Notre Dame Press, 1972.

Schell, Patience A. *Church and State Education in Revolutionary Mexico City.* Tucson: University of Arizona Press, 2003.

Schmitt, Karl M. "Catholic Adjustment to the Secular State: The Case of Mexico, 1867–1911." *Catholic Historical Review* 48 (July 1962): 182–204.

———. "Church and State in Mexico: A Corporatist Relationship." *The Americas* 40 (January 1984): 349–376.

Schwaller, John Frederick. "The Cathedral Archives of Mexico." *The Americas* 42 (October 1985): 229–242.

Sheerin, John B., CSP. *Never Look Back: The Career and Concerns of John J. Burke.* New York: Paulist Press, 1975.

Slawson, Douglas J., CM. "The National Catholic Welfare Conference and the Church-State Conflict in Mexico, 1925–1929." *The Americas* 47 (July 1990): 55–93.

Sloan, John W. "United States Policy Responses to the Mexican Revolution: A Partial Application of the Bureaucratic Politics Model." *Journal of Latin American Studies* 10 (November 1978): 283–308.

Small, Melvyn. "Historians Look At Public Opinion." In Melvyn Small, ed., *Public Opinion and Historians: Interdisciplinary Perspectives.* Detroit: Wayne State University Press, 1970.

———. "Public Opinion." In Michael J. Hogan and Thomas G. Paterson, eds., *Explaining the History of American Foreign Relations.* Cambridge: Cambridge University Press, 1991.

Snow, Sinclair. "Protestant versus Catholic: U.S. Reaction to the Mexican Church-State Conflict of 1926–1929." *The North Dakota Quarterly* 39:3 (Summer 1971): 68–80.

Spalding, Thomas W. *The Premier See: A History of the Archdiocese of Baltimore, 1789–1989.* Baltimore: Johns Hopkins University Press, 1989.

Spenser, Daniela. "Encounter of the Mexican and the Bolshevik Revolutions in the U.S. Sphere of Interests, 1917–1930." Ph.D. dissertation, University of North Carolina, 1994.

Steel, Ronald. *Walter Lippmann and the American Century.* Boston: Little, Brown and Co., 1980.

Tannenbaum, Frank. *Mexico: The Struggle for Peace and Bread.* New York: Alfred A. Knopf, 1951.

———. *Peace by Revolution: Mexico after 1910.* New York: Columbia University Press, 1933, 1966.

Thomas, Clive S., and Ronald Hrebnar. "Who's Got Clout? Interest Group Power in the States." *State Legislatures* 25:4 (April 1999): 30–35.

Uslaner, Eric M. "All in the Family? Interest Groups and Foreign Policy." In Allan J. Cigler and Burdett A. Loomis, eds., *Interest Group Politics.* 5th ed. Washington, DC: Congressional Quarterly Press, 1998.

Vaillancourt, Jean-Guy. *Papal Power: A Study of Vatican Control over Lay Catholic Elites.* Berkeley: University of California Press, 1980.

Vera Estañol, Jorge. *Historia de la Revolucion Mexicana: Orígines y resultados.* 4th ed. Mexico: Editorial Porcúa, S. A., 1983.

Wolfskill, George, and Douglas Richmond, eds. *Essays on the Mexican Revolution: Revisionist Views of the Leaders.* Austin: University of Texas Press, 1979.

Womack, John, Jr. *Zapata and the Mexican Revolution.* New York: Knopf, 1969.

Wood, Bryce. *The Making of the Good Neighbor Policy.* New York: Columbia University Press, 1961.

Wootten, Graham. *Interest Groups.* Englewood Cliffs, NJ: Prentice-Hall, 1970.

Yoho, James. "The Evolution of a Better Definition of 'Interest Group' and Its Synonyms." *The Social Science Journal* 35:2 (April 1998): 231–246.

INDEX

MATTHEW A. REDINGER

is professor of history at Montana State University, Billings.